Evgeny Matusov

Advantages of System Combination for Spoken Language Translation

Evgeny Matusov

Advantages of System Combination for Spoken Language Translation

Combining Natural Language Processing Systems to Improve Machine Translation of Speech

Südwestdeutscher Verlag für Hochschulschriften

Imprint
Any brand names and product names mentioned in this book are subject to trademark, brand or patent protection and are trademarks or registered trademarks of their respective holders. The use of brand names, product names, common names, trade names, product descriptions etc. even without a particular marking in this work is in no way to be construed to mean that such names may be regarded as unrestricted in respect of trademark and brand protection legislation and could thus be used by anyone.

Publisher:
Südwestdeutscher Verlag für Hochschulschriften
is a trademark of
Dodo Books Indian Ocean Ltd., member of the OmniScriptum S.R.L Publishing group
str. A.Russo 15, of. 61, Chisinau-2068, Republic of Moldova Europe
Printed at: see last page
ISBN: 978-3-8381-2012-6

Zugl. / Approved by: Aachen, RWTH, Diss., 2009

Copyright © Evgeny Matusov
Copyright © 2010 Dodo Books Indian Ocean Ltd., member of the OmniScriptum S.R.L Publishing group

To my father

Abstract

Machine translation of spoken language is a challenging task that involves several natural language processing (NLP) software modules. Human speech in one natural language has to be first automatically transcribed by a speech recognition system. Next, the transcription of the spoken utterance can be translated into another natural language by a machine translation system. In addition, it may be necessary to automatically insert sentence boundaries and punctuation marks.

In recent years, a tremendous progress in improving the quality of automatic speech translation could be observed. In particular, statistical approaches to both speech recognition and machine translation have proved to be effective on a large number of translation tasks with both small and large vocabularies. Nevertheless, many unsolved problems remain. In particular, the systems involved in speech translation are often developed and optimized independently of each other.

The goal of this thesis is to improve speech translation quality by enhancing the interface between various statistical NLP systems involved in the task of speech translation. The whole pipeline is considered: automatic speech recognition (ASR); automatic sentence segmentation and prediction of punctuation marks; machine translation (MT) using several systems which take either single best or multiple ASR hypotheses as input and employ different translation models; combination of the output of different MT systems. The coupling between the various components is reached through combination of model scores and/or hypotheses, development of new and modifications of existing algorithms to handle ambiguous input or to meet the constraints of the downstream components, as well as through optimization of model parameters with the aim of improving the final translation quality.

The main focus of the thesis is on a tighter coupling between speech recognition and machine translation. To this end, two phrase-based MT systems based on two different statistical models are extended to process ambiguous ASR output in the form of word lattices. A novel algorithm for lattice-based translation is proposed that allows for exhaustive, but efficient phrase-level reordering in the search. Experimental results show that significant improvements in translation quality can be obtained by avoiding hard decisions in the ASR system and choosing the path in the lattice with the most likely translation according to the combination of recognition and translation model scores. The conditions under which these improvements are to be expected are identified in numerous experiments on several small and large vocabulary MT tasks.

Another important part of this work is combination of multiple MT systems. Different MT systems tend to make different errors. To take advantage of this fact, a method for computing a consensus translation from the outputs of several MT systems is proposed. In this approach, a consensus translation is computed on the word level and includes a novel statistical approach for aligning and reordering the translation hypotheses so that a confusion network for weighted majority voting can be created. A consensus translation is expected to contain words and phrases on which several systems agree and which therefore have a high probability of being correct. In the application to speech translation, the goal can be to combine MT systems which translate only the single best ASR output and those systems which can translate word lattices. The proposed system combination method resulted in highly significant improvements in translation quality over the best single system on a multitude of text and speech translation tasks. Many of these improvements were obtained in official and highly competitive evaluation campaigns, in which the quality of the translations was evaluated using both automatic error measures and human judgment.

Contents

1 **Introduction**   1
    1.1   Machine translation 1
    1.2   Structure of this document 3
    1.3   Statistical machine translation 4
        1.3.1   Statistical machine translation of text 4
             1.3.1.1   Decision criterion 4
             1.3.1.2   Alignment training 5
             1.3.1.3   Phrase pair extraction 6
             1.3.1.4   Log-linear translation model 7
             1.3.1.5   Search 12
        1.3.2   Statistical machine translation of speech 16
             1.3.2.1   System architecture 16
    1.4   Related work on speech translation 22

2 **Scientific goals**   27

3 **Automatic evaluation of speech translation**   31
    3.1   Introduction 31
    3.2   Evaluation measures 32
        3.2.1   WER 33
        3.2.2   PER 34
        3.2.3   BLEU and NIST 34
        3.2.4   TER 35
    3.3   Automatic segmentation algorithm 35
        3.3.1   Notation 36
        3.3.2   Dynamic programming 36
        3.3.3   Complexity of the algorithm 38
    3.4   Applications 38

Contents

4 Coupling of speech recognition and machine translation — **45**
- 4.1 Introduction 45
- 4.2 Bayes decision rule 45
  - 4.2.1 Source-channel paradigm 46
  - 4.2.2 Direct modeling 47
- 4.3 Tuple-based context-dependent speech translation model 50
  - 4.3.1 Model definition 50
  - 4.3.2 Model training 53
    - 4.3.2.1 Bilingual corpus transformations 54
    - 4.3.2.2 Avoiding heuristics for training corpus transformation 57
  - 4.3.3 Search 59
  - 4.3.4 Reordering 64
    - 4.3.4.1 GIATI monotonization technique 64
    - 4.3.4.2 Reordering in training based on word alignment information . 66
    - 4.3.4.3 Target language reordering after search 69
- 4.4 Phrase-based speech translation using a log-linear model 71
  - 4.4.1 Advantages over the tuple-based model 71
  - 4.4.2 Model features and training 72
  - 4.4.3 Search 74
    - 4.4.3.1 Preparing word lattices 74
    - 4.4.3.2 Phrase matching for lattice input 76
    - 4.4.3.3 Monotonic lattice-based search 77
    - 4.4.3.4 Extension to allow limited reordering 78
    - 4.4.3.5 Source cardinality-synchronous search 79
  - 4.4.4 Combination with the tuple-based model 82
- 4.5 Experimental results 84
  - 4.5.1 Corpus statistics 85
  - 4.5.2 Translation of word lattices 88
    - 4.5.2.1 BTEC Italian-to-English task 88
    - 4.5.2.2 TC-STAR Spanish-to-English task 93
    - 4.5.2.3 LC-STAR Spanish-to-English and Spanish-to-Catalan task . . 98
    - 4.5.2.4 Discussion 100
  - 4.5.3 Comparison of input types and search strategies for speech translation 102
    - 4.5.3.1 BTEC Chinese-to-English task 102
    - 4.5.3.2 BTEC Italian-to-English task 104
  - 4.5.4 Oracle experiments 105

		4.5.5	Reordering in the context of lattice translation	108

  4.6 Other applications of lattice-based search 111
  4.7 Conclusions 114

5 Sentence segmentation and punctuation prediction for speech translation 115
  5.1 Sentence segmentation 115
      5.1.1 Related work 116
      5.1.2 Explicit sentence length modeling 116
      5.1.3 Decision rule 117
      5.1.4 Additional features 119
      5.1.5 Search algorithm 120
      5.1.6 Phrase coverage feature 122
      5.1.7 Sentence segmentation for word lattices 123
  5.2 Punctuation prediction 123
      5.2.1 Alternative punctuation prediction strategies 124
          5.2.1.1 Target-side punctuation prediction 125
          5.2.1.2 Source-side punctuation prediction 126
          5.2.1.3 Punctuation prediction by the MT system 127
      5.2.2 Using sentence-internal punctuation as reordering constraints 128
  5.3 Experimental results 130
      5.3.1 Sentence segmentation 130
          5.3.1.1 IWSLT Chinese-to-English task 131
          5.3.1.2 TC-STAR English-to-Spanish task 132
          5.3.1.3 GALE Chinese-to-English and Arabic-to-English tasks 134
      5.3.2 Punctuation prediction 137
          5.3.2.1 Translation quality in the context of punctuation prediction . 137
          5.3.2.2 Sentence-internal punctuation marks in reordering for MT . . 140
  5.4 Conclusions 142

6 Combination of multiple machine translation systems 143
  6.1 Introduction 144
  6.2 Related work 145
  6.3 Word alignment algorithm 148
  6.4 Confusion network generation and scoring 152
      6.4.1 Single confusion network 152
      6.4.2 Union of confusion networks 153
  6.5 Extensions 155

		6.5.1	Using a language model	155

        6.5.1   Using a language model 155
        6.5.2   Handling of sentence segmentation differences 156
        6.5.3   TrueCasing 157
  6.6   Experimental results 158
        6.6.1   TC-STAR Spanish↔English task 158
        6.6.2   GALE Chinese-to-English and Arabic-to-English tasks 165
        6.6.3   BTEC speech translation tasks 168
                6.6.3.1   Chinese-to-English translation 169
                6.6.3.2   Arabic-to-English translation 172
                6.6.3.3   Multi-source translation 174
        6.6.4   Word lattice translation in context of MT system combination 175
  6.7   Conclusions 177

7 Scientific contributions   179

8 Future directions   181

A Corpora   183
  A.1   LC-STAR Spanish-to-English and Spanish-to-Catalan tasks 183
  A.2   BTEC speech translation tasks 184
  A.3   TC-STAR Spanish-English speech translation tasks 187
  A.4   GALE Arabic-to-English and Chinese-to-English tasks 189

B Additional examples   191

C Symbols and acronyms   195
  C.1   Key mathematical symbols 195
  C.2   Acronyms 197

Bibliography   199

List of Tables

3.1 Corpus statistics of the data used to assess the quality of speech translation evaluation using the segmentation algorithm in Section 3.3. 39
3.2 Comparison of the evaluation measures as calculated using the correct and the automatic segmentation (TC-STAR task). 41
3.3 Comparison of the BLEU and NIST scores on document level with the same scores computed using correct and automatic segmentation. 42

4.1 Corpus statistics of the development and test data for the BTEC Italian-to-English and Chinese-to-English translation tasks. 85
4.2 Corpus statistics of the LC-STAR Spanish development and test corpora used for translation to English and Catalan. 86
4.3 Corpus statistics of the development and test data for the TC-STAR Spanish-to-English speech translation task. 87
4.4 Translation results on the BTEC Italian-to-English task. Comparison of the log-linear model approach with the joint probability approach. 89
4.5 Examples of improvements with the integrated speech translation approach (BTEC Italian-to-English task, PBT system). 91
4.6 Speech translation results on the TC-STAR Spanish-to-English task. 94
4.7 Improvements in BLEU due to word lattice translation using lattices produced by ASR systems of different quality. Comparison with the approach of [Bertoldi & Zens+ 07]. 95
4.8 Improvements due to lattice-based translation: comparison of the error rates for those segments, for which the lattice-based translation produced results different from the translations of the single best output (TC-STAR 2007 EPPS test set). 96
4.9 Examples of translation quality improvements due to the lattice-based translation (TC-STAR Spanish-to-English task). The recognition errors are marked in bold. 97

List of Tables

4.10 ASR lattice translation: the role of translation model combination for the case when the source LM feature is not used in the log-linear model (TC-STAR Spanish-to-English task). 98

4.11 Translation results for the LC-STAR Spanish-to-English and Spanish-to-Catalan tasks (FSA system, see Section 4.3). 99

4.12 Estimation of the potential for translation quality improvement due to considering multiple ASR hypotheses. 100

4.13 Lattice vs. confusion network translation on the BTEC Chinese-to-English task. 103

4.14 Comparison of the proposed lattice-based translation approach with the CN-based translation approach of [Shen & Delaney+ 08]. 104

4.15 Comparison of the word lattice and confusion network input for the phrase-based source cardinality-synchronous search (BTEC Italian-to-English task). . 105

4.16 Word error rates for some hypotheses extracted from the ASR word lattices on the BTEC Italian-to-English task (development + test set). 106

4.17 Oracle experiments on the test set of the BTEC Italian-to-English task. 107

4.18 The role of target language reordering as postprocessing (lattice-based translations with the FSA system, BTEC Italian-to-English task). 109

4.19 Comparison of reordering approaches for lattice- and CN-based search (BTEC Chinese-to-English task). 110

4.20 Comparison of reordering approaches for lattice- and CN-based search (BTEC Italian-to-English task). 111

5.1 Quality of sentence segmentation on the IWSLT Chinese-English task. Comparison of the RWTH approach with the approach of SRI. 131

5.2 Quality of sentence segmentation on the TC-STAR English ASR output. 132

5.3 Translation quality on the TC-STAR English-to-Spanish task using various sentence segmentation and punctuation prediction settings. 133

5.4 Segmentation and translation results for different sentence segmentation settings on the GALE Chinese-to-English task. 135

5.5 Segmentation and translation results for different sentence segmentation settings on the GALE Arabic-to-English task. 137

5.6 Translation quality for the IWSLT 2006 Chinese-to-English task (evaluation set).138

5.7 Translation quality on the TC-STAR English-to-Spanish task (ASR output) using different punctuation prediction strategies. 140

5.8 Comma prediction and translation results for the different SU and soft boundary settings on the GALE Chinese-to-English task. 141

List of Tables

5.9 Examples of improved MT quality by using automatically predicted commas as soft boundaries (GALE Chinese-to-English task). 141

6.1 TC-STAR 2007 evaluation results for the English-to-Spanish translation direction (including system combination). 159

6.2 The influence of individual system combination components on the quality of the consensus translation. 160

6.3 The influence of language model scores on the quality of the system combination translation 162

6.4 TC-STAR 2007 evaluation results for the Spanish-to-English translation direction. 163

6.5 The potential of the presented system combination approach. 164

6.6 Examples of translation quality improvements resulting from system combination (TC-STAR Spanish-to-English verbatim evaluation condition). 165

6.7 System combination results for the Arabic-to-English translation of the broadcast news portion of the GALE 2007 evaluation data. 166

6.8 System combination results for the Chinese-to-English translation of the broadcast news portion of the "Nightingale" blind test data. Comparison with the system combination approach of [Ayan & Zheng[+] 08] (SRI). 167

6.9 System combination of 5 RWTH-internal systems on the BTEC Chinese-to-English task (correct transcripts of read speech), official IWSLT 2008 evaluation results. 170

6.10 Potential of the described system combination approach. BTEC Chinese-to-English task, IWSLT 2005 development corpus. 171

6.11 System combination of 4 RWTH-internal systems on the BTEC Chinese-to-English task (ASR of spontaneous speech), official IWSLT 2008 evaluation results. 172

6.12 System combination of 4 RWTH-internal systems on the BTEC Arabic-to-English task (correct transcripts and ASR of read speech), official IWSLT 2008 evaluation results. 173

6.13 Multi-source translation: improvements in translation quality when combining the output of 4 Chinese-to-English and 4 Arabic-to-English systems. 174

6.14 The results of the human system combination evaluation at the Workshop on Statistical Machine Translation 2009. 175

6.15 Improvements in translation quality on the BTEC Italian-to-English task due to computing a consensus translation from the output of two MT systems which translate either single best ASR output or ASR word lattices. 176

6.16 Examples of the errors made by a speech translation system which can be corrected after system combination. 177

vii

List of Tables

A.1 Training corpus statistics of the LC-STAR Spanish-to-English and Spanish-to-Catalan speech translation tasks (MT systems for word lattice translation experiments described in Chapter 4). 183

A.2 Corpus statistics of the MT training data for the Italian-to-English and Chinese-to-English BTEC tasks (MT systems for word lattice translation experiments described in Chapter 4). 184

A.3 Corpus statistics of the IWSLT 2006 training data and development, test and evaluation corpora after preprocessing (MT system for sentence segmentation and punctuation prediction experiments described in Chapter 5). 185

A.4 Corpus statistics of the IWSLT 2008 development and evaluation data for the Chinese-to-English task (as used for the system combination experiments in Chapter 6). 186

A.5 Corpus statistics of the IWSLT 2008 development and evaluation data for the Arabic-to-English task (as used for the system combination experiments in Chapter 6). 186

A.6 Corpus statistics of the TC-STAR English-to-Spanish MT training data (MT system used for the sentence segmentation and punctuation prediction experiments described in Chapter 5). 187

A.7 Corpus statistics of the TC-STAR Spanish-to-English MT training data (MT system used in word lattice translation experiments described in Chapter 4). . 187

A.8 Corpus statistics of the TC-STAR Spanish-to-English development and test corpora used for the system combination experiments in Chapter 6. 188

A.9 Corpus statistics for the bilingual training data of the Chinese-to-English and Arabic-to-English MT systems (GALE large data track). These systems were used for sentence segmentation and soft boundary experiments in Chapter 5. . 189

A.10 Corpus statistics of the development (DEV07) and evaluation (EVAL07) data used by the Nightingale team in the GALE 2007 evaluation to perform system combination experiments (Arabic-to-English task, see Chapter 6). 189

A.11 Corpus statistics of the development and test data used by the Nightingale team in the GALE 2008 evaluation to perform system combination experiments (Chinese-to-English task, see Chapter 6). 190

List of Figures

1.1	Example of alignment and selected phrase pairs extracted from a training sentence pair.	7
1.2	Architecture of the classical source-channel approach to statistical machine translation.	8
1.3	Illustration of Bayes architecture for machine translation with a phrase-based log-linear model.	9
1.4	Illustration of a phrasal segmentation.	10
1.5	Non-monotonic search algorithm from [Zens 08] for text input (without pruning).	14
1.6	Illustration of the search for a German input sentence.	15
1.7	Speech recognition architecture.	16
1.8	General speech translation architecture.	18
1.9	Machine translation architecture for translation of ASR word lattices.	19
3.1	Pearson's correlation coefficients for the human adequacy judgments (IWSLT task).	40
3.2	Pearson's correlation coefficients for the human fluency judgments (IWSLT task).	40
3.3	Kendall's correlation coefficients for the human ranking of translation systems (IWSLT task).	41
4.1	Relations between the alignment indices i,j and k.	52
4.2	Example of a transformed sentence pair.	55
4.3	Example of an alignment cost matrix.	58
4.4	Example of a transducer that maps source words to bilingual tuples.	60
4.5	Example of a transducer that maps bilingual tuples to target words.	61
4.6	Example of a transducer that implements a smoothed bigram LM.	61
4.7	Example of a linear acceptor.	62
4.8	Example of a word lattice (acyclic finite-state acceptor). The weights of the lattice arcs are omitted for better readability.	62

List of Figures

4.9 Example of applying the GIATI monotonization technique to a non-monotonic alignment. 65
4.10 Example of target sentence reordering based on a full-coverage alignment that is a function of target words. 67
4.11 Examples of constrained permutations. 70
4.12 An example word lattice in which arcs are labeled with slot information. . . . 76
4.13 Non-monotonic source cardinality-synchronous search algorithm for word lattice input (without pruning). 81
4.14 Dependency of the translation edit rate for WFST-based ASR translation on the scaling factor for the translation model (BTEC Italian-to-English task, development and test sets). 90

5.1 Illustration of the search algorithm for sentence segmentation with explicit optimization over segment length. 121
5.2 Three different strategies for predicting punctuation in the process of speech recognition and machine translation. 125
5.3 Example of reordering penalties computed using automatically predicted commas. 129

6.1 The system combination architecture. 144
6.2 Examples of the TER-based alignment in comparison with the alignment produced by the enhanced alignment and reordering algorithm of [Matusov & Ueffing[+] 06]. 147
6.3 Example of creating a confusion network for system combination. 151
6.4 Union of several confusion networks. 153

1 Introduction

1.1 Machine translation

Among the multitude of natural language processing (NLP) tasks, the task of machine translation (MT) has become more important in recent years. With the continuing globalization of economies and societies, the demand for high-quality and cost-efficient translation from one natural language into another is steadily growing.

Effective solutions for MT of both text and speech are expected, among others, in the following areas:

- Translation of webpage content into several languages to enable cross-lingual search and information extraction.

- Translation of technical documents such as manuals and patents for professional use in the foreign countries where the technology they describe is exported.

- Translation of documents and speeches which concern alliances of several countries with multiple official languages. The most prominent example of such alliances is the European Union (EU) with its 23 official languages. In the European Parliament, every parliament member can speak his or her native language, and the speech transcripts have to be translated into all of the other EU languages. Another example is the United Nations where all documents are translated into 6 most widely used languages: English, Chinese, Arabic, Spanish, Russian, French.

- Continuous translation of television and radio broadcasts, newswire feeds, weblogs, etc. with the goal of collecting information for general-public or intelligence use.

- Efficient translation capabilities for use in portable devices, with the goal of e.g. aiding tourists visiting foreign countries, or enabling reliable personal communication of military, medical or emergency personnel in overseas deployments.

Whereas with the current state of MT technology perfect translations can rarely be expected for any of the above tasks, the continuous improvements to the state-of-the-art make it possible to use automatic translations for subsequent information extraction. Also, post-editing of the

1 Introduction

MT output by human translators can often be faster than creating human translations "from scratch".

Different approaches exist to address the machine translation problem. The first attempts to build MT systems relied on *rule-based* methods. In a rule-based system, the source language sentence is analyzed with morphological tools, part-of-speech taggers, parsers, etc.. Given this information, the sentence is usually transformed into an intermediate representation, from which the target translation is generated using rules designed by human experts. In most cases, these rules do not cover all language phenomena; their creation is a time-consuming process.

The *statistical* approach to MT has become increasingly popular in the last 20 years. A statistical MT (SMT) system uses bilingual parallel corpora and monolingual corpora as the main source of knowledge. In a SMT system, machine translation is treated as a decision problem: given a sentence in the source language, its target language translation has to be chosen according to the prediction of probabilistic models. The statistical decision theory and, in particular, the Bayes decision rule, are used to formulate the theoretical basis for SMT.

The statistical approach to MT has roots in automatic speech recognition (ASR). Nowadays, the state-of-the-art speech recognition systems always employ statistical models. The decision problem in ASR is similar to that of MT: given the speech utterance represented as a sequence of acoustic observations, the best word sequence for this utterance has to be determined.

The focus of this thesis is on translation of speech using statistical phrase-based MT systems. For this task, it is natural to consider speech translation as a joint decision problem where the best target language word sequence has to be determined given the speech signal. Thus, we are not interested in the best source language word sequence representing the speech signal, but only in the final quality of the translation of the spoken utterance.

Beyond the coupling of ASR and MT in a statistical framework, this thesis considers all of the NLP systems which are normally involved in speech translation. The aim was to improve the whole speech translation pipeline, which consists of the following successive steps:

- automatic speech recognition,
- automatic sentence segmentation and punctuation prediction,
- machine translation using different statistical models,
- combination of multiple speech translation systems.

The improvement of the ultimate speech translation quality is reached by introducing mechanisms for a tighter coupling and sharing of knowledge between all of the components of this pipeline.

1.2 Structure of this document

This thesis is organized as follows. The following section of this chapter is dedicated to the description of the statistical approach to phrase-based MT of text and speech that is followed and extended in this work. Also, the problem of speech translation and the architecture of the proposed system for its solution is presented. At the end of the chapter, we give an overview of the related work on speech translation.

Chapter 2 summarizes the scientific goals of this work.

In Chapter 3, the established automatic MT evaluation measures are presented and their usability for evaluating translations of spoken utterances is analyzed. Then, the chapter presents an algorithmic solution for dealing with the (possibly automatic) sentence segmentation of the translation hypotheses which may be different from the segmentation of the human reference translations.

Chapter 4 builds the core of this work. There, the theoretical base for coupling speech recognition and MT is first presented. Then, two translation models which are designed to process multiple ASR hypotheses are described and compared. Furthermore, a novel algorithm for translating word lattices with full phrase reordering capabilities is proposed. The advantage of using this algorithm, as well as the improvement in MT quality through the use of multiple ASR hypotheses in MT search is supported by the experimental results presented at the end of the chapter.

Chapter 5 describes how ASR output can be annotated with additional information useful for MT, such as segment boundaries and punctuation marks. An algorithm for sentence segmentation that explicitly considers MT requirements is presented and evaluated in terms of segmentation and translation quality. Different strategies for predicting punctuation marks in translations of spoken utterances are analyzed and compared experimentally.

Chapter 6 shows that speech translation quality can be improved not only by coupling ASR and MT but also by combining the outputs of several MT systems with different qualities. A comprehensive summary of the previous work on this subject is presented, followed by a detailed description of an algorithm for computing the system combination translation based on the enhanced hypotheses alignment. The quality of the algorithm is confirmed experimentally on several different speech translation tasks.

Chapter 7 summarizes the main scientific contributions of this work. It is followed by a discussion of the possible future research directions in Chapter 8.

1 Introduction

1.3 Statistical machine translation

The statistical approach to machine translation was introduced by the IBM research group in the late eighties [Brown & Cocke[+] 88]. Since then, it has received growing interest. In various comparative evaluations, it has been proved competitive or superior to other (e. g. rule-based) approaches. The crucial extension of the original approach which lead to such good results was the concept of phrase-based translation where, instead of single words, groups of words are translated so that context is taken into account.

In this section, the main concepts of the phrase-based statistical MT are described. This includes the search algorithm and the probabilistic models that are used for translation of text and can be adjusted for translation of spoken language. Then, the problem of speech translation and, in particular, the task of tighter coupling of ASR and MT is formulated, followed by an introduction to some of the techniques which will be used in this thesis to address this task.

1.3.1 Statistical machine translation of text

1.3.1.1 Decision criterion

In statistical machine translation of text, we are given a source language sentence $f_1^J = f_1 \ldots f_j \ldots f_J$, which is to be translated into a target language sentence $e_1^I = e_1 \ldots e_i \ldots e_I$. Among all possible target language sentences, we will choose the sentence with the highest probability:[a]

$$\hat{e}_1^I = \operatorname*{argmax}_{e_1^I} \left\{ Pr(e_1^I | f_1^J) \right\} \quad (1.1)$$

$$= \operatorname*{argmax}_{e_1^I} \left\{ Pr(e_1^I) \cdot Pr(f_1^J | e_1^I) \right\} \quad (1.2)$$

The decomposition into two knowledge sources in Equation 1.2 is known as the source-channel approach to Statistical Machine Translation [Brown & Cocke[+] 90]. It allows an independent modeling of target language model $Pr(e_1^I)$ and translation model $Pr(f_1^J | e_1^I)$. The target language model describes the well-formedness of the target language sentence. The translation model links the source language sentence to the target language sentence.

---

[a]The notational convention will be as follows. We use the symbol $Pr(\cdot)$ to denote general probability distributions with (nearly) no specific assumptions. In contrast, for model-based probability distributions, we use the generic symbol $p(\cdot)$.

1.3 Statistical machine translation

1.3.1.2 Alignment training

In training, the translation model is further decomposed into a lexicon model, which gives the probability for word-to-word translations, and an alignment model, which connects the word positions in the source and target sentences. The alignment is introduced as a hidden variable A:

$$Pr(f_1^J|e_1^I) = \sum_A Pr(f_1^J, A|e_1^I) = \sum_A Pr(f_1^J|e_1^I, A) \cdot Pr(A|e_1^I) \tag{1.3}$$

The probability $Pr(f_1^J|e_1^I, A)$ is the lexicon probability, and the probability $Pr(A|e_1^I)$ is the alignment probability. In general, the alignment is a relation $A \subset \{1, \ldots, J\} \times \{1 \ldots, I\}$ which links words from the source sentence to their translations in the target sentence. Since one source word can correspond to several target words and vice versa (e.g. the German word "übermorgen" is translated with "the day after tomorrow"), we allow for one-to-many and many-to-one word alignments. In addition, an artificial source and target position zero may be introduced for mapping source words that do not have any equivalence in the target sentence, as well as target words which do not have any equivalence in the source sentence. Alignment points (j, i) can be numbered by an index k. An alignment can then be regarded as a function of k:

$$A : \{1, \ldots, K\} \rightarrow \{1, \ldots, J\} \times \{1, \ldots, I\} \tag{1.4}$$

$$A_k = (j(k), i(k)) \tag{1.5}$$

Here, $(j(k), i(k))$ is the pair of source and target word positions which are aligned with the alignment connection number k. The alignments used for extracting bilingual phrase translations are usually *symmetric* alignments, i.e. one-to-many and many-to-one connections are allowed at the same time. However, for efficient word alignment model training restricted alignments are usually used. These alignments can be viewed as mappings $a : j \rightarrow a_j \in \{0, \ldots, I\}$ assigning a target position a_j to each source position j [Brown & Della Pietra+ 93]. The resulting alignment for the whole source sentence is then denoted with $A = a_1^J$.

The most widely used alignment models are the IBM models 1 through 5 [Brown & Della Pietra+ 93] and the HMM alignment model of [Vogel & Ney+ 96]. All of these models assume that the lexicon probability $Pr(f_1^J|e_1^I, A)$ is decomposed into the product of single-word based probabilities over the source positions:

$$Pr(f_1^J|e_1^I, A) = Pr(f_1^J|e_1^I, a_1^J) \cong \prod_{j=1}^{J} p(f_j|e_{a_j}) \tag{1.6}$$

The difference between the models is in the assumptions made about the alignment probability $Pr(A|e_1^I)$. A detailed comparison of the alignment models is given in [Och & Ney 03].

1 Introduction

The parameters of the statistical models are estimated on the available parallel sentence-aligned training data, normally using the *maximum likelihood* criterion. The maximum likelihood criterion states that we should choose the set of parameters $\hat{\vartheta}$ that maximizes the term

$$\hat{\vartheta} = \underset{\vartheta}{\operatorname{argmax}} \sum_s \log p_\vartheta((f_s)_1^{J_s} | (e_s)_1^{I_s}), \tag{1.7}$$

where s is a running index over the training sentence pairs $((f_s)_1^{J_s}, (e_s)_1^{I_s})$. That is, we try to maximize the probability that our statistical model gives to the observed training sentences. In the particular example of the HMM alignment model [Vogel & Ney[+] 96], the set of parameters is composed of the alignment probabilities $p_\vartheta(a_j|a_{j-1}, I, J)$ and the lexicon probabilities $p_\vartheta(f_j|e_{a_j})$. The maximization process is carried out with a modified version of the EM algorithm [Brown & Della Pietra[+] 93] implemented in the GIZA++ alignment tool [Och & Ney 03]. The GIZA++ training yields the *Viterbi* alignment, i.e. the alignment for which the following equation holds:

$$\hat{A} = \underset{A}{\operatorname{argmax}}\{Pr(f_1^J, A|e_1^I)\} \tag{1.8}$$

1.3.1.3 Phrase pair extraction

The lexicon models in Equation 1.6 are called *single-word based* models because the lexicon probabilities are formulated for single words only. One major disadvantage of single-word based approaches to MT is that contextual information is not taken into account. The translation of a given word, however, depends heavily on the surrounding words. In the single-word based translation approach, this disambiguation is addressed by the language model only, which is often not capable of performing this task.

One way to incorporate context into the translation model is to learn translations for whole phrases. Here, a phrase is simply a sequence of words, without any other linguistic meaning. The basic idea of phrase-based translation is to segment a given source sentence into phrases, then translate each phrase and finally compose the target sentence from these phrase translations.

First an alignment between the words in the source and target sentence is found by training a chain of single-word based models such as IBM model 1, HMM, IBM model 4 (see Section 1.3.1.2). The training is performed in both directions (source-to-target and target-to-source). The two restricted Viterbi alignments obtained are combined using a heuristic [Och & Ney 03]. The resulting alignment generally allows for many-to-one, one-to-many or even many-to-many connections. Alternatively, a symmetric alignment can be computed directly [Matusov & Zens[+] 04]. Given an alignment, the extraction of phrase pairs

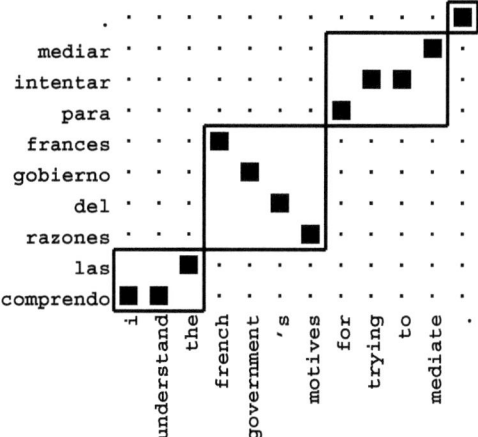

Figure 1.1: Example of alignment and selected phrase pairs extracted from a training sentence pair.

is carried out as in [Zens & Ney 04]. The phrase extraction criterion is identical to the alignment template criterion described in [Och & Tillmann⁺ 99]. Two phrases are considered to be translations of each other, if the words are aligned only within the phrase pair and not to words outside. Each phrase has to be contiguous. All possible phrase pairs fulfilling this criterion are extracted. An example of an alignment between two sentences and a possible subset of phrases that can be extracted using this alignment is shown in Figure 1.1.

1.3.1.4 Log-linear translation model

The argmax operation in Equation 1.1 denotes the search problem, i.e. the generation of the output sentence in the target language. We have to maximize over all possible target language sentences. An illustration of this process is given in Figure 1.2.

An alternative to the classical source-channel approach is the direct modeling of the posterior probability $Pr(e_1^I|f_1^J)$. Using a log-linear model [Och & Ney 02], we obtain:

$$Pr(e_1^I|f_1^J) = \exp\left(\sum_{m=1}^{M} \lambda_m h_m(e_1^I, f_1^J)\right) \cdot Z(f_1^J) \qquad (1.9)$$

Here, the terms $h_m(e_1^I, f_1^J)$ are the features of the model, and the values λ_m are their scaling factors. $Z(f_1^J)$ denotes the appropriate normalization constant. As a decision rule, we obtain:

$$\hat{e}_1^I = \underset{e_1^I}{\operatorname{argmax}}\, Pr(e_1^I|f_1^J) = \underset{e_1^I}{\operatorname{argmax}} \left\{ \sum_{m=1}^{M} \lambda_m h_m(e_1^I, f_1^J) \right\} \qquad (1.10)$$

1 Introduction

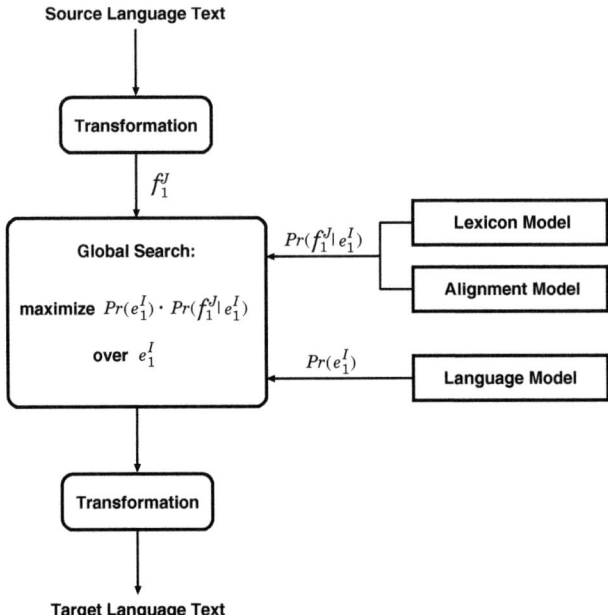

Figure 1.2: Architecture of the classical source-channel approach to statistical machine translation.

This approach is a generalization of the source-channel approach. It has the advantage that additional models or feature functions can be easily integrated into the overall system, including the phrase-based models. The model scaling factors λ_1^M can be trained according to the maximum entropy principle, e. g. using the GIS algorithm. Alternatively, one can train them with respect to the final translation quality measured by some error criterion [Och 03]. To this end, a development set is translated multiple times with different sets of scaling factors. The process is controlled by an optimization algorithm like the Powell's implementation of the Downhill Simplex algorithm [Press & Teukolsky[+] 02].

The architecture for machine translation using a phrase-based log-linear model is shown in Figure 1.3. In the following, we describe the basic models used as features $h_m(e_1^I, f_1^J)$ in Equation 1.10. These models are widely used by most phrase-based SMT systems and are: phrase translation model, single word based translation model, target language model, phrase distortion penalty model, as well as a word and phrase penalty.

1.3 Statistical machine translation

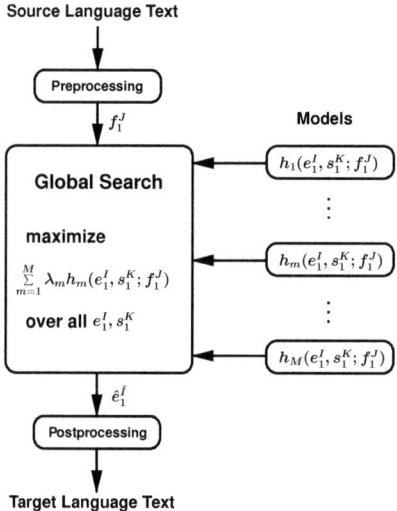

Figure 1.3: Illustration of Bayes architecture for machine translation with a phrase-based log-linear model.

Phrase-based model To use bilingual phrase pairs in the translation model, we define a segmentation of a given sentence pair (f_1^J, e_1^I) into K non-empty non-overlapping contiguous blocks:

$$k \quad \rightarrow \quad s_k := (i_k; b_k, j_k), \text{ for } k = 1 \ldots K. \tag{1.11}$$

Here, i_k denotes the last word position of the kth target phrase; we set $i_0 := 0$. The pair (b_k, j_k) denotes the start and end positions of the source phrase that is aligned to the kth target phrase; we set $j_0 := 0$. We constrain the segmentation so that all words in the source and the target sentence are covered by exactly one phrase (see Figure 1.4).

For a given sentence pair (f_1^J, e_1^I) and a segmentation s_1^K, we define the bilingual phrases as:

$$\tilde{e}_k := e_{i_{k-1}+1} \ldots e_{i_k} \tag{1.12}$$

$$\tilde{f}_k := f_{b_k} \ldots f_{j_k} \tag{1.13}$$

9

1 Introduction

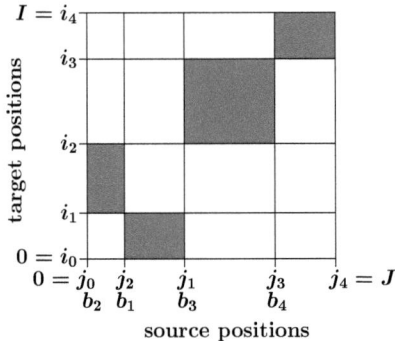

Figure 1.4: Illustration of a phrasal segmentation.

Note that the segmentation s_1^K contains the information on the phrase-level reordering. It is introduced as a hidden variable in the translation model. Therefore, it would be theoretically correct to sum over all possible segmentations. In practice, we use the maximum approximation for this sum. As a result, the models $h(\cdot)$ in Equation 1.10 depend not only on the sentence pair (f_1^J, e_1^I), but also on the segmentation s_1^K, i.e. we have models $h(f_1^J, e_1^I, s_1^K)$.

The phrase translation probabilities $p(\tilde{f}|\tilde{e})$ are estimated by relative frequencies:

$$p(\tilde{f}|\tilde{e}) = \frac{N(\tilde{f}, \tilde{e})}{N(\tilde{e})} \tag{1.14}$$

Here, $N(\tilde{f}, \tilde{e})$ is the number of co-occurrences of a phrase pair $(\tilde{f}, \tilde{e})$ in training. As in [Zens & Ney 04], we count all possible phrase pairs which are consistent with the word alignment. The marginal count $N(\tilde{e})$ in Equation 1.14 is the number of occurrences of the target phrase $\tilde{e}$ in the training corpus. The resulting feature function is:

$$h_{\text{Phr}}(f_1^J, e_1^I, s_1^K) = \log \prod_{k=1}^{K} p(\tilde{f}_k|\tilde{e}_k) \tag{1.15}$$

To obtain a more symmetric model, the inverse phrase-based model $p(\tilde{e}|\tilde{f})$ is also used. Its feature is denoted with $h_{\text{iPhr}}(f_1^J, e_1^I, s_1^K)$.

Word-based lexicon model Relative frequencies are used to estimate the phrase translation probabilities (Equation 1.14). Most of the longer phrases occur only once in the training corpus. Therefore, pure relative frequencies overestimate the probability of those phrases. To overcome this problem, word-based lexicon models are used to smooth the phrase translation probabilities.

1.3 Statistical machine translation

The score of a phrase pair is computed in a way similar to the IBM model 1 [Brown & Della Pietra+ 93], but here, the summation is carried out only within a phrase pair and not over the whole target language sentence:

$$h_{\text{Lex}}(f_1^J, e_1^I, s_1^K) = \log \prod_{k=1}^{K} \prod_{j=b_k}^{j_k} \sum_{i=i_{k-1}+1}^{i_k} p(f_j|e_i) \qquad (1.16)$$

The word translation probabilities $p(f|e)$ are estimated as relative frequencies from the word-aligned bilingual training corpus. The word-based lexicon model is also used in both directions $p(f|e)$ and $p(e|f)$. The expression $\sum_{i=i_{k-1}+1}^{i_k} p(f_j|e_i)$ can also be denoted by $p(f_j|\tilde{e}_k)$.

Word and phrase penalty Two simple heuristics, namely word penalty and phrase penalty are often used in statistical phrase-based MT:

$$h_{\text{WP}}(f_1^J, e_1^I, s_1^K) = I, \quad h_{\text{PP}}(f_1^J, e_1^I, s_1^K) = K \qquad (1.17)$$

In practice, these two models affect the average sentence and phrase lengths. The model scaling factors can be adjusted to prefer longer sentences and/or longer phrases.

Target language model A standard n-gram language model is an important feature of a statistical MT system. Its feature function is:

$$h_{\text{LM}}(f_1^J, e_1^I, s_1^K) = \log \prod_{i=1}^{I} p(e_i|e_{i-n+1}^{i-1}) \qquad (1.18)$$

The smoothing technique applied is in most cases the modified Kneser-Ney discounting with interpolation [Kneser & Ney 95].

Distortion penalty model The phrase reordering in translation can be scored using a simple *distortion penalty* model. This model assigns costs based on the distance from the end position of the previous phrase to the start position of the current phrase.

$$h_{\text{Dist}}(f_1^J, e_1^I, s_1^K) = \sum_{k=1}^{K+1} |j_{k-1} - b_k + 1| \qquad (1.19)$$

The sum in Equation 1.19 includes a jump to the position b_{K+1} which we define as the position "one after the sentence end", as well as the jump from the beginning of a source sentence denoted by j_0 to the start of the first translated phrase. In case of monotonic translation, the distortion penalty model assigns costs of zero. The more phrases are reordered and the bigger the "jump" distance is, the higher is the distortion penalty.

A more sophisticated lexicalized reordering model can be used in combination with the distortion penalty model to improve translation word order and quality [Zens & Ney 06].

1 Introduction

1.3.1.5 Search

As described in [Zens 08], the search for the best translation according to criterion 1.10 can be interpreted as a sequence of decisions $(\tilde{e}_k, b_k, j_k)$ for $k = 1, \ldots, K$. At each step the source phrase $\tilde{f}_k$ with its start and end positions (b_k, j_k) is translated by a target phrase $\tilde{e}_k$. To ensure the constraints of the phrase segmentation, i.e. that there is no overlap and all source words are covered, we have to keep track of the already translated (covered) source positions. To memorize these positions, we will use the *coverage* sets $C \subset \{1, \ldots, J\}$ for each partial translation hypothesis. The final translation of the whole source sentence is the concatenation of the phrases $\tilde{e}_k$ in the order they were generated.

To make a translation decision for each phrase, we employ two types of model costs. The first type does not have dependencies across phrase boundaries and can be computed for each phrase pair without context. Typically, these costs are computed as the weighted sum of the phrase-based and word-based translation models in both directions, as well as word and phrase penalty:

$$\begin{aligned}q_{TM}(\tilde{e}_k, b_k, j_k) &= \lambda_{\text{Phr}} \cdot \log p(\tilde{f}_k | \tilde{e}_k) + \lambda_{\text{iPhr}} \cdot \log p(\tilde{e}_k | \tilde{f}_k) \\ &+ \lambda_{\text{Lex}} \cdot \sum_{j=b_k}^{j_k} \log p(f_j | \tilde{e}_k) + \lambda_{\text{iLex}} \cdot \sum_{i=i_{k-1}+1}^{i_k} \log p(e_i | \tilde{f}_k) \\ &+ \lambda_{\text{WP}} \cdot (i_k - i_{k-1}) + \lambda_{\text{PP}} \end{aligned} \quad (1.20)$$

Two models described in Section 1.3.1.4 are not included in Equation 1.20, namely the language model and the distortion penalty model. Both of these models include dependencies on the previous phrase translation decisions. The language model history is required to compute the LM score of an expansion; the end position of the last phrase is required to compute the distortion model score. Therefore, separate auxiliary quantities for these two models are introduced:

$$q_{LM}(\tilde{e}|\tilde{e}') = \lambda_{\text{LM}} \cdot \sum_{i=1}^{|\tilde{e}|} \log p(\tilde{e}^i | \tilde{e}^{i-1}, \ldots, \tilde{e}^1, \tilde{e}') \quad (1.21)$$

Here, $\tilde{e}^i$ denotes the ith word of the phrase $\tilde{e}$, and $\tilde{e}'$ stands for the words of the previous phrase(s) which are considered in the case when i is smaller than the context length n of the n-gram language model.

A similar auxiliary function is defined for the distortion penalty model. The weighted score of a jump from source position j to source position j' is denoted with $q_{DM}(j, j')$:

$$q_{DM}(j, j') = \lambda_{\text{Dist}} \cdot |j - j' + 1| \quad (1.22)$$

The states in the search space are identified by a triple $(C, \tilde{e}, j)$, where C denotes the coverage set, $\tilde{e}$ denotes the language model history, and j denotes the end position of the last source

1.3 Statistical machine translation

phrase. The language model history $\tilde{e}$ consists typically of the last $(n-1)$ words of the target hypothesis. The LM history is usually not identical with the target phrase $\tilde{e}_k$ of the last decision $(\tilde{e}_k, b_k, j_k)$. It may be shorter if the phrase $\tilde{e}_k$ is longer than $n-1$ words. It may also include words from predecessor phrases $\tilde{e}_{k-1}, \tilde{e}_{k-2}, \ldots$ if $\tilde{e}_k$ is shorter than $n-1$ words.

The *hypothesis expansion* is performed by computing the successor states of a given state $(C, \tilde{e}, j)$. The score of such an expansion with a phrase pair $(\tilde{e}', j', j'')$ that covers the positions starting at j' and ending at j'' is calculated as:

$$q_{TM}(\tilde{e}', j', j'') + q_{LM}(\tilde{e}'|\tilde{e}) + q_{DM}(j, j') \qquad (1.23)$$

The successor state is $(C \cup \{j', \ldots, j''\}, \tilde{e} \oplus \tilde{e}', j'')$. The symbol $\oplus$ denotes concatenation of the two phrases. Of course, we have to ensure that there is no overlap, i.e. that $C \cap \{j', \ldots, j''\} = \emptyset$.

The search is performed using dynamic programming in combination with beam pruning [Zens 08]. The auxiliary quantity $Q(C, \tilde{e}, j)$ for dynamic programming is defined as the maximum score of a partial hypothesis leading from the initial state to the state $(C, \tilde{e}, j)$. The dynamic programming recursion equations are formulated as follows (L_s denotes the maximum phrase length in the source language):

$$Q(\emptyset, \$, 0) = 0 \qquad (1.24)$$

$$Q(C, \tilde{e}'', j'') = \max_{\substack{j, j' : j' \leq j'' < j' + L_s \wedge \{j', \ldots, j''\} \subseteq C \\ \tilde{e}, \tilde{e}' : \tilde{e} \oplus \tilde{e}' = \tilde{e}''}} \Big\{ Q(C \setminus \{j', \ldots, j''\}, \tilde{e}, j) + q_{TM}(\tilde{e}', j', j'')$$

$$+ q_{LM}(\tilde{e}'|\tilde{e}) + q_{DM}(j, j') \Big\} \qquad (1.25)$$

$$\hat{Q} = \max_{\tilde{e}, j} \Big\{ Q(\{1, \ldots, J\}, \tilde{e}, j) + q_{LM}(\$|\tilde{e}) + q_{DM}(j, J+1) \Big\} \qquad (1.26)$$

The recursion implies that the search graph should be traversed in topological order. Thus, before a hypothesis is expanded, we have to make sure that all predecessor nodes have been covered. The number of covered source positions of a partial hypothesis is called its *cardinality* c. The topological order of processing can be ensured if the nodes are processed according to their source cardinality. Therefore this processing scheme is also called *source cardinality-synchronous search (SCSS)*.

There are multiple ways to implement a solution to the dynamic programming equations 1.24 through 1.26. The pseudo-code for the non-monotonic search algorithm presented in Figure 1.5 is one such solution, first described in [Zens 08]. Let $E(j', j'')$ denote the set of possible phrase translations of the source phrase $\tilde{f} = f_{j'}, \ldots, f_{j''}$. The input is the source sentence f_1^J, the translation options $E(j', j'')$ for all source phrases, with $1 \leq j' \leq j'' \leq J$. The auxiliary quantity $Q(C, \tilde{e}, j)$ has the same meaning as in the dynamic programming recursion, i.e. the maximum score of a partial translation with coverage C, language model history $\tilde{e}$ and end

13

1 Introduction

> INPUT: source sentence f_1^J, translation options $E(j', j'')$ for $1 \leq j' \leq j'' \leq J$,
> models $q_{TM}(\cdot)$, $q_{LM}(\cdot)$ and $q_{DM}(\cdot)$
>
> 0 $Q(\emptyset, \$, 0) = 0$; all other $Q(\cdot, \cdot, \cdot)$ entries are initialized to $-\infty$
> 1   FOR cardinality $c = 1$ TO J DO
> 2   FOR source phrase length $l = 1$ TO $\min\{L_s, c\}$ DO
> 3   FOR ALL coverages $C \subset \{1, ..., J\} : |C| = c - l$ DO
> 4   FOR ALL start positions $j' \in \{1, ..., J\} : C \cap \{j', ..., j'+l\} = \emptyset$ DO
> 5   coverage $C' = C \cup \{j', ..., j'+l\}$
> 6   FOR ALL states $\tilde{e}, j \in Q(C, \cdot, \cdot)$ DO
> 7   FOR ALL phrase translations $\tilde{e}' \in E(j', j'+l)$ DO
> 8   score $= Q(C, \tilde{e}, j) + q_{TM}(\tilde{e}', j', j'+l) + q_{LM}(\tilde{e}'|\tilde{e}) + q_{DM}(j, j')$
> 9   language model state $\tilde{e}'' = \tilde{e} \oplus \tilde{e}'$
> 10   IF score $> Q(C', \tilde{e}'', j'+l)$
> 11   THEN $Q(C', \tilde{e}'', j'+l) =$ score
> 12 $B(C', \tilde{e}'', j'+l) = (C, \tilde{e}, j)$
> 13 $A(C', \tilde{e}'', j'+l) = \tilde{e}'$

Figure 1.5: Non-monotonic search algorithm from [Zens 08] for text input (without pruning).

position of the last source phrase j. In addition, we store backpointers $B(\cdot)$ to the previous best decision as well as the maximizing arguments $A(\cdot)$, i.e. the best target phrases. For each cardinality c, there is a loop over all possible source phrase lengths l. Then, there is a loop over the possible predecessor coverages C with cardinality $c-l$. The next loop goes over all possible start positions j', thus effectively we select a source phrase $\tilde{f} = f_{j'}, ..., f_{j'+l}$. The "no overlap" constraint is checked in line 4. The coverage after the expansion is $C' = C \cup \{j', ..., j'+l\}$. Then, there is a loop over all existing predecessor states $\tilde{e}, j$ and all translation options $\tilde{e}' \in E(j', j'+l)$ in lines 6 and 7. Eventually, the score of the expansion is computed in line 8. If this score is better than the existing one, we update the auxiliary quantity Q as well as the backpointer and the pointer to the maximizing argument.

Phrase pairs $(\tilde{f}, \tilde{e})$ are usually used multiple times in line 8. To avoid repeated computations, the set of possible translations $E(j', j'')$ is generated for each phrase in the source sentence before the search along with their phrase model scores $q_{TM}(\tilde{e}', j', j'')$.

Further details of the search implementation, including the various pruning strategies and

1.3 Statistical machine translation

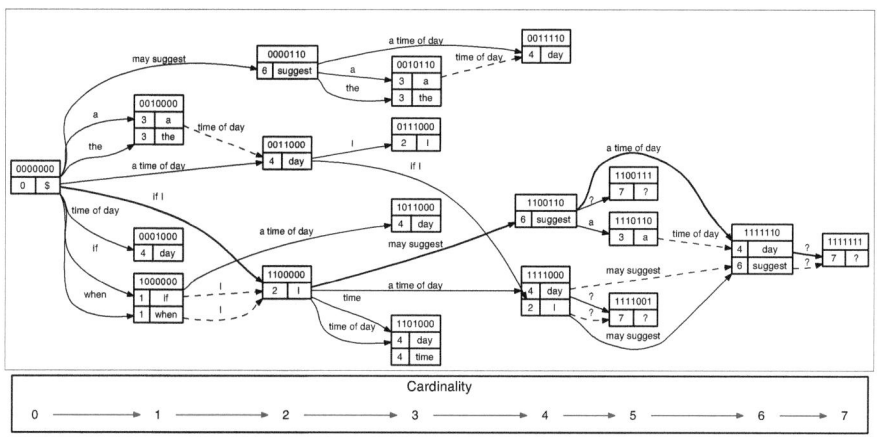

Figure 1.6: Illustration of the search (from [Zens 08]). German input sentence: 'Wenn ich eine Uhrzeit vorschlagen darf?'. English translation: 'If I may suggest a time of day?'. In each node, we store the coverage (here as bitvector), the end position of the current phrase and the language model history (here: bigram). Dashed edges are recombined. Best path is shown in bold. Scores are omitted.

reordering constraints, are described in [Zens 08]. Here, we conclude the description of the search with the illustration of the search graph that can be constructed by the algorithm in Figure 1.5. This graph is generated from left to right, i.e. with increasing cardinality, as illustrated in Figure 1.6. Each node contains hypotheses with the same covered source positions, but different translations of these positions (the so called *lexical hypotheses*). The coverage is represented using bitvectors. Each lexical hypothesis is identified by the end position of the current phrase in the left part of the node and the language model state in the right part of the node. The edges are labeled with the target phrases. Dashed edges indicate recombination. Each lexical hypothesis, except for the root node, has exactly one non-dashed inbound edge, which connects it with the previously best partial hypothesis. This edge is used as a backpointer $B(\cdot)$ and the label is the maximizing argument $A(\cdot)$. Pruning is applied for each cardinality. The pruned nodes are not expanded and, thus, do not have outbound edges. In addition, we can prune the lexical hypotheses by limiting their maximum number in each node of the search graph.

The models described in this section, and in particular the search algorithm based on Equations 1.24 through 1.26 will be used for most MT experiments in this thesis. In addition,

15

1 Introduction

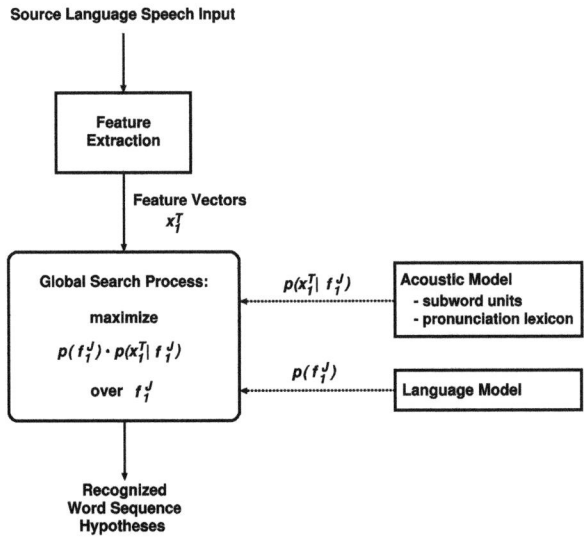

Figure 1.7: Speech recognition architecture.

in Chapter 4 the algorithm in Figure 1.5 will be extended to process not only a single source sentence, but also multiple speech recognition hypotheses for an utterance represented in word lattices.

1.3.2 Statistical machine translation of speech

1.3.2.1 System architecture

A statistical MT system for translation of text can be also used for translation of spoken language. Usually, it is implied that a spoken language utterance is first automatically transcribed using a speech recognition system. Then, the transcribed word sequence is translated by the MT system as if it were a normal sentence.

The majority of the state-of-the-art speech recognition systems follow a statistical approach to speech recognition. This approach is based on the following decision rule:

$$\hat{f}_1^{\hat{J}} = \underset{f_1^J}{\operatorname{argmax}} \left\{ Pr(x_1^T | f_1^J) \cdot Pr(f_1^J) \right\} \tag{1.27}$$

The search is performed over all possible source word hypotheses for a spoken utterance f_1^J. The decision is made based on the conditional probability $Pr(x_1^T|f_1^J)$ for the sequence of acoustic observations x_1^T that represent the speech signal and a prior probability for the word sequence $Pr(f_1^J)$ that is used to ensure the well-formedness of the recognized utterance. The architecture of a statistical speech recognition system is depicted in Figure 1.7.

A speech recognition system can make a number of errors due to many reasons, which can include e. g. adverse acoustic conditions or undertrained models. The translation model can serve as an additional knowledge source which can help to avoid some of these errors. By considering multiple speech recognition hypotheses in the translation process, the decision on the best transcription of the spoken utterance can be deferred until the end of the MT search and can be modeled jointly using speech recognition and translation models. Thus, an improvement in translation quality in comparison with the translation of the single best recognizer output is to be expected.

An example of a case where an MT system can help to disambiguate between several ASR hypotheses is when a word in an established phrase is misrecognized in the first-best ASR output as some other frequent (and thus probable) word, but which completely changes the meaning of the phrase. If the correct phrase has a good and probable translation, the MT system may be able to choose another ASR hypothesis for the phrase without the error.

A possible general speech translation system architecture is shown in Figure 1.8. The speech recognition system provides automatic transcriptions for a speech utterance. First, this utterance has to be automatically divided into sentences or sentence-like units (SUs). It can be also enriched with automatically predicted punctuation marks such as commas. Ideally, the automatic sentence segmentation and punctuation prediction methods should be developed with the goal of improving the quality of the final system output, i. e. MT quality. At the same time, the acoustic/prosodic features provided by the ASR system (e. g. pause duration) should also be included. In Chapter 5, we propose an automatic sentence segmentation algorithm that fulfills these criteria. We also investigate which punctuation prediction strategies are most suitable for optimal performance of the MT system.

After the sentence-like units have been determined, the ASR hypotheses for these units are fed into the machine translation system. The following representations of multiple recognizer hypotheses for a single speech utterance can be considered:

1 Introduction

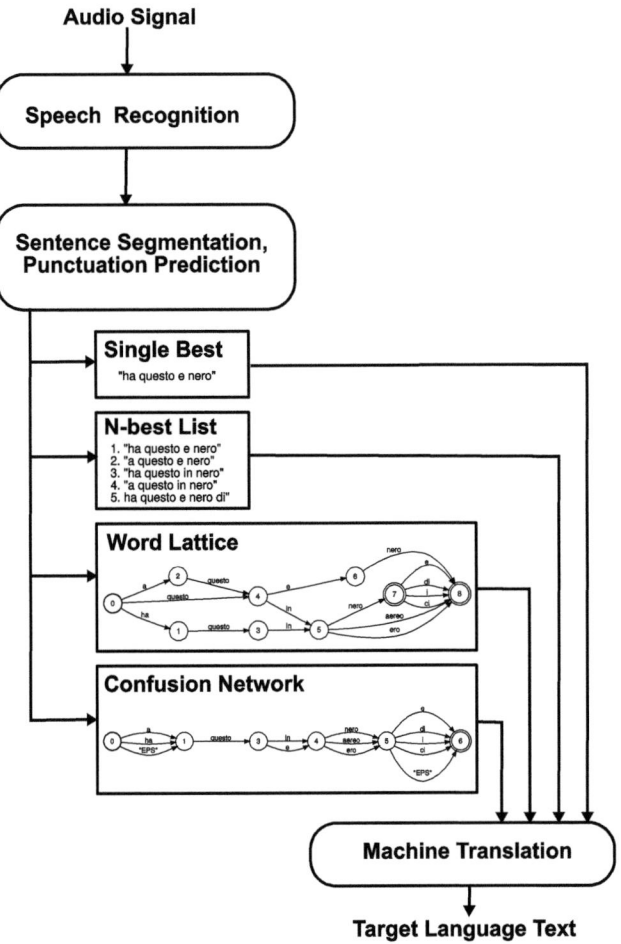

Figure 1.8: General speech translation architecture.

Single best automatic transcript: The translation of the single best ASR hypothesis of each SU is the most simple case of automatic speech translation. The advantage of this approach is that there is no additional computational overhead involved. Also, some MT algorithms such as e. g. sophisticated reordering methods may have some properties which only allow their application to a single input sequence. The obvious disadvantage of this approach is that

1.3 Statistical machine translation

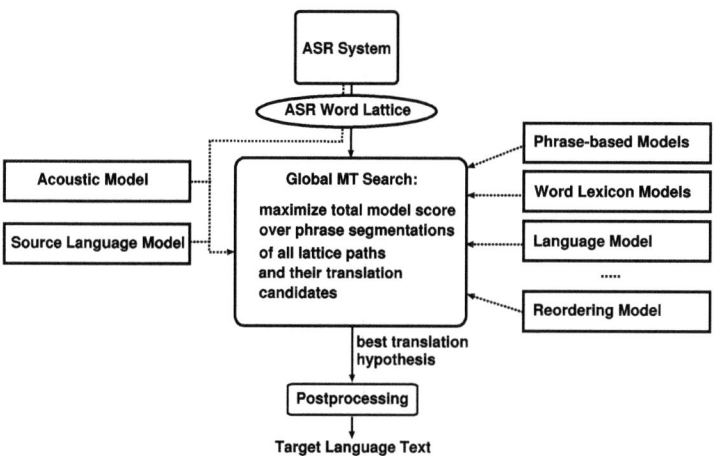

Figure 1.9: Machine translation architecture for translation of ASR word lattices.

the hard decisions made by the ASR system can not be corrected anymore in the translation process.

N-best lists: Instead of the single best ASR output, the list of N ASR hypotheses with the best scores can be used to couple speech recognition and machine translation (see Figure 1.8). Each hypothesis can be translated by the MT system, and the best translation can be selected based on the combination of the translation model score and the ASR score for the whole sentence. This approach has the advantage that (similar to the translation of single best ASR output), no modifications to the involved MT algorithms have to be made. However, the approach is not efficient. The size of the N-best list usually has to be large (e.g. 1000) to include those hypotheses which have significantly lower word error rate than the single best ASR output. Most of these hypotheses are different from each other in 1 or 2 words. Thus, the translation process is often redundant, since the same word sequences have to be translated over and over again. In order to avoid the translation being e.g. $N = 1000$ times slower, the size N is usually chosen to be smaller, e.g. 100 [Bozarov & Sagisaka+ 05]. With such small N-best lists, significant improvements of translation quality can hardly be expected. For these reasons, this work leaves the translation of ASR N-best lists out of its scope and concentrates on translation of word lattices.

1 Introduction

Word lattices: An ASR word lattice is a data structure used to represent a subspace of the search network in speech recognition.

Formally, a lattice $L = (V, E, \Sigma)$ is a directed acyclic graph, where V is a set of nodes (or states) and E is a set of edges (or arcs). Each edge connects two nodes (tail node and head node) and is annotated with a symbol from a finite alphabet Σ or the empty word ε. Each edge is also assigned a weight such that the edges form a semiring. Exactly one node has no incoming edges and is designated as a start node. The lattice must also have a non-empty set of *final* nodes with no outgoing edges. A lattice L is equivalent to a weighted acyclic finite-state automaton (see Section 4.3.3 for details on the finite-state search implementation and semirings). Thus, a word lattice is guaranteed to describe a finite set of strings. The number of such strings encoded in a lattice is exponential in the number of nodes, and the base of the exponent is dependent on the number of edges.

In speech recognition, the finite alphabet Σ is the set of words which form the vocabulary of the ASR system. Thus, each lattice arc encodes a word hypothesis. The weight of such a hypothesis is its ASR word posterior probability (see Chapter 4 for details). It can be decomposed into the acoustic model probability and the language model probability. In practice, the negative logarithms of these probabilities are used, referred to as acoustic and language model scores.

A possible architecture of a machine translation system that can process ASR word lattices is shown in Figure 1.9. Here, a log-linear model is used that combines both the translation model features (e. g. the ones described in Section 1.3.1.4) and the speech recognition features. This model is presented in detail in Chapter 4. In the search, phrase extraction is performed efficiently from the multitude of existing lattice subpaths. For each subpath with a phrasal translation, the acoustic and source LM scores saved in the arcs of the subpaths are combined with the translation model features for the phrase pair. Given all possible phrase segmentations and their translation candidates, the best translation hypothesis is determined using also the target LM scores and possibly a distortion model. For all features involved, appropriate scaling factors are included.

For this type of MT search, the representation of multiple recognizer hypotheses in word lattices has a number of advantages in comparison with the other representation forms:

- The lattices provide an efficient way of exploring the ASR search space in translation. Partial hypotheses can be built and the hypotheses with a low total score can be discarded early in the MT search using pruning techniques.
- The lattice representation allows the MT system to explore a much larger number of alternative word hypotheses than the N-best representation. For instance, the average

lattice density (i.e. the average number of word alternatives at each source sentence position) often exceeds 50 for the experiments in this thesis. At the same time, the lattice-based system is usually only 3-10 times slower than the system translating single best ASR output.

- The ASR word lattices represent a portion of the true ASR search space. Thus, no approximations are made. Such approximations have to be accepted in the case of e.g. confusion networks, as mentioned below.

A drawback of the lattice-based translation is that the existing algorithms for translation of text have to be modified in order to efficiently cope with the ambiguous input. A special challenge is the reordering, which, if not constrained, has exponential complexity even when only a single sentence is considered. A large part of this thesis is dedicated to the algorithmic advances which allow for robust and efficient processing of ASR word lattices.

Confusion networks: A confusion network (CN) is a special case of a word lattice with the property that every path from its start to its single final node goes through all other nodes (see an example in Figure 1.8). A confusion network preserves the linear structure of a sentence, but may have multiple edges between adjacent nodes, thereby encoding a multitude of paths. Since an edge may be labeled with the empty word ε, the word sequences encoded may be of different length.

A confusion network can be obtained from an ASR word lattice through merging of nodes and introduction of ε-arcs. Usually, this is done using the information on the beginning and end time of a word hypothesis. The hypotheses with the same or overlapping times are put into a *slot* between two adjacent nodes. The details of this procedure are described in e.g. [Mangu & Brill+ 00]. Note that the transformation of a word lattice into a confusion network is an approximation that introduces extra paths into the lattice which have not been part of the original search space.

The advantage of using CNs for translation is based on their linear structure. Given the well-defined CN slots, it is possible to efficiently perform phrase extraction and reordering from the CN subpaths corresponding to a sequence of the slots. However, as we will show in Chapter 4, it is possible to utilize the slot information also for translation of the original ASR word lattices. A possible disadvantage of the CN representation are the extra hypotheses introduced in the process of its construction. These may be both good-quality and very much erroneous hypotheses. The MT system may not be powerful enough to differentiate between them. Also, since word hypotheses from different lattice edges are merged in the process of the CN construction, the original acoustic and source LM scores can not be used anymore, but a word posterior probability is computed [Bertoldi & Zens⁺ 07]. This may be suboptimal for machine translation, where it may be of advantage to keep the acoustic and source LM scores separate and use scaling factors for them which are optimal for MT quality and possibly different from the scaling factors used in the ASR search.

The details of the proposed models and algorithms for translation of word lattices and confusion networks are described in Chapter 4.

Fully integrated translation: A fully integrated speech translation approach has been proposed and evaluated in [Matusov & Kanthak⁺ 05b]. In that work, both speech recognition and machine translation models were implemented using weighted finite-state transducers (WFSTs). The search space of speech recognition and machine translation was represented in a single finite-state search network. Building the network follows the description of [Mohri & Pereira⁺ 00] where the ASR language model was substituted by the translation model. The fully integrated system has shown a significant improvement in terms of MT error measures over the translation of single best ASR output. However, the translation of ASR word lattices resulted in translation quality improvements of the same range, since high-density word lattices provide a good approximation of the full ASR search space. On the other hand, using WFSTs for speech recognition requires a careful and non-trivial optimization of the search network on state-level, especially if it has to be applied to large vocabulary tasks. Thus, the implementation overhead with regard to the ASR system is substantial. Here, we focus on improvements and changes to the MT system to process word lattices or confusion networks; the topic of preparing an ASR system for the task of fully integrated speech translation is beyond the scope of this work.

1.4 Related work on speech translation

In this section, the related work on speech translation will be reviewed. We will concentrate on the related research in the area of tighter coupling of ASR and MT. The related work on sentence segmentation and punctuation prediction, as well as on MT system combination will be reviewed in chapters 5 and 6, respectively.

Speech translation has been a popular research topic in the recent years. Several authors have presented statistical word-based and phrase-based translation models, the structure of which was motivated by the structure of an n-gram language model in speech recognition. Therefore, they could be most conveniently applied to the output of an ASR system, either to the single best ASR output or to ambiguous output in the form of word lattices.

1.4 Related work on speech translation

A simple word-based translation system that implemented the IBM translation models [Brown & Cocke[+] 90] has been applied to translation of single best ASR output within the German Verbmobil project [Nießen & Vogel[+] 98]. This system was already competitive with the rule-based MT systems on this task, and its phrase-based extension outperformed them significantly [Vogel & Och[+] 00].

In the following research, more sophisticated translation models which include context dependency (e.g. in the form of bilingual phrase pairs) have been applied to translation of speech. An implementation of a joint probability translation model with WFSTs was proposed by [Vidal 97]. In this model, the translation units are tuples of the form (single source word, target word sequence), and the context-dependent translation model is a WFST representation of an m-gram language model trained on the sequences of tuples. These sequences are obtained by transforming each pair of sentences in the parallel bilingual training corpus based on word alignment. A similar model with a different definition of bilingual tuples has been proposed and used for single best ASR output translation by [Bangalore & Riccardi 00b], as well as by [de Gispert & Mariño 02]. At RWTH, a joint probability model based on the one presented by [Vidal 97] had been implemented by Stephan Kanthak [Kanthak & Ney 04] using his FSA WFST toolkit. This model was then further improved by the author of this thesis, as it will be described in Chapter 4.

A better choice for high-quality MT is usually a phrase-based log-linear translation model that combines word-based and phrase-based translation features, as well as the target language model and possibly a reordering model. This model has been described in Section 1.3.1.4 for text translation. It can be modified to take into account the ambiguity of speech recognition. A WFST implementation of such a model is possible with cascaded transducers, where each WFST represents a certain model (e.g. phrase segmentation, phrase translation, language model and reordering transducers). This type of a MT system is described most thoroughly in [Kumar & Byrne 03]; it was successfully applied to word lattice translation by e.g. [Mathias & Byrne 06], [Shen & Delaney[+] 08], and [Zhou & Besacier[+] 07].

A phrase-based log-linear model for speech translation can be also implemented using a dedicated dynamic programming algorithm. In [Bertoldi 05], this model was implemented using multi-stack decoding and applied to confusion networks. Another phrase-based open-source MT decoder MOSES was developed at the 2006 summer workshop at Johns Hopkins University [Koehn & Hoang[+] 07]. It also uses a log-linear model and is able to process ambiguous ASR output in the form of confusion networks. Since the appearance of this decoder, it has been used by several research groups for speech translation [Besacier & Mahdhaoui[+] 07, Shen & Delaney[+] 07].

1 Introduction

The attempts to improve speech translation quality through coupling ASR and MT were first made in the late nineties. In 1997, [Vidal 97] presented an integrated speech translation system for tasks from the Eutrans project. However, the experimental results were inconsistent as the integrated speech translation performed much worse than the serial approach on real-world data. [Ney 99] presented the theory of integrated speech translation, but lacked experimental results. The WFST-based system of [Bangalore & Riccardi 00b] was only applied to the single best recognizer output.

The most elegant and theoretically well-grounded way of coupling ASR and MT is to use word lattices which represent a large portion of the true ASR search space. First improvements on real-word data due to the consideration of alternative ASR recognition hypotheses in the form of word lattices were obtained by [Saleem & Jou$^+$ 04]. However, [Saleem & Jou$^+$ 04] concluded that improvements from tighter coupling may only be observed when lattices are sparse, i. e. when there are only few hypothesized words per spoken word in the lattice. This is inconsistent with the theory of [Ney 99] and would mean that integrated speech translation would not work at all.

A number of research publications also very tightly restrict the ambiguity of the ASR output by using N-best hypotheses (with e. g. $N = 100$). Moderate improvements with this approach were reported by e. g. [Bozarov & Sagisaka$^+$ 05] and [Utiyama & Finch$^+$ 08]. However, many authors [Saleem & Jou$^+$ 04, Bertoldi & Zens$^+$ 07] comment that N-best list translation is redundant, inefficient, and does not have the potential for significant improvements of translation quality.

As already mentioned, recent research has shown that a more tighter coupling of ASR and MT can be reached when ASR word lattices or confusion networks are translated. The translation quality can be improved if the recognition model scores and the translation model scores are combined with optimal scaling factors. A theoretical basis for the score combination was given in [Ney 99]. As recognition features, either the acoustic and source language model scores [Matusov & Ney$^+$ 05, Shen & Delaney$^+$ 07], or the word posterior probability [Alabau & Sancis 07, Bertoldi & Zens$^+$ 07] were used. The best effect is reached when the recognition features are included directly in the search, and their scaling factors are optimized jointly with the translation model scaling factors on a held-out tuning set with the goal of improving an automatic MT error measure.

At RWTH Aachen, we have developed two state-of-the-art speech translation systems which can take ASR word lattices as input. The first system implements a joint probability approach to speech translation using weighted finite-state transducers [Matusov & Kanthak$^+$ 05b]. With this system, we were able to show consistent and significant improvements in translation quality on three different tasks using lattices of high density with acoustic model scores. The translation system of [Matusov & Kanthak+ 05b] evaluated translation hypotheses with a single score; it was stressed that the optimization of a scaling factor for this score is crucial for good performance when it is combined with the acoustic model scores of the lattice hypotheses.

A more sophisticated system that combines multiple translation features was developed and presented in [Matusov & Ney+ 05]. In this approach, translation models, e.g. phrase-based and single word based lexica or the target language model, as well as features from speech recognition can be directly integrated into the decoding process. The optimization of scaling factors for the features is performed with respect to an objective error measure in a minimum error training framework. An improvement of this approach that allows for more exhaustive phrase-level reordering was presented in [Matusov & Hoffmeister+ 08]. In this thesis, the two models will be described in detail and compared experimentally in Chapter 4.

The word and phrase-level reordering that has to be applied in the translation process can not be applied directly to lattice input for efficiency reasons. A word lattice can contain an exponential number of alternative speech recognition paths for an utterance, and the distance-based reordering of each of those paths also has exponential complexity. Therefore, most of the previous work either translated word lattices monotonically [Casacuberta & Llorens+ 01], or applied reordering to the single best MT hypotheses in a postprocessing step [Bangalore & Riccardi 00a]. More recent implementations included a very limited word or phrase reordering, e.g. by allowing the search algorithm to skip one word or phrase and translate it at a later stage [Zens & Bender+ 05]. In the case of WFST implementations, such reordering is realized with a special reordering transducer [Mathias & Byrne 06, Saon & Picheny 07].

In order to solve the reordering problem, translation of confusion networks has been proposed [Bertoldi & Zens+ 07]. In a confusion network, the recognized word hypotheses are aligned to specific positions, or slots. At each slot, there are several word alternatives, including the empty word. The structure of a CN allows for an MT search that is similar to the established search for text input. Thus, even long-range reordering becomes possible. Significant improvements due to confusion network translation with the MOSES decoder were reported on a small vocabulary Arabic-to-English translation task by [Besacier & Mahdhaoui+ 07]. In [Shen & Delaney+ 07], the performance of the MOSES decoder on the ASR confusion networks is compared to the quality of a FST-based lattice decoder (using only local phrase-level reordering) on three different tasks. However, in contrast to similar experiments presented in this thesis, each decoder used different translation models and had different reordering capabilities so that it is hard to conclude, which representation

1 Introduction

of multiple ASR hypotheses has more advantages.

With a clear definition of word positions, or slots, in a general word lattice, coverage vectors for MT search can be defined in terms of these slots. This enables cardinality-synchronous search and other, more sophisticated types of decoding e.g. using hierarchical phrases (CYK-style search), as mentioned in [Dyer & Muresan[+] 08]. Both [Dyer & Muresan[+] 08] and [Saon & Picheny 07] show that by using coverage vectors defined in terms of topologically ordered lattice states it is possible to perform even long-range reordering using the original ASR lattices as input. Independent of that research, [Matusov & Hoffmeister[+] 08] presented an approach that makes use of CN slots to define spans for original word lattices and translate them with exhaustive phrase-level reordering. Chapter 4 will present the details of this algorithm.

Improving of the interface between speech recognition and machine translation is not limited to the translation of multiple ASR hypotheses, but also may involve automatic methods for sentence segmentation (as e.g. in [Fügen & Kolss 07]) and punctuation mark prediction [Lee & Roukos[+] 06]. In [Cattoni & Bertoldi[+] 07], confusion networks are used to encode optional punctuation marks together with multiple ASR hypotheses. A detailed overview of the related work on sentence segmentation and punctuation prediction will be given in Chapter 5.

Finally, in [Matusov & Ueffing[+] 06] it was shown that an improvement in speech translation quality can be larger than the one obtained through word lattice translation. This is possible if the output of MT systems translating either single best or word lattice input is combined using a confusion-network-based word-level MT system combination method. The details of this experiment will be described in Chapter 6. This chapter also includes a thorough review of the related work on system combination for machine translation of speech and text.

2 Scientific goals

Improving interfaces between NLP systems involved in speech translation

The overall goal of this thesis is to improve speech translation quality by enhancing the interface between various NLP systems involved in the task of speech translation. The whole pipeline is considered: automatic speech recognition, sentence segmentation, prediction of punctuation marks, machine translation with several systems taking either single best or multiple ASR hypotheses as input and employing different translation models, combination of the output of different translation systems. The coupling between the various components is reached through combination of model scores and/or hypotheses, development of new and modifications of existing algorithms to handle ambiguous input or to meet the constraints of the downstream components, as well as through optimization of model parameters with the aim of improving the final translation quality.

Improving MT quality by using multiple ASR hypotheses in the search

One of the main goals of this thesis was to modify existing statistical MT algorithms to benefit from processing multiple ASR hypotheses in the form of word lattices or confusion networks. It was important to investigate under what conditions the translation quality can be improved by avoiding a hard decision in the ASR system and choosing the path in the lattice with the most likely translation according to the combination of acoustic, source LM, and translation probabilities.

Extension of the non-monotonic translation search to work on ASR word lattices

One of the advantages of the state-of-the art phrase-based MT algorithms is the ability to perform reordering on word and phrase level. When the input source sentence is replaced by a lattice with multiple ASR hypotheses, the challenge is to apply the same type of reordering to the paths of the lattice without dramatically increasing search complexity. The novel algorithm developed to meet this challenge makes use of confusion network slot information to organize the search, but at the same time works with the original ASR lattices and ASR scores of the word hypotheses in them.

Comparison and combination of phrase-based and tuple-based translation models

The two translation models which are often used to translate ASR word lattices are either the joint probability tuple-based context-dependent translation model, or a phrase-based log-linear translation model. The first model has advantages from the implementation point of view because it can simply act as a language model in the rescoring of ASR lattices using weighted finite-state transducer tools. The phrase-based log-linear model allows for a more effective combination of ASR and MT features and includes better ways of modeling reordering. The goal was to propose a more consistent training of a tuple-based model than previously presented in the literature, and then to analyze the performance of the improved model in direct comparison with the phrase-based model. Finally, the aim was to combine the two models in the phrase-based search.

Development of algorithms for accurate sentence segmentation and punctuation prediction in the context of speech translation

Most speech translation systems are trained to translate sentence-like units and expected to produce translations with proper punctuation marks. However, the automatically recognized utterances are usually transcriptions of whole speeches and have to be automatically divided into sentence-like units. The existing methods for sentence segmentation were developed independently of any subsequent application like machine translation. The goal was to develop a sentence segmentation algorithm that would explicitly include MT requirements, such as minimum and maximum sentence length constraints. This algorithm makes decisions based on combination of prosodic and lexical features and includes an explicit sentence length model. Another goal was to investigate what automatic punctuation prediction strategy works best in terms of MT quality.

Effective combination of multiple MT systems

Different MT systems tend to make different errors. The goal was to significantly improve translation quality of both speech and text by combining the output of multiple translation systems. To this end, an algorithm was to be developed that combines system outputs on the word level using statistical alignment, and computes a consensus translation based on system weights and language model information. This translation is expected to contain words and phrases on which several systems agree and which therefore have a high chance of being correct. In the application of speech translation, the goal was to combine MT systems which translate only the single best ASR output and those systems which can translate word lattices.

Enabling segment-wise automatic evaluation of speech translation

Automatic speech recognition systems usually produce transcriptions of utterances which are not segmented into sentences. Yet the state-of-the-art evaluation of speech translation is performed on sentence level. Automatic sentence segmentation methods have to be applied, and they may segment the transcripts differently than the manual segmentation used for the evaluation. To enable evaluation on the sentence level, the translation output has to be re-segmented to match the reference translation sentence units. The goal was to solve this problem by developing an efficient algorithm for re-segmentation which is based on the edit distance but takes multiple reference translations into account.

3 Automatic evaluation of speech translation

3.1 Introduction

Evaluation of the produced results is important for machine translation in general and in particular for speech translation. Human evaluation of MT system output is a time consuming and expensive task. This is why automatic evaluation is preferred to human evaluation in the research community. A variety of automatic evaluation measures have been proposed and studied over the last years. All of the wide-spread evaluation measures like BLEU [Papineni & Roukos+ 02], TER [Snover & Dorr+ 06], and word error rate compare translation hypotheses with (multiple) human reference translations. Since a human translator usually translates one sentence of a source language text at a time, all of these measures include the concept of sentences or more generally, segments. Each evaluation algorithm expects that a machine translation system will produce exactly one target language segment for each source language segment. Thus, the total number of segments in the automatically translated document must be equal to the number of reference segments in the manually translated document.

In case of speech translation, the concept of sentences is in general not well-defined. A speaker may leave a sentence incomplete, make long pauses, or speak for a long time without making a pause. A human transcriber of speech is usually able to subjectively segment the raw transcriptions into sentence-like units (SUs). In addition, if he or she was instructed to produce meaningful units, each of which has clear semantics, then these sentence-like units can be properly translated into sentence-like units in the target language.

However, an automatic speech translation system is expected to translate automatically recognized utterances. In some of the past speech translation evaluations, an automatic speech recognition (ASR) system was forced to generate segment boundaries in the timeframes which had been defined by a human transcriber. This restriction implied that a manual transcription and segmentation of the test speech utterances had to be performed in advance. A drawback of this type of evaluation is that it does not reflect real-life conditions. In an on-line speech translation system, the correct utterance transcription is unknown to the ASR component, and segmentation is done automatically based on prosodic or language model features. This automatic segmentation should define the initial sentence-like units for translation.

In recent years, automatic SU detection was successfully used in large-scale speech translation evaluations within the international research projects TC-STAR [TC-STAR 07] and GALE [GALE 07]. One possible method for automatic sentence segmentation will be presented in Chapter 5.

A given automatic segmentation of ASR output may be partially erroneous. Therefore, the segment boundaries in the produced translations of these SUs may not correspond to the segment boundaries in the manual reference translations. As we will show in Section 3.2, most of the existing MT error measures will not be applicable for evaluation under these conditions.

In this chapter we propose a solution to the problem. In Section 3.3 we describe an algorithm that is able to find an optimal re-segmentation of the MT output based on the segmentation of the human reference translations. The algorithm is based on the Levenshtein edit distance algorithm [Levenshtein 66], but is extended to take into account multiple human reference translations for each segment. As a result of this re-segmentation we obtain a novel evaluation measure – *automatic segmentation word error rate* (AS-WER, [Matusov & Leusch[+] 05]).

In Section 3.4 we will show how the new algorithm can be used as a starting point for computing the established automatic error measures. We will compare the error rates calculated based on automatic segmentation with the error rates calculated based on human segmentation and show that the new evaluation measures give accurate estimates of translation quality for different tasks and systems. We will also briefly describe how the algorithm can be utilized for an effective human evaluation of MT output in the context of post-editing.

3.2 Evaluation measures

Here, we shortly describe the most popular MT evaluation measures and analyze their suitability for evaluation of translation output with possibly incorrect segment boundaries. The measures that are widely used in research and evaluation campaigns are WER, PER, BLEU, TER, and NIST.

Let a test document consist of $k = 1, \ldots, K$ candidate segments E_k generated by an MT system. We also assume that we have R reference translation documents. Each reference document has the same number of segments. Each segment is a translation of the "correct" segmentation of the manually transcribed speech input. If the segmentation of the MT output corresponds to the segmentation of the manual reference translations, then for each candidate segment E_k, we have R reference sentences[a] $\tilde{E}_{rk}$, $r = 1, \ldots, R$. Let I_k denote the length of a candidate segment E_k, and N_{rk} the reference lengths of each reference segment $\tilde{E}_{rk}$. From the reference lengths, an optimal reference segment length N_k^* is selected as the length of the reference with the lowest segment-level error rate or best score [Leusch & Ueffing[+] 05].

With this, we write the total candidate length over the document as $I := \sum_k I_k$, and the total reference length as $N^* := \sum_k N_k^*$.

3.2.1 WER

The segment-level word error rate is defined as the Levenshtein distance $d_L(E_k, \tilde{E}_{rk})$ between a candidate segment E_k and a reference segment $\tilde{E}_{rk}$, divided by the reference length N_k^* for normalization.

For a whole candidate corpus with multiple references, the segment-level scores are summed, and the WER is defined to be:

$$\text{WER} := \frac{1}{N^*} \sum_k \min_r d_L\left(E_k, \tilde{E}_{rk}\right) \tag{3.1}$$

It is also possible to evaluate MT output *at document level*. When evaluating at document level, we consider the whole candidate document and the documents of reference translations to be single segments (thus, K is equal to 1 in Equation 3.1). This is different from the usual interpretation of the term which implies the average over segment-level scores.

Word error rate on document level without segmentation into sentences is often computed for the evaluation of ASR performance. In ASR research, where there is a unique reference transcription for an utterance, such document-level evaluation is acceptable. In machine translation evaluation, many different, but correct translations are possible; thus, multiple references are commonly used. However, the document-level *multiple-reference* WER calculation is not possible. According to Equation 3.1, such a calculation will always degenerate to a single-reference WER calculation, because the reference document with the smallest Levenshtein distance to the candidate document will be selected.

---

[a] Here, the assumption is that each segment has the same number of reference translations. This is not a real restriction since the same translation can appear in several reference documents.

3.2.2 PER

The position independent error rate [Tillmann & Vogel[+] 97] ignores the ordering of the words within a segment. Independent of the word position, the minimum number of deletions, insertions and substitutions to transform the candidate segment into the reference segment is calculated. Using the counts n_{ek}, $\tilde{n}_{erk}$ of a word e in the candidate segment E_k and the reference segment $\tilde{E}_{rk}$ respectively, we can calculate this distance as

$$d_{\text{PER}}\left(E_k, \tilde{E}_{rk}\right) := \frac{1}{2}\left(\left|I_k - N_{rk}\right| + \sum_e \left|n_{ek} - \tilde{n}_{erk}\right|\right) \qquad (3.2)$$

This distance is then normalized to obtain an error rate, the PER, as described in section 3.2.1.

Calculating PER on document level results in clearly too optimistic estimates of the translation quality since, e. g. the first word in the candidate document will be counted as correct if the same word appears as the last (e. g. 500th) word in a reference translation document. Therefore, meaningful sentence-like units are necessary for the PER measure.

3.2.3 BLEU and NIST

BLEU [Papineni & Roukos[+] 02] is a precision measure based on m-gram count vectors. The precision is modified such that multiple references are combined into a single m-gram count vector. Multiple occurrences of an m-gram in the candidate sentence are counted as correct only up to the maximum occurrence count within the reference sentences. Typically, the m-grams of size $m = 1, \ldots, 4$ are considered. To avoid a bias towards short candidate segments consisting of "safe guesses" only, segments shorter than the reference length are penalized with a brevity penalty.

The NIST score [Doddington 02] extends the BLEU score by taking information weights of the m-grams into account. The NIST score is the sum over all information counts of the co-occurring m-grams, which are summed up separately for each $m = 1, \ldots, 5$ and normalized by the total m-gram count. As in BLEU, there is a brevity penalty to avoid a bias towards short candidates. Due to the information weights, the value of the NIST score depends highly on the selection of the reference documents.

Both measures can be computed at document level. However, as in the case of PER, the resulting scores will be too optimistic (see Section 3.4), since incorrect m-grams appearing in one portion of a candidate document will be matched against the same m-grams in completely different portions in the reference translation document.

3.2.4 TER

The translation edit rate (TER) described by [Snover & Dorr[+] 06] is an extension of WER. The measure attempts to compute the minimum number of edit operations necessary to transform a candidate MT hypothesis into a reference translation. In addition to deletions, insertions and substitutions, shifts of word blocks are considered to be edit operations.

Since the problem of finding the minimum number of edits is NP-complete, the authors of TER use a greedy algorithm to compute the alignment between the candidate hypothesis and a reference translation. Shifts are constrained with various heuristics. For instance, only blocks that fully match a reference block in another position can be shifted. Nevertheless, the computation of TER has shown to be time-consuming.

TER can not be efficiently calculated on document level. Moreover, this calculation is not reasonable because, for instance, block shifts could be performed by matching them across several reference SU boundaries. Thus, well-defined segments in the translation output are necessary for computing TER.

3.3 Automatic segmentation algorithm

The main idea of the proposed automatic re-segmentation algorithm is to make use of the Levenshtein alignment between the candidate translations and human references on document level. The Levenshtein alignment between the sequence of candidate words for the whole document and a sequence of reference translation words can be found by backtracing the decisions of the Levenshtein edit distance algorithm. Based on this automatic alignment, the segment boundaries of the reference document can be transferred to the corpus of candidate translations. This is illustrated by the following example:

```
HYP: a    b b a c d a b d    c
     -    - -   - - *   - -
REF: a a b b    c d c    d a c
                  ^
```

Here, the reference contains two segments with a segment boundary between **d** and **c** shown with symbol ^. The alignment matches are shown with symbol -, the substitutions with symbol *. Insertion and deletion errors are shown with whitespace in the corresponding sequence. From the alignment, it is clear that the reference segment boundary is to be inserted into the hypothesis between **d** and **a**.

35

3.3.1 Notation

More formally, given a reference document $w_1, \ldots, w_n, \ldots, w_N$ with a segmentation into K segments defined by the sequence of indices $n_1, \ldots, n_k, \ldots, n_K := N$, and a candidate document $e_1, \ldots, e_i, \ldots, e_I$, we find a Levenshtein alignment between the two documents with minimal costs and obtain the segmentation of the candidate document, denoted by $i_1, \ldots, i_k, \ldots, i_K := I$, by marking words which are Levenshtein-aligned to reference words w_{n_k}.

This procedure has to be extended to work with multiple reference documents $r = 1, \ldots, R$. To simplify the algorithm, we assume that a reference translation of a segment k has the same length across reference documents. To obtain such a set of reference documents, we apply a preprocessing step. First, for each segment, the reference translation with the maximum length is determined. Then, to the end of every other reference translation of the segment, we attach a number of "empty word" symbols $ so that the segment would have this maximum length. In addition, at each segment boundary (including the document end) we insert an artificial segment end symbol. This is done to make the approach independent of the punctuation marks, which may not be present in the references or do not always stand for a segment boundary.

After this transformation, each reference document has the same length (in words), given by:

$$N := K + \sum_{k=1}^{K} \max_r N_{r,k} \qquad (3.3)$$

3.3.2 Dynamic programming

The proposed algorithm is similar to the algorithm for speech recognition of connected words with whole word models [Rabiner & Juang 93]. In that dynamic programming algorithm, there are two distinct recursion expressions, one for within-word transitions, and one for transitions across a word boundary. Here, we differentiate between the alignment within a segment and the recombination of hypotheses at segment boundaries.

For the within-segment alignment, we determine the costs of aligning a portion of the candidate translation to a predefined reference segment. As in the usual Levenshtein distance algorithm, these are recursively computed using the auxiliary quantity $D(i, n, r)$ in the dynamic programming:

$$\begin{aligned} D(i,n,r) &= \min\{D(i-1, n-1, r) + 1 - \delta(e_i, w_{nr}), \\ &\quad D(i-1, n, r) + 1, D(i, n-1, r) + 1\} \end{aligned} \qquad (3.4)$$

3.3 Automatic segmentation algorithm

Here, given the previously aligned words, we determine what possibility has the lowest costs: either the candidate word e_i matches the word w_{nr} in the r-th reference document, or it is a substitution, an insertion or a deletion error. A special case here is when a reference translation that does not have the maximum length has already been completely processed. Then the current word w_{nr} is the empty word $, and it is treated as a deletion with no costs:

$$D(i, n, r) = D(i, n-1, r), \text{ if } w_{nr} = \$. \tag{3.5}$$

The index of the last candidate word of the previous segment is saved in a backpointer $B(i, n, r)$; the backpointer of the best predecessor hypothesis is passed on in each recursion step.

The hypotheses are recombined at reference segment boundaries. This type of recombination allows for two consecutive candidate segments to be aligned and scored with segments from different reference documents. Assuming that a boundary for the k-th segment is to be inserted after the candidate word e_i, we determine the reference which has the smallest edit distance $D(i, n_k, r)$[b] to the hypothesized segment that ends with e_i. We memorize this locally optimal reference in a backpointer $BR(i, k)$:

$$D(i, n = n_k, r) = \min_{r'=1,\ldots,R} D(i, n-1, r') \tag{3.6}$$

$$BR(i, k) = \hat{r} = \operatorname*{argmin}_{r'=1,\ldots,R} D(i, n-1, r') \tag{3.7}$$

$$BP(i, k) = B(i, n-1, \hat{r}) \tag{3.8}$$

In a backpointer $BP(i, k)$, we save the index of the last word of the hypothesized segment $k-1$, which was propagated in the recursive evaluation. Note that in contrast to speech recognition, where any number of words can be recognized, the number of segments here is fixed. That is why the backpointer arrays BR and BP have the second dimension k in addition to the dimension i (which corresponds to the time frame index in speech recognition).

The algorithm terminates when the last word in each reference document and candidate corpus is reached. The optimal number of edit operations is then given by

$$d_L = \min_r D(I, N, r) \tag{3.9}$$

With the help of the backpointer arrays BP and BR, the sentence boundary decisions $i_1, \ldots, i_K$ are recursively backtraced from $i_K = I$, together with the optimal sequence of reference segments $\hat{r}_1, \ldots, \hat{r}_K$. These reference segments can be viewed as a new single-reference document $\hat{E}$ that contains, for each segment, a selected translation from the original

---
[b] The word $w_{n_k r}$ is always the artificial segment end symbol.

reference documents. Let $\hat{N}$ be the number of words in $\hat{E}$. Then the automatic segmentation word error rate (AS-WER) is given by:

$$\text{AS-WER} = \frac{d_L}{\hat{N}} \qquad (3.10)$$

3.3.3 Complexity of the algorithm

Since the decisions of the algorithm in the recursive evaluation depend, in each step, only on the previous words e_{i-1} and w_{n-1}, the memory complexity can be reduced with the so called "one column" solution. Here, for each reference document index $r = 1, \ldots, R$, we keep only an array A of length N. The element $A[n]$ in this array represents the calculation of $D(i-1, n, r)$ and is overwritten with $D(i, n, r)$ based on the entry $A[n-1]$ which holds the value $D(i, n-1, r)$ and on the value of a buffer variable which temporarily holds $D(i-1, n-1, r)$. Thus, the total memory complexity of the algorithm is $O(N \cdot R + I \cdot K)$: two arrays of size $I \times K$ are required to save backpointers with optimal segmentation boundaries and sequences of reference segments.

The time complexity of the algorithm is dominated by the product of the reference document length, the candidate corpus length and the number of references, i.e. it is $O(N \cdot I \cdot R)$.

Experimentally, our C++ implementation of the algorithm using integer word indices and costs is rather efficient. For instance, it takes less than 2 minutes and max. 400 MB of memory on a desktop PC to align a corpus of 20K words using two reference documents with 2643 segments.

3.4 Applications

To assess the novel evaluation measure and the effect of automatic segmentation for the candidate translations, we performed the following experiments. First, we calculated the scores for several automatic evaluation measures – WER, PER, BLEU, NIST – using the available candidate translation documents with correct segmentation[c]. Note that the correct segmentation of these documents was obtained by translating the source language documents which already had the same segmentation as the manual reference translations. This is an approximation of a real-life application of the proposed evaluation strategy, but it eliminates the need for a costly manual re-segmentation of the translated data.

---

[c]The scores were calculated using the internal C++ implementations, but preprocessing of the hypotheses was done as in the NIST MT evaluation [Papineni 02].

Table 3.1: Corpus statistics of the data used to assess the quality of speech translation evaluation using the segmentation algorithm in Section 3.3.

	TC-STAR	IWSLT
Source language	Spanish	Chinese
Target language	English	English
Segments	2 643	500
Running words	20 164	3 632
Ref. translations	2	16
Avg. ref. length	7.8	7.3
Candidate systems	4	20

Then, we removed the segment boundaries from the candidate translations and determined the segmentation automatically using the Levenshtein distance based algorithm as described in Section 3.3. As a consequence of the alignment procedure we obtained the AS-WER. In addition, using the resulting automatic segmentation which corresponds to the segmentation of the reference documents, we recomputed the other evaluation measures. In the following, we denote these measures by AS-PER, AS-BLEU, and AS-NIST. The goal was to compute the correlation with human judgment between these measures and the same measures using the correct segmentation.

We calculated all of the evaluation measures on two different tasks. The first task is the 2004 Chinese-to-English evaluation of the International Workshop on Spoken Language Translation (IWSLT, [Akiba & Federico[+] 04]). The task consists of translation of tourism-related spoken utterances usually found in phrase books for tourists going abroad. Here, we evaluated translation output on a corpus of twenty MT systems which had participated in this public evaluation. The evaluation was case-insensitive, and the translation hypotheses and references did not include punctuation marks. Additionally, we scored the translations of four MT systems from different research groups which took part in the first MT evaluation in the framework of the European research project TC-STAR [TC-STAR 07]. We addressed only the condition of translating verbatim (exactly transcribed) speech from Spanish to English. Here, the evaluation was case-sensitive, but again without considering punctuation. The evaluation corpus statistics for both tasks are given in Table 3.1.

In both tasks, we evaluated translations of spoken language, i.e. a translation system had to deal with incomplete/not well-formed sentences, hesitations, repetitions, etc. In the experiments with the automatic segmentation measures, we considered the whole document

3 Automatic evaluation of speech translation

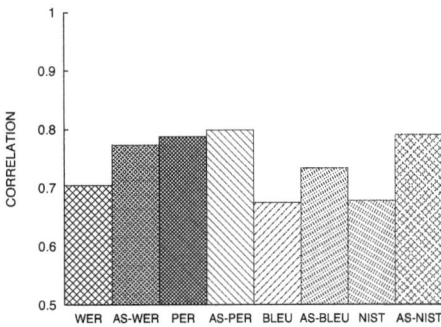

Figure 3.1: Pearson's correlation coefficients for the human adequacy judgments (IWSLT task).

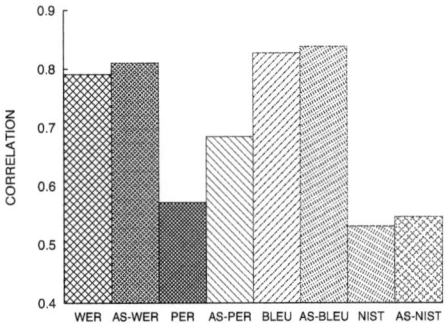

Figure 3.2: Pearson's correlation coefficients for the human fluency judgments (IWSLT task).

(e. g. more than 20K words on the TC-STAR task) as a single text stream in which K segment boundaries (e. g. $K = 2643$ on the TC-STAR task) are to be inserted automatically.

For the IWSLT task, a human evaluation of translation quality had been performed; its results were made publicly available. We compared automatic evaluation results with human evaluation of adequacy and fluency by computing the correlation between human and automatic evaluation at system level. We chose Pearson's r to calculate the correlation. Figures 3.1 and 3.2 show the correlation with adequacy and fluency, respectively. The even columns of the graph show the correlation for the error measures using automatic segmentation. It can be observed that the correlation of these measures with the human judgments regarding adequacy or fluency is better than when manual segmentation is used.

In addition, the Kendall's τ for rank correlation [Kendall 70] was calculated. Figure 3.3

3.4 Applications

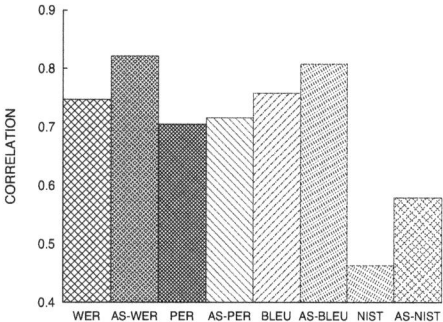

Figure 3.3: Kendall's correlation coefficients for the human ranking of translation systems (IWSLT task).

Table 3.2: Comparison of the evaluation measures as calculated using the correct and the automatic segmentation (TC-STAR task).

Error measure:	System			
	A	B	C	D
WER [%]	37.4	40.4	41.4	47.9
AS-WER [%]	36.2	39.1	40.0	45.7
PER [%]	30.7	33.7	33.9	40.6
AS-PER [%]	30.6	33.4	33.9	39.7
BLEU [%]	51.1	47.8	47.4	40.6
AS-BLEU [%]	50.9	47.5	47.2	40.6
NIST	10.34	9.99	9.74	8.65
AS-NIST	10.29	9.92	9.68	8.65
Segmentation ER [%]	6.5	8.0	7.8	9.5

shows that the evaluation measures based on automatic segmentation can rank the systems as well as the measures based on manual segmentation, or even better. The improvements in correlation with the automatic segmentation should not be overestimated since only 20 observations are involved. Nevertheless, it is clear that the AS-WER and other measures which use the re-segmentation algorithm described in Section 3.3 are as suitable for the evaluation and ranking of MT systems as the measures which require correct segmentation.

On the TC-STAR task, no human evaluation of translation output had been performed.

3 Automatic evaluation of speech translation

Table 3.3: Comparison of the BLEU and NIST scores on document level with the same scores computed using correct and automatic segmentation (TC-STAR task).

| Error | System | | | |
measure :	A	B	C	D
BLEU [%]	51.1	47.8	47.4	40.6
AS-BLEU [%]	50.9	47.5	47.2	40.6
BLEU doc. level [%]	55.3	50.5	50.9	47.5
NIST	10.34	9.99	9.74	8.65
AS-NIST	10.29	9.92	9.68	8.65
NIST doc. level	11.57	11.23	11.12	10.89

Here, in a contrastive experiment, we present the absolute values for the involved error measures using correct/automatic segmentation in Table 3.2. First, it is important to note that re-segmentation of the translation outputs with our algorithm does not change the ranking of the four systems A,B,C,D as given e.g. by the word error rate.

The values for the AS-WER are somewhat lower here than those for WER, but can also be higher, as the experiments on the IWSLT task have shown. This can be explained by different normalization. In the case of AS-WER, the Levenshtein distance d_L is divided by the length of an optimal sequence of reference segments. For each segment, a reference with the lowest number of substitution, insertion and deletion errors is selected. This optimal reference is determined when computing Levenshtein alignment for the whole document. Thus, it is not always the same as in the case of sentence-wise alignment, where (and this is another difference) the reference with the lowest *normalized* error count is selected [Leusch & Ueffing[+] 05].

Another interesting observation is the fact that the values of the other measures PER, BLEU, and NIST are not seriously affected by automatic segmentation. This suggests that Levenshtein distance based segmentation produces reliable segments not only for calculation of the WER, but also for calculation of error measures not based on this distance. In contrast, when we compute BLEU/NIST scores on document level (see Section 3.2.3), the obtained values differ dramatically from the values with correct segmentation and overestimate the performance of the translation systems (see Table 3.3). Moreover, the difference between systems in terms of e.g. the BLEU score may be significantly underestimated. For example, the difference in the BLEU scores at document level between systems B and D is only 6% (vs. 15% as given by the BLEU scores using correct segmentation).

3.4 Applications

Finally, for the introduced error measures with automatic segmentation, we observe that even if the word error rate is high (about 50% or more, like for system D in the TC-STAR evaluation and most of the systems in the IWSLT evaluation), the difference between the error rates using manual and automatic segmentation is still not very big. Thus, the proposed algorithm is able to produce an acceptable segmentation even if the number of matched words between a candidate and a reference document is small. This statement is supported by the *segmentation error rate*. We define this error rate as the word error rate between a document with candidate translations and manual (correct) segmentation and *the same* document with automatic segmentation, computed on segment level. Thus, this error rate is 0 if the automatic segmentation is correct. In Table 3.2, the segmentation error rate is below 10% for all systems, and degrades only slightly with the degrading WER. The robustness of automatic segmentation is important for evaluating translations of automatically recognized speech which at present usually have high error rates.

Several examples of candidate translations of ASR output for the TC-STAR Spanish-to-English task are provided in Appendix B. These candidate translations were automatically aligned with two reference translations using the algorithm proposed in this chapter; one of the two references is shown in the examples for comparison.

The initial version of the algorithm in Section 3.3 was proposed in [Matusov & Leusch[+] 05]. The implementation of this algorithm was successfully used for scoring of speech translation results in the official TC-STAR evaluations in 2006 and 2007. It will be also used for the speech translation experiments on the TC-STAR data presented in this thesis.

In the GALE project evaluations in 2006 and 2007, the evaluation of speech translation was done manually by post-editing the MT output to have correct English syntax and express the meaning of a "gold standard" reference translation. The post-editing was performed on a sentence-by-sentence basis, but the context (2-3 sentences before and after the current one) was shown in a graphical user interface. Since the sentence segmentation of the evaluated automatically translated document was different from the segmentation of the reference document, the human post-editor often had to adjust the sentence boundaries. However, the segmentation differences were sometimes so severe, that it was often not possible to synchronize the two documents on the screen. Therefore, the algorithm presented in this chapter was selected for initial re-segmentation of the translation hypotheses which could be additionally corrected by a human. In the process of post-editing, some editors observed that sometimes 1-3 words in the beginning of a sentence were wrongly assigned to the previous segment. Our analysis showed that these words were insertion errors and therefore placing them in the current or the previous segment did not affect the AS-WER nor would have significantly affected any

43

3 Automatic evaluation of speech translation

other automatic MT error measures calculated after the re-segmentation. However, they do affect the human judgment and make the post-editing more difficult. To make sure that these words are aligned correctly, the algorithm was extended by word-dependent edit operation costs which took into account the punctuation marks that marked the segment end. Whereas the standard cost for an edit operation is 1, the insertion/deletion error of a punctuation mark, as well as a substitution of a punctuation mark with a word which is not a punctuation mark was assigned a cost of 2. Also, if the previously aligned word was a punctuation mark in the reference translation, or the next word of the reference is the last word in the segment, the insertion costs for all words were set to 2. These heuristics subjectively improved the correspondence between the hypotheses and the reference translation and were used in the official post-editing process.

4 Coupling of speech recognition and machine translation

4.1 Introduction

In this chapter, we will propose solutions for a better coupling of automatic speech recognition and machine translation. It will be described how a speech translation system can take advantage of the uncertainty of speech recognition results in the form of multiple recognition hypotheses. We will present novel ideas and algorithms which enable machine translation of ASR word lattices with state-of-the-art phrase-based translation models. We will investigate experimentally under which conditions an improvement in translation quality can be expected by considering alternative ASR hypotheses and thus avoiding some recognition errors. We will compare and combine two different translation models and show how word and phrase reordering can be performed in each of the models in the case of word lattice input.

The structure of this chapter is as follows. In Section 4.2, we will first give an overview of the theoretical base for speech translation and thus motivate the applicability of the joint probability tuple-based model (Section 4.3) and the log-linear phrase-based model (Section 4.4) for translation of ASR word lattices. The two latter sections will give a detailed description of the two models, the training procedures, and the lattice-based search algorithms. Section 4.5 will present experimental results for lattice translation on four different translation tasks. Some ideas on other applications of the proposed lattice translation techniques will be shortly discussed in Section 4.6. The conclusions on the experimental findings will finish this chapter in Section 4.7.

4.2 Bayes decision rule

In speech translation, we are looking for a target language sentence e_1^I which is the translation of a speech utterance represented by acoustic vectors x_1^T. In order to minimize the number of

4 Coupling of speech recognition and machine translation

sentence errors, we apply the Bayes decision rule that maximizes the posterior probability of the target language translation given the speech signal (see [Ney 99]):

$$(\hat{I}, \hat{e}_1^{\hat{I}}) = \underset{I, e_1^I}{\operatorname{argmax}} \left\{ Pr(e_1^I | x_1^T) \right\} \tag{4.1}$$

Equation 4.1 implies the search over all possible target language sentences which are candidate translations for the spoken utterance.

In the following, we will provide a theoretical motivation for two different speech translation models which realize a tighter coupling of ASR and MT. In both approaches, the automatic transcription of the speech utterance is introduced as a hidden variable f_1^J representing the recognized source word sequence. Given a source word sequence, the translation, i.e. the probabilistic mapping of source words and phrases to their target language counterparts can be performed under specific modeling assumptions.

4.2.1 Source-channel paradigm

Following the approaches which use the *source-channel* paradigm, we transform the probability $Pr(e_1^I | x_1^T)$ in Equation 4.1 as follows:

$$\begin{aligned}(\hat{I}, \hat{e}_1^{\hat{I}}) &= \underset{I, e_1^I}{\operatorname{argmax}} \left\{ Pr(e_1^I | x_1^T) \right\} \\ &= \underset{I, e_1^I}{\operatorname{argmax}} \left\{ Pr(e_1^I) \cdot Pr(x_1^T | e_1^I) \right\} \end{aligned} \tag{4.2}$$

Here, $Pr(e_1^I)$ is the *prior* language model probability for the target language word sequence. The source words are then introduced as a hidden variable into the *conditional* probability $Pr(x_1^T | e_1^I)$:

$$\begin{aligned}(\hat{I}, \hat{e}_1^{\hat{I}}) &= \underset{I, e_1^I}{\operatorname{argmax}} \left\{ Pr(e_1^I) \cdot Pr(x_1^T | e_1^I) \right\} \\ &= \underset{I, e_1^I}{\operatorname{argmax}} \left\{ Pr(e_1^I) \cdot \sum_{f_1^J} \left(Pr(f_1^J | e_1^I) \cdot Pr(x_1^T | f_1^J, e_1^I) \right) \right\} \end{aligned} \tag{4.3}$$

In the next step, we make two natural assumptions which are common to all current speech translation approaches. We assume that there is no direct dependency between the speech signal x_1^T and the target sentence e_1^I, but rather there is a strong dependency between the speech signal and its source language transcription f_1^J. We also approximate the sum over all possible source language transcriptions by the maximum. With these assumptions, we formulate Equation 4.4.

$$(\hat{I}, \hat{e}_1^{\hat{I}}) \cong \underset{I, e_1^I}{\operatorname{argmax}} \underset{f_1^J}{\max} \left\{ Pr(e_1^I) \cdot Pr(f_1^J | e_1^I) \cdot Pr(x_1^T | f_1^J) \right\} \tag{4.4}$$

4.2 Bayes decision rule

Here, $Pr(f_1^J|e_1^I)$ refers to the translation model while $Pr(x_1^T|f_1^J)$ may be a standard acoustic model.

As already mentioned in the description of related work in Section 1.4, there are two source-channel approaches used for coupling ASR and MT. The most straightforward approach for fully integrated speech translation is the approach which uses the joint probability translation model. Formally, this model is derived from Equation 4.4 by multiplying the conditional translation probability with the language model probability:

$$(\hat{I}, \hat{e}_1^{\hat{I}}) = \operatorname*{argmax}_{I,e_1^I} \max_{f_1^J} \left\{ Pr(f_1^J, e_1^I) \cdot Pr(x_1^T|f_1^J) \right\} \quad (4.5)$$

According to Equation 4.5, the joint translation probability $Pr(f_1^J, e_1^I)$ replaces the usual (source) language model in the decision criterion for speech recognition. Thus, the translation model is expected not only to provide probabilities for word and phrase correspondences, but also to model the well-formedness of the source and target language. A variant of this model is described in Section 4.3. The advantages of the model are its relatively simple structure, the implementation which relies on established language modeling algorithms, and effortless application to both single sentence or lattice input.

If the language model probability $Pr(e_1^I)$ and the conditional translation model probability $Pr(f_1^J|e_1^I)$ are to be modelled separately, the translation model has to include context dependency on the previously recognized source words. Such a model is presented e.g. in [Schmidt & Vilar+ 08], but is beyond the scope of this work. Here, we choose a more flexible direct modeling approach that allows the use of a source LM for modeling the source sentence structure.

4.2.2 Direct modeling

An alternative to the source-channel approaches above is to model the posterior probability $Pr(e_1^I|x_1^T)$ directly using a log-linear model combination. Here, we also introduce the source sentence as a hidden variable and make the maximum approximation, arriving at the following decision criterion:

$$(\hat{I}, \hat{e}_1^{\hat{I}}) = \operatorname*{argmax}_{I,e_1^I} \max_{f_1^J} \left\{ Pr(e_1^I, f_1^J|x_1^T) \right\} \quad (4.6)$$

The probability $Pr(e_1^I, f_1^J|x_1^T)$ can be determined using the well-established log-linear framework in which we combine real-valued feature functions $h_m(e_1^I, f_1^J, x_1^T)$ and real-valued parameters $\lambda_m; m = 1, \ldots, M$. The same framework for translation of text was described in

4 Coupling of speech recognition and machine translation

Section 1.3.1.4. The final decision criterion is formulated as:

$$(\hat{I}, \hat{e}_1^{\hat{I}}) = \underset{I, e_1^I}{\operatorname{argmax}} \max_{f_1^J} \left\{ \sum_{m=1}^{M} \lambda_m h_m(e_1^I, f_1^J, x_1^T) \right\} \qquad (4.7)$$

The advantage of the log-linear model in Equation 4.7 is the possibility to use any kind of features which are helpful for translation. The parameters λ_m can be e.g. optimized on held-out data to reduce the number of translation errors as computed by an automatic MT evaluation measure. In practice, the features h_m do not include the dependency on all three variables. Instead, the features used in the log-linear model for text translation (see Section 1.3.1.4) are used together with features from speech recognition which depend only on the acoustic utterance and the source word sequence. When the alternative recognition hypotheses are represented using word lattices, these features may be the acoustic and source language model scores for each arc (word hypothesis) in the lattice. Another possibility is to use *word posterior probabilities* of the form $p(f|x_1^T)$. In the following, a *theoretical motivation* for using these features is provided.

Taking the decision criterion in Equation 4.5, we decompose the joint translation probability $Pr(f_1^J, e_1^I)$ as follows:

$$\begin{aligned}(\hat{I}, \hat{e}_1^{\hat{I}}) &= \underset{I, e_1^I}{\operatorname{argmax}} \max_{f_1^J} \left\{ Pr(f_1^J, e_1^I) \cdot Pr(x_1^T|f_1^J) \right\} \\ &= \underset{I, e_1^I}{\operatorname{argmax}} \max_{f_1^J} \left\{ Pr(x_1^T|f_1^J) \cdot Pr(f_1^J) \cdot Pr(e_1^I|f_1^J) \right\} \end{aligned} \qquad (4.8)$$

According to Equation 4.8, the decision is made based on three models. The probability $Pr(e_1^I|f_1^J)$ can be estimated as the phrase-based log-linear translation model described in Section 1.3.1.4 that combines different MT features. The probability $Pr(x_1^T|f_1^J)$ is approximated with the acoustic model probability, and $Pr(f_1^J)$ with a source n-gram language model. Since in practice the last two models are only approximations of the true probability distributions, it is a standard procedure to include scaling factors for these models. Therefore, the logarithms of these two probabilities can be interpreted as two features added to the log-linear model $Pr(e_1^I|f_1^J)$ with an additional dependency on the sequence of acoustic observations x_1^T. This is equivalent to using the two models as features in the log-linear combination as given by Equation 4.7.

Interestingly, one can derive an analogous theoretical justification for using the ASR word posterior probabilities. Starting from the posterior probability $Pr(e_1^I|x_1^T)$ in Equation 4.1, we add the hidden variables corresponding to a recognized word sequence directly into this probability:

$$\begin{aligned}
(\hat{I}, \hat{e}_1^{\hat{I}}) &= \underset{I, e_1^I}{\operatorname{argmax}} \left\{ Pr(e_1^I | x_1^T) \right\} \\
&\cong \underset{I, e_1^I}{\operatorname{argmax}} \underset{f_1^J}{\max} \left\{ Pr(e_1^I, f_1^J | x_1^T) \right\} \\
&= \underset{I, e_1^I}{\operatorname{argmax}} \underset{f_1^J}{\max} \left\{ Pr(f_1^J | x_1^T) \cdot Pr(e_1^I | x_1^T, f_1^J) \right\} \\
&\cong \underset{I, e_1^I}{\operatorname{argmax}} \underset{f_1^J}{\max} \left\{ Pr(f_1^J | x_1^T) \cdot Pr(e_1^I | f_1^J) \right\}
\end{aligned} \quad (4.9)$$

In Equation 4.9 we apply the usual maximum approximation and again assume that there is no direct dependency of the target sentence e_1^I on the acoustic utterance x_1^T. Next, we factorize the probability $Pr(f_1^J | x_1^T)$ using the chain rule and assume a *unigram* model on the level of source words f_1^J:

$$Pr(f_1^J | x_1^T) = \prod_{j=1}^{J} Pr(f_j | f_1^{j-1}, x_1^T) \cong \prod_{j=1}^{J} Pr(f_j | x_1^T) \quad (4.10)$$

Given a word hypothesis f, a good approximation for the probability distribution $Pr(f | x_1^T)$ from Equation 4.10 is the local word posterior probability $p_j(f | x_1^T)$, i.e. the probability that f appears on position j in the source sentence. The use of such probabilities is motivated by the minimum-Bayes-risk decoding in ASR [Evermann & Woodland 00], where the goal is to minimize the number of word errors. These probabilities can be interpreted as confidence measures: the probability that the ASR system makes an error by hypothesizing f on position j is $1 - p_j(f | x_1^T)$. The word posterior probability can be computed as follows [Wessel & Schlüter+ 01]:

$$p_j(f | x_1^T) = \frac{1}{Pr(x_1^T)} \sum_{\tilde{J}, \tilde{f}_1^{\tilde{J}} : \tilde{f}_j = f} \left(Pr(\tilde{f}_1^{\tilde{J}}) \cdot Pr(x_1^T | \tilde{f}_1^{\tilde{J}}) \right) \quad (4.11)$$

The sum in Equation 4.11 is carried over all sentence hypotheses in a word lattice which have the word f on position j on a lattice path. It can be computed over a (general) lattice using the forward-backward algorithm. In practice, this sum is often computed in the process of constructing a confusion network from the general lattice [Mangu & Brill+ 00]. The summation is performed over the arcs hypothesizing the same word in a certain time period; these arcs are assigned to the same slot of the CN. The word posterior probabilities are thus available as a byproduct of the CN construction algorithm. This means that they can be used in CN translation as mentioned in Section 1.3.2.

With the above motivation, we substitute the posterior probability $Pr(f_1^J | x_1^T)$ in Equation 4.9 with the product of the word posterior probabilities over the source word

4 Coupling of speech recognition and machine translation

sequence f_1^J:

$$Pr(f_1^J|x_1^T) \cong \prod_{j=1}^{J} p_j(f_j|x_1^T) \qquad (4.12)$$

This approximation justifies the use of a scaling factor for the probability $Pr(f_1^J|x_1^T)$ in the decision criterion 4.9. In Equation 4.9, this scaled probability is multiplied with the probability $Pr(e_1^I|f_1^J)$ which is, as mentioned above, a log-linear translation model combining multiple features with their own scaling factors. Thus, the logarithm of $Pr(f_1^J|x_1^T)$, which is, according to Equation 4.12, the sum of the logarithms of the word posterior probabilities, can be again interpreted as a feature added to the log-linear model $Pr(e_1^I|f_1^J)$, which has an additional dependency on the acoustic observations x_1^T. Thus, the use of word posterior probabilities in the more generally formulated log-linear model combination in Equation 4.7 is also well-grounded.

In the next two sections, we will describe the speech translation models for which we gave a theoretical motivation above.

4.3 Tuple-based context-dependent speech translation model

This section describes context-dependent speech translation models which are trained using *tuples* of the type (source phrase, target phrase) *of the smallest possible length* as translation units. Such models are popular in MT since they are easily applicable to both text and speech input, and can easily be used to process multiple speech recognition hypotheses. In particular, we focus here on the joint probability tuple-based translation model that fits the decision criterion in Equation 4.5.

4.3.1 Model definition

The joint probability $Pr(f_1^J, e_1^I)$ can be modeled as a *bilingual m-gram* model. Variants of a bilingual *m*-gram model are described in [Casacuberta & Vidal 04, Mariño & Banchs[+] 06, Matusov & Kanthak[+] 05a]. The popularity of the model can be explained by the following:

- As already mentioned, the joint translation model probability $Pr(f_1^J, e_1^I)$ as in Equation 4.5 replaces the usual source LM in the decision criterion for statistical speech recognition. In case of word lattice input, the translation model can thus be interpreted simply as a lattice rescoring model.

4.3 Tuple-based context-dependent speech translation model

- The model allows for a left-to-right generation of translation candidates that is synchronous with the generation of the ASR hypotheses. In an ASR system, the source word hypotheses are generated monotonically (from left to right). The translation model extends such an ASR system by associating one or several target words with each produced source word. The probability of this association depends on the previously observed source words and their corresponding target words.

- The model can be effortlessly trained using standard language modeling techniques, including smoothing of the m-gram probabilities. The smoothing is performed by backing-off to shorter LM histories all the way to the unigram probabilities, which is equivalent to reducing the size of the translation context from m words to no context (single word translation).

- The search for word lattice input using this model can be easily implemented with weighted finite state transducers (WFSTs) [Kanthak & Ney 04]. The representation of an m-gram LM with a WFST is canonical [Mohri & Pereira+ 00]. The coupling of ASR and MT can be most effectively realized by composition of an ASR word lattice represented as a weighted acceptor with the WFST for the translation model (see Section 4.3.2).

In the following, the bilingual m-gram model will be discussed in detail.

Similarly to Equation 1.3, we introduce word alignments between the source and the target words as the hidden variable $A = a_1^K$:

$$Pr(f_1^J, e_1^I) = \sum_{a_1^K} Pr(a_1^K) \cdot Pr(f_1^J, e_1^I | a_1^K) \tag{4.13}$$

In general, the hidden alignment A represents all possible interpretations of source words by target words. In this section we assume that these alignments are monotonic, i.e.

$$\forall k, k' : 1 \leq k < k' \leq K \Rightarrow j(k) \leq j(k') \text{ and } i(k) \leq i(k')$$

We also consider only full-coverage alignments, i.e. the alignments in which each source word is aligned to at least one target word and vice versa.

A monotonic full-coverage alignment has the property that the alignment points can be ordered and numbered using an index k. This indexing is done consecutively as shown in Figure 4.1. In this (canonical) ordering, for two alignment indices k and $k+1$ ($k = 1, \ldots, K-1$), the following holds:

$$j(k+1) = j(k) + 1 \text{ and } i(k+1) = i(k) + 1 \quad \text{or}$$
$$j(k+1) = j(k) \text{ and } i(k+1) = i(k) + 1 \quad \text{or}$$
$$j(k+1) = j(k) + 1 \text{ and } i(k+1) = i(k) \tag{4.14}$$

4 Coupling of speech recognition and machine translation

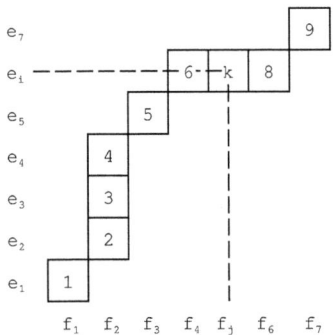

Relations between i,j and k in the figure:

- $k = 7$
- $a_k = (5,6)$
- $i(k) = 6$
- $j(k) = 5$
- $(i,j)_k = (6,5)$

Figure 4.1: Relations between the alignment indices i,j and k.

The ordering of the monotonic alignment points allows for a straightforward definition, training, and application of the model. In Section 4.3.4, we will show that non-monotonic alignments can be transformed to monotonic ones using several techniques. Thus, the joint probability translation model described in this section is also applicable to languages with substantial differences in word order.

The full-coverage constraint on the alignment is not a real constraint either since during the construction of the translation units for model training some of the words will be aligned to the empty word (see Section 4.3.2).

The alignment probability $Pr(a_1^K)$ in Equation 4.13 is assumed to be uniform; the sum over all alignments is approximated by the alignment that maximizes the translation model probability. This probability $Pr(f_1^J, e_1^I | a_1^K)$ is transformed under the assumption that the translation model is a Markov chain of order m:

$$\begin{aligned}
Pr(f_1^J, e_1^I) &= \sum_{a_1^K := (i,j)_1^K} \prod_{k=1}^K Pr(f_{j(k)}, e_{i(k)} | f_1^{j(k-1)}, e_1^{i(k-1)}) \\
&\cong \max_{(i,j)_1^K} \prod_{k=1}^K p(f_{j(k)}, e_{i(k)} | f_{j(k-m+1)}^{j(k-1)}, e_{i(k-m+1)}^{i(k-1)})
\end{aligned} \quad (4.15)$$

The alignment information is contained in the functions $j(k)$ and $i(k)$, therefore the explicit dependency on the alignment a_1^K is omitted. The optimization over the alignment a_1^K is reformulated in terms of alignment connections $(i,j)_1^K$. The assumption in Equation 4.15 is similar to that in n-gram language models where the probability of a word depends on its $n-1$ predecessor words. Here, the dependency is restricted to the last $m-1$ alignment points and the words associated with those points. Thus, the value m can be referred to as *model order*. However, depending on the alignment type used to create bilingual tuples (see Section 4.3.2.1),

4.3 Tuple-based context-dependent speech translation model

the length of the actual source word and target word context used in the model may vary. It should be emphasized here that the joint m-gram probability $p(f_{j(k)}, e_{i(k)}|f_{j(k-m+1)}^{j(k-1)}, e_{i(k-m+1)}^{i(k-1)})$ contains dependencies on the predecessor source words $f_{j(k-m+1)}^{j(k-1)}$ and therefore also plays the role of a source language model.

The training of the model in Equation 4.15, including several alternative representations of the events modeled by the bilingual m-gram, will be described in Section 4.3.2.

The acoustic model probability $Pr(x_1^T|f_1^J)$ from Equation 4.5 is modeled depending on the representation of the multiple ASR hypotheses. Here, we consider the case of word lattices which is the main focus of this work. Each arc in a word lattice is scored with the conditional probability of the acoustic signal given a source word hypothesis

$$Pr(x_1^T|f_1^J) \cong \prod_{j=1}^{J} p(x_{\tau_{j-1}}^{\tau_j}|f_j) \tag{4.16}$$

where τ_{j-1} is the starting time and τ_j is the end time of the hypothesized acoustic realization of f_j.

Inserting Equations 4.15 and 4.16 into Equation 4.5, we arrive at the following search criterion for the joint probability translation model:

$$(\hat{I}, \hat{e}_1^{\hat{I}}) = \underset{I, \tilde{e}_1^I}{\operatorname{argmax}} \underset{(i,j)_1^K, f_1^J}{\max} \left\{ \prod_{k=1}^{K} p(f_{j(k)}, e_{i(k)}|f_{j(k-m+1)}^{j(k-1)}, e_{i(k-m+1)}^{i(k-1)}) \cdot p(x_{\tau_{j(k)-1}}^{\tau_{j(k)}}|f_{j(k)}) \right\} \tag{4.17}$$

In practice, the search can be conveniently implemented using WFSTs [Matusov & Kanthak+ 05b, Kanthak & Ney 04]. This will be discussed in more detail in Section 4.3.3.

4.3.2 Model training

The joint probability translation model in Equation 4.15 is trained as follows:

1. transform each bilingual sentence pair in the training corpus into a representation with bilingual translation units (*tuples*) $t_k := (f_{j(k)}, e_{i(k)}), k = 1, \ldots, K$ based on the word alignment;

2. train an m-gram language model on the transformed corpus;

3. build a weighted finite-state automaton (acceptor) for this language model.

The transformation mentioned in point 1. is performed based on a specific type of full-coverage monotonic word alignment. Some of the widely-used alignment types are described in Section 4.3.2.1. Given a transformed corpus where each sentence pair is represented with bilingual tuples, the translation model is trained by estimating an m-gram language model over the vocabulary of tuples. The joint probability in Equation 4.15 can be re-written using the tuple notation as follows:

$$Pr(f_1^J, e_1^I) = \max_{t_1^K} \prod_{k=1}^{K} p(t_k | t_{k-m+1}^{k-1}) \tag{4.18}$$

Here, the maximization is performed over all possible word alignments that induce a transformation of the source sentence f_1^J and target sentence e_1^I into a valid tuple sequence t_1^K.

An example of a word alignment and variants of a transformed sentence pair are shown in Figure 4.2. The goal of these transformations is to keep the translation units as small as possible to limit the size of the tuple vocabulary and allow for robust training of the m-gram language model using long contexts (m=4 and higher). Whereas in case of one-to-one alignment correspondence of a word f to a word e the resulting smallest tuple is naturally $\text{f}|\text{e}^a$, the cases of many-to-one and one-to-many correspondences are more complicated. Different variants of the alignment-based corpus transformations exist in research publications. The three depicted in Figure 4.2 are most widely used and are described below.

4.3.2.1 Bilingual corpus transformations

In the work of [Bangalore & Riccardi 00b], the corpus of *bilingual pairs* is created based on a *one-to-one* alignment. This means that for every source and every target word there exists at most one alignment connection to a non-empty word. Given these restrictions, each pair of training sentences is written with bilingual tuples $t_k = f_{j(k)} | e_{i(k)}$ where either $f_{j(k)}$ or $e_{i(k)}$ can be a normal word or an artificially introduced "empty word" which we denote with $ (see representation 1 in Figure 4.2; the unshaded boxes from a general monotonic alignment are omitted here to obtain the one-to-one alignment). The number of bilingual pairs K can vary from $\max(I, J)$ to $(I + J)$. Whereas the vocabulary size of the corpus in this representation is relatively limited, m-gram models with a long history m have to be built to capture enough phrasal context. Also, the complexity of the search increases since there exist tuples of the type $|\text{e}$. Such tuples imply that a target word has to be inserted without observing a source word, and this can happen at any point in the search.

---

[a] "|" is a separator symbol.

4.3 Tuple-based context-dependent speech translation model

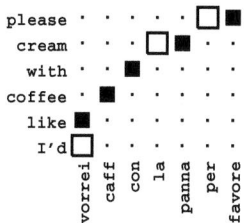

1. $|I'd vorrei|like caffe|coffee con|with la|$ panna|cream per|$ favore|please

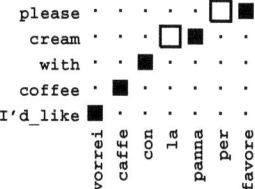

2. vorrei|I'd_like caffe|coffee con|with la|$ panna|cream per|$ favore|please

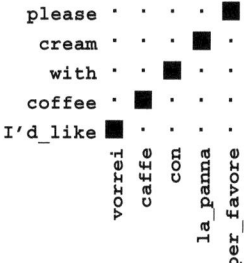

3. vorrei|I'd_like caffe|coffee con|with la_panna|cream per_favore|please

Figure 4.2: Example of a transformed sentence pair using three transformation techniques: bilingual pairs, GIATI, and the transformation of [de Gispert & Mariño 02], respectively. The alignment for the bilingual pairs is used to transform the target sentence in the GIATI approach and both the source and the target sentence in the approach of [de Gispert & Mariño 02]. The transformation merges words in a many-to-one or one-to-many alignment link group into a new word using the underscore symbol. Alignment links which in the first two approaches result in tuples with the "empty word" of the type f|$ and/or $|e are shown with empty boxes.

4 Coupling of speech recognition and machine translation

In the $GIATI^b$ transformation of [Casacuberta & Vidal 04] which was also used in [Matusov & Kanthak$^+$ 05b], *one-to-many* alignments which are functions of target words are used. There is only one difference to one-to-one alignments, namely for the case when $n \geq 2$ target words are aligned to one source word. In such cases, we perform a transformation of the target sentence, mapping the sequence of target words $e_i, \ldots e_{i'}$ aligned to the same word f_j to a new "word" $\bar{e}_j$ written as the concatenation of all these target words using the auxiliary underscore symbol: $e_i\_e_{i+1}\_\ldots\_e_{i'}$. The corresponding tuple has the form $f_j|\bar{e}_j$. This is illustrated in the representation 2 in Figure 4.2: the English words I'd and like aligned to the same Italian word vorrei are merged into one word.

The advantage of the GIATI representation is that a partial translation in the search is generated only when a single word is read from the input. Thus, the search effort is proportional to the length of the source sentence. This is especially important for word lattice translation where the possibility to arbitrary insert a target word between reading two source words would result in high computational complexity. However, the vocabulary size of the "bi-language" increases, since the vocabulary is extended by the tuples of the form $f_j|\bar{e}_j$ (e. g. vorrei|I'd_like in representation 2 in Figure 4.2). This may result in data sparseness problems, which at least partially can be solved with LM smoothing techniques.

Finally, [de Gispert & Mariño 02] and later [Mariño & Banchs$^+$ 06] use "one-to-many", "many-to-one", and even "many-to-many" bilingual tuples. They perform an analogous transformation of the source sentence for the cases where a sequence of source words is aligned to the same target word. This representation is directly derived from the alignment with one-to-many and many-to-one connections, i. e. the full-coverage alignment with all words aligned. The target sentence is transformed as in the GIATI representation. The transformation of the source sentence is similar: every sequence of source words $f_j, \ldots f_{j'}$ aligned to the same word e_i is mapped to a new "word" $\tilde{f}_i$ which is the concatenation of the sequence using the underscore: $f_j\_f_{j+1}\_\ldots\_f_{j'}$. The resulting tuple is $\tilde{f}_i|e_i$. In example 3 in Figure 4.2, these are the tuples la_panna–cream and per_favore–please. The drawback of this representation is that the tuple vocabulary size increases once again, making a reliable LM estimation a hard task, especially on a limited amount of training data. Another disadvantage is the inability to translate individual words in $\tilde{f}_j$, if e. g. they do not appear in the training corpus in another context. On the other hand, introducing tuples of the type $\tilde{f}_i|e_i$ may be advantageous for the cases when n source words are always translated with one target word (e. g. translating an English phrase "the day after tomorrow" into a German word "übermorgen"). In cases of $n > m$, where m is the order of the bilingual LM, the context information contained in the

---

[b]GIATI: Grammatical Inference and Alignments for Transducer Inference.

model may not be sufficient for a correct translation of such phrases if they are not explicitly memorized in the bilingual tuples.

The representation of [de Gispert & Mariño 02] also allows for tuples of the type $\tilde{f}|\tilde{e}$ where both $\tilde{f}$ and $\tilde{e}$ are sequences of more than 1 word. These tuples can be derived from an alignment with *many-to-many* connections[c]. Such tuples may be used to represent non-literal phrase-to-phrase translations, when translating individual source words does not convey the meaning of the source phrase.

4.3.2.2 Avoiding heuristics for training corpus transformation

The three described corpus transformation techniques rely on different types of alignments. The alignments used by the first two transformations can be obtained from the full coverage monotonic alignment by dropping all but one link in a many-to-one or one-to-many link group. The words which loose their alignment links then build a tuple with the empty word $. However, given a word alignment represented as a set of alignment links, it is not clear which links should be dropped, and which should remain i.e. which links are more probable than the others. In previous work, the links were dropped heuristically (e.g. only the first (most left) link was kept). In [Matusov & Kanthak+ 05a], we introduced a method for a more consistent removal of such links. With this method, the original monotonic full-coverage alignment, as well as the alignments required for the other tuple representations are computed using an alignment cost matrix C for each training sentence pair (f_1^J, e_1^I). The size of this matrix is $I \times J$, and its elements $C(i,j)$ are the local costs of aligning a source word f_j to a target word e_i. We compute these local costs as follows.

First, the marginal probability for a target word e_i to occur on the sentence position i as the translation of the source word f_j on position j is estimated with the following sum:

$$p_j(i, f_1^J | e_1^I) = \sum_{\mathbf{a}: a_j = i} Pr(f_1^J, \mathbf{a} | e_1^I) \tag{4.19}$$

This value represents the likelihood of aligning f_j to e_i via every possible functional alignment $\mathbf{a} := a_1^J$ that includes the alignment connection $a_j = i$. By normalizing it over the positions i' in e_1^I, we arrive at the *state occupation probability* $p_j(i|f_1^J, e_1^I)$. The probability distribution $Pr(f_1^J, \mathbf{a}|e_1^I)$ can be estimated using either HMM or IBM-4 alignment models as trained by the GIZA++ toolkit [Och & Ney 03].

To obtain the local alignment costs $C(i,j)$, we interpolate the negative logarithms of the state occupation probability $p_j(i|f_1^J, e_1^I)$ from the source-to-target alignment training and the

---
[c]This type of alignment can not be canonically numbered with indices k as in Equation 4.13.

4 Coupling of speech recognition and machine translation

Figure 4.3: An example of an alignment cost matrix. Darker boxes represent lower local alignment costs.

corresponding probability $p_i(j|f_1^J, e_1^I)$ from the target-to-source alignment training:

$$C(i,j) = -(\alpha \cdot \log p_j(i|f_1^J, e_1^I) + (1-\alpha) \cdot \log p_i(j|f_1^J, e_1^I)) \qquad (4.20)$$

An example of an alignment cost matrix with local alignment costs determined according to Equation 4.20 is shown in Figure 4.3.

For a given alignment $A \subseteq I \times J$, we define the costs of this alignment $C(A)$ as the sum of the local costs of all aligned word pairs:

$$C(A) = \sum_{(i,j) \in A} C(i,j) \qquad (4.21)$$

The goal is to find an alignment with the minimum costs which fulfills certain constraints. Typical constraints would be that each source and target word has to be aligned at least once, the monotonicity, or the functional form of the alignment. Equations describing some of these alignment types will be presented in Section 4.3.4. Assuming that a monotonic full-coverage alignment is given, we can obtain the alignment that is as function of target words as follows.

4.3 Tuple-based context-dependent speech translation model

All links in e. g. a many-to-one link group of several source words aligned to a target word e' on position i' are dropped except the word f' on position j' which has the lowest alignment costs:

$$j' = \operatorname*{argmin}_{j:\ \exists k:\ j(k)=j \text{ and } i(k)=i'} C(i', j) \qquad (4.22)$$

A similar equation holds for the case when only one link from a one-to-many link group must be kept.

For translation of ASR word lattices, we found the GIATI representation based on the consistent alignment computation described above to be the most useful. As mentioned above, with this representation the search can be very efficiently realized using operations on WFSTs. Following a path in an ASR lattice from the initial state to one of its final states labeled with the source words f_1^J, for each source word we can produce $n \geq 0$ target words. This allows us to produce translations of length I possibly different from J. At the same time, since the number of candidate translations for each word f_j is limited (i.e. there are only a few tuples of the type $f_j|*$), the search effort remains proportional to the number of arcs in the ASR lattice.

The GIATI transformation used in this work is based on the functional alignment determined as in Equation 4.22. This alignment was computed based on well-defined alignment costs and without heuristics from a monotonic full-coverage alignment. The latter can also be obtained consistently using alignment cost matrices computed during a general (non-monotonic) alignment training, as it will be shown in Section 4.3.4.

4.3.3 Search

In the previous section, we described the training of a monotonic translation model. In this section, we will describe the monotonic search algorithm for this model. A joint probability model which can handle reordering can be trained after monotonization of the alignment. Several monotonization techniques and their realization in training and search will be described in Section 4.3.4.

The search using the joint probability translation model as given by Equation 4.17 is most conveniently realized with weighted finite-state transducers (WFSTs). The basic theory of weighted finite-state automata and transducers is well known in theoretical computer science and is described in a number of publications [Mohri 97, Allauzen & Mohri[+] 03]. Here, we will review the main definitions.

A WFST T is a weighted finite-state automaton with output symbols. It is defined by the

4 Coupling of speech recognition and machine translation

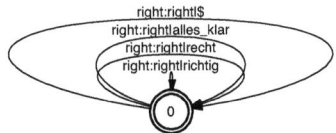

Figure 4.4: Example of a transducer C_1 that maps source words to bilingual tuples.

tuple $(Q, \Sigma, \Omega, K, q_0, \lambda, E, F, \rho)$ where:

- Σ is a finite set of source symbols, Ω is a finite set of output (or *target*) symbols (Σ and Ω are also called source and target *alphabets*, respectively),
- $K = (I\!K, \oplus, \otimes, \bar{0}, \bar{1})$ is a weight semiring,
- Q is a finite set of states with $q_0 \in Q$ being the initial state with weight λ,
- $E \subseteq Q \times (\Sigma \cup \{\varepsilon\}) \times (\Omega \cup \{\varepsilon\}) \times I\!K \times Q$ is a set of arcs (transitions),
- $F \subseteq Q$ is a set of final states weighted by the function $\rho : F \to I\!K$.

A weighted finite-state *acceptor* is a WFST without the output alphabet.

The arcs, the initial state, and the final state in a WFST are assigned weights which are the elements of the semiring K. The two semirings used in speech recognition and speech translation are the *log-semiring* which is a positive real semiring ($I\!R \cup \{-\infty, +\infty\}, \oplus_{log}, +, +\infty, 0$) with $a \oplus_{log} b = -log(e^{-a} + e^{-b})$, and the *tropical semiring* ($I\!R \cup \{-\infty, +\infty\}, \min, +, +\infty, 0$). The two semirings represent the sum and maximum weighted path criteria, respectively. The search using WFSTs takes advantage of the well-known composition operation for transducers. Let $T_1 : \Sigma^* \times \Omega^* \to I\!K$ and $T_2 : \Omega^* \times \Gamma^* \to I\!K$ be two transducers defined over the same semiring $K = (I\!K, \oplus, \otimes, \bar{0}, \bar{1})$, with the output alphabet of T_1 identical to the input alphabet of T_2. Their weighted composition $T = T_1 \circ T_2$ realizes a function $T : \Sigma^* \times \Gamma^* \to I\!K$. The details of the composition algorithm are described in [Pereira & Riley 96]. In the application of machine translation, we can use the composition to map sequences of source words to bilingual translation units, as well as to map sequences of bilingual translation units to sequences of target words.

To implement the decision criterion 4.17, we construct the following four weighted finite-state automata:

- A finite-state transducer C_1 outputs for each input source word f a bilingual translation unit of the form f|*. An example of a transducer C_1 with only one word *right* as input is given in Figure 4.4. This transducer has no weights.

4.3 Tuple-based context-dependent speech translation model

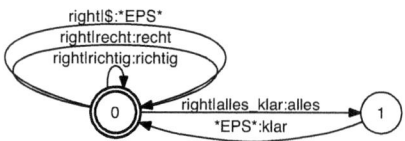

Figure 4.5: Example of a transducer C_2 that maps bilingual tuples to target words.

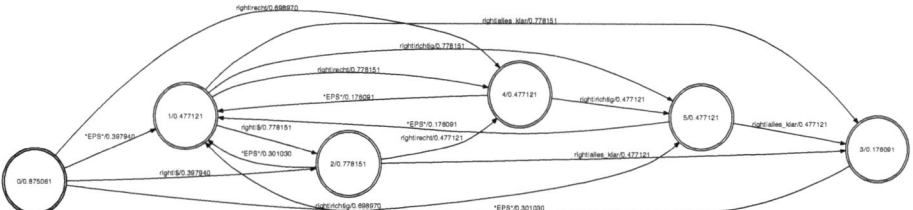

Figure 4.6: Example of a transducer T that implements a smoothed bigram LM over the vocabulary of bilingual tuples right|richtig, right|alles_klar, right|$, right|recht.

- A finite-state-transducer C_2 is a trivial transducer that maps every bilingual translation unit to its target part. As described in Section 4.3.2, the target part of a bilingual tuple can contain the empty word symbol $. In this case, the transducer outputs the ε-symbol. In other cases the target part can contain a sequence of target words separated by the underscore symbol. In this case, the transducer outputs this whole sequence by taking ε-symbols as input for all except the first word in the sequence. An example of the transducer C_2 is given in Figure 4.5. C_2 is also an unweighted transducer.

- A weighted finite-state acceptor A realizes a smoothed m-gram language model over the vocabulary of bilingual tuples and is used to score sequences of such tuples with context-dependent LM probabilities. The construction of this acceptor is described in detail in [Mohri & Pereira[+] 00]. Figure 4.6 gives an example of such an acceptor for a bigram translation model with a 4-word vocabulary. Note that the automaton includes many ε-arcs which are necessary for backing off to shorter contexts (in this case, to unigram probabilities).

- Finally, the (speech) input to the search is represented in a lattice L which is also an acyclic weighted finite-state acceptor as mentioned in Section 1.3.2. When only the first-best ASR output is to be translated, the lattice L is a trivial unweighted linear

4 Coupling of speech recognition and machine translation

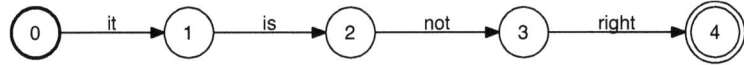

Figure 4.7: Example of a linear acceptor.

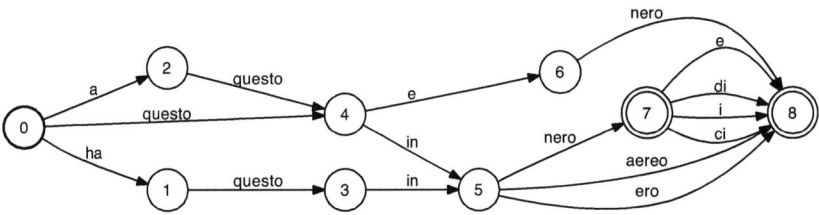

Figure 4.8: Example of a word lattice (acyclic finite-state acceptor). The weights of the lattice arcs are omitted for better readability.

acceptor (see Figure 4.7). If multiple ASR hypotheses are considered, L can be a lattice that represents all those hypotheses in a compact form, as in Figure 4.8. In this case, each arc of the lattice represents a word hypothesis f_j and is weighted with the negative logarithm of the acoustic model probability $p(x_{\tau_{j-1}}^{\tau_j}|f_j)$ (see Equation 4.16). In Figure 4.8, the arc weights are omitted for better readability.

The search space is defined by the composition of all four automata:

$$\hat{e}_1^I = \texttt{project-output}(\texttt{best}(L \circ C_1 \circ A \circ C_2))\,. \tag{4.23}$$

By extracting from this search space the path with the minimum weight (assuming a tropical semiring) using the best operation and considering only the resulting target symbol sequence (with the project-output operation), we obtain the best translation of the given speech utterance.

In practice, we perform the composition $T := C_1 \circ A \circ C_2$ only once, and save the resulting WFST T. Then, the search problem as given by Equation 4.17 is equivalent to a single composition operation:

$$\hat{e}_1^I = \texttt{project-output}(\texttt{best}(L \circ T))\,. \tag{4.24}$$

Since both the acoustic probabilities specified in L and the translation probabilities encoded in T are only approximations to the true probability distributions given by Equation 4.5, it is reasonable to include a scaling factor for one of the models, i.e. to multiply all weights in e.g. T with a scaling factor γ. In our experiments, we manually optimized the factor γ with the goal of obtaining the best translation quality on a given development set (see Section 4.5.2).

4.3 Tuple-based context-dependent speech translation model

For performing the search as in Equation 4.24, we used the finite-state toolkit FSA [Kanthak & Ney 04]. In this toolkit, the composition operation is very efficiently realized using on-demand computation. This means that only those paths in the composed WFST are considered which are necessary for determining the globally best path.

WFST operations can be used to prepare the original word lattices for translation. A speech recognition system usually produces word lattices where arcs are labeled with start and end time, the recognized entity (word, noise, hesitation, silence), the negative log probability of acoustic vectors between start and end time given the entity[d]. In a first step we map all entities that are not spoken words onto the empty arc label ε. As the time information is not used in the translation process, we remove it from the lattices and compress the structure by applying ε-removal, determinization, and minimization. For all of these operations, we also employ the finite-state transducer toolkit of [Kanthak & Ney 04] which efficiently implemented them on-demand.

Alternative implementations of the search with a joint probability translation model. Weighted finite state transducer toolkits provide a useful generic framework for a fast implementation of a tuple-based context-dependent translation model. However, such a model can also be realized with a dynamic programming algorithm that does not explicitly use the concept of weighted automata. This has been done by [Mariño & Banchs⁺ 06]. Their dedicated implementation allows them to combine the tuple-based m-gram model with other features such as word-based lexica, word penalty, and a standard target language model. Thus, they perform a log-linear combination of several features. This is similar to the log-linear combination presented in Chapter 1, but the main feature is not the conditional probability for a source phrase of variable length memorized in training given its target phrasal translation candidate, but the tuple LM probability.

Other WFST search implementations. On the other hand, WFSTs can be used not only to implement the search with the tuple-based translation model, but also with phrase-based and other, more complicated models. In [Kumar & Byrne 03], a translation system is proposed that is based on a cascade of WFSTs, each of which implements a particular model such as a word-to-phrase segmentation transducer, a transducer that maps source phrases to target phrases, a phrase permutation transducer, etc. The translation is performed by composing the linear acceptor for the input sentence with the successive composition of all these WFSTs. The latter can be partially computed in advance. Whereas [Kumar & Byrne 03] apply this model

---

[d]and possibly the negative log language model probability of the entity which is not used in translation with the tuple-based model.

to translation of text, other authors [Mathias & Byrne 06, Saon & Picheny 07] use an ASR lattice instead of the linear acceptor to perform translation with a similar kind of cascaded WFST translation model. In such systems, all of the transducers are composed with optimized scaling factors for their weights, which again leads to a log-linear model combination.

4.3.4 Reordering

Natural languages exhibit a variety of sentence structures and word orders. To obtain good-quality translations from one language to another, a possibility for reordering must be included in the translation models and algorithms. When a speech recognition system is to be effectively combined with a MT system, the challenge is to perform word and phrase reordering given the multiple recognition hypotheses represented in a word lattice.

In the previous section, the context-dependent tuple-based translation model has been defined for monotonic word alignments and therefore could produce translations only without reordering. To estimate the model with non-monotonic alignments, we have to modify either the non-monotonic alignment itself or the word order of the source or the target sentence in training. This section will describe the main approaches for reordering in training, including a novel consistent approach that avoids some of the widely used monotonization heuristics. The proposal is to perfrom reordering of the words in the target sentences during training. Such reordering simplifies the translation of ASR lattices, since the paths in such a lattice do not have to be explicitly or implicitly reordered. However, the produced sequence of target words has the structure of the source sentence. The words in this sequence have to be additionally permuted to obtain a more fluent sentence. Section 4.3.4.3 describes how these permutations can be implemented.

4.3.4.1 GIATI monotonization technique

The first method of dealing with non-monotonicity in word alignments was presented as a part of the GIATI framework [Casacuberta & Llorens[+] 01]. Casacuberta et al. also implemented their tuple-based model using WFSTs; thus, they were bound to the sequential reading of the input word sequence f_1^J. As described in Section 4.3.2, the main idea was to emit $n \geq 0$ target words for each consumed source word; to this end, the considered alignments b_1^I which were functions of target words e_1^I, i.e. did not contain many-to-one or many-to-many source-to-target word connections. All target words were aligned to real source words in these alignments.

To follow the same approach using a non-monotonic alignment, each violation of the

4.3 Tuple-based context-dependent speech translation model

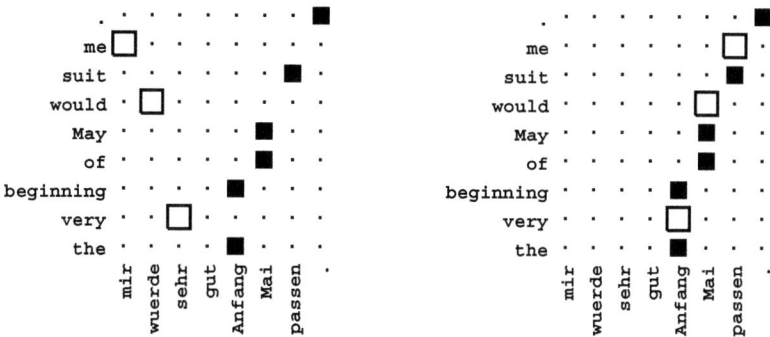

Figure 4.9: Example of applying the GIATI monotonization technique to a non-monotonic alignment. The unshaded boxes represent alignment connections which violate the monotonicity and have to be replaced.

sequential order in the alignment had to be corrected. The following alignment $\tilde{b}_1^I$ was computed recursively:

$$\begin{aligned} \tilde{b}_1 &= b_1 \\ \tilde{b}_i &= \begin{cases} b_{i-1} & : \ b_{i-1} > b_i \\ b_i & : \ \text{otherwise} \end{cases} \end{aligned} \quad (4.25)$$

Thus, for each target word e_i aligned to a source word f_j, if its predecessor word e_{i-1} was aligned to a source word $f_{j'}$ following f_j, the alignment has to be corrected to j'. An example of a non-monotonic alignment and its corrected monotonic version is given in Figure 4.9. When bilingual tuples are extracted from the modified alignment as described in Section 4.3.2, the tuple containing the target word sequence with non-monotonic original alignment will be generated with the last source word that is aligned to this sequence. All other words originally aligned to this sequence will be paired with the empty word $. Here is the tuple sequence resulting from the monotonic version of the alignment in Figure 4.9:

mir|$ wuerde|$ sehr|$ gut|$ Anfang|the_very_beginning
             Mai|of_May_would passen|suit_me .|.

One advantage of this representation is that reordering with such tuples can be performed in the search without any explicit computational overhead. However, this heuristic has many disadvantages. First, the source and target parts of the tuples linguistically may not be translations of each other. Therefore, if the source part occurs in a test sentence in a different context, it can be translated wrongly. Also, very long contexts have to be memorized by the translation model in order to first read several source words without output, and then produce several target words with one source word. This means that m-gram tuple LMs with long context m have to be built. Such models may be unreliable given a limited amount of parallel data for training. Finally, due to reordering, a large number of source words is paired in tuples with the empty word (e.g. the 4 words `mir wuerde sehr gut` in Figure 4.9). This can lead to omission of these words in translation if they appear in a different context than in training.

Another solution for handling non-monotonicity in the alignment is to use "many-to-many" tuples (see Section 4.3.2), extracting non-monotonic alignment regions as single tuples [Mariño & Banchs[+] 06]. Since phrase pairs are thus saved explicitly in the tuple vocabulary, the non-monotonic sequences can be better translated than when the GIATI technique is employed. However, this happens at the expense of a much larger tuple vocabulary; data sparseness may be a problem in estimating a tuple LM with such a vocabulary. Also, the information on how to translate individual words within a non-monotic alignment region is lost. To overcome this problem, [Crego & Mariño[+] 05] described a "tuple unfolding" strategy which resembles the reordering of source words in training based on word alignment as published earlier in [Matusov & Kanthak[+] 05a]. The last method is presented in detail in the next section, but applied to the reordering of target words.

4.3.4.2 Reordering in training based on word alignment information

A non-monotonic word alignment between a source sentence and its translation can be transformed into a monotonic one not only by modifying the alignment function as described above, but also by reordering the words of either the source or the target sentence. Then, the tuples built with the GIATI technique will be small, and the estimation of the translation model will improve. However, in the search, either the input source word sequence would have to have the target word order, or the produced target translation will have the order of the source sentence and will have to be postprocessed. Both solutions are feasible, but changing the order of multiple source word sequences represented in an ASR word lattice is not trivial and very inefficient if we would consider multiple reorderings of each lattice path. Therefore, here we describe reordering of target sentences in training, which is coupled with postprocessing of the produced translations using word-level permutations under certain constraints, as described in Section 4.3.4.3.

4.3 Tuple-based context-dependent speech translation model

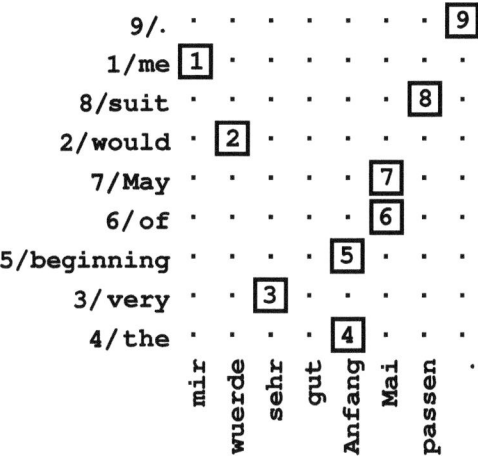

Figure 4.10: Example of target sentence reordering based on a full-coverage alignment that is a function of target words. The reordering is performed by numbering the alignment links and the corresponding target words in the source word order.

The decision on how to permute target words in training can be made based on the word alignment links of those words. However, Viterbi alignments or their heuristic combination may contain alignments with the empty word, many-to-one, one-to-many, and even many-to-many alignments. In the past, various heuristics were used for reordering source or target sentences based on those alignments. In [Kanthak & Vilar+ 05], we suggested the following consistent source sentence reordering and alignment monotonization approach in which we compute optimal, minimum-cost alignments. In this approach we avoid choosing heuristics for handling non-aligned words and general alignments that are not functions. Here, we modify this approach to work for target sentence reordering.

First, we estimate a cost matrix C for each sentence pair (f_1^J, e_1^I). The elements of this matrix $C(i,j)$ are the local costs of aligning a source word f_j to a target word e_i. The costs are computed using state occupation probabilities from the HMM and IBM-4 alignment training as described in Section 4.3.2.

To reorder a target sentence, we require the alignment to be a *function* of *target* words B:

67

$\{1,\ldots,I\} \rightarrow \{1,\ldots,J\}$, easily computed from the cost matrix C as:

$$B(i) = \operatorname*{argmin}_{j} C(i,j) \qquad (4.26)$$

We do not allow non-aligned target words. The alignment B naturally defines a permutation of the target words e_1^I which we denote by $\breve{e}_1^I$. By computing this permutation for each pair of sentences in training and applying it to each target sentence, we create a corpus of reordered target sentences. Since the alignment is monotonic after the permutation and is still a function of target words, we can directly extract the tuple sequence for training the m-gram tuple LM.

An example is given in Figure 4.10. In the example, the initial word alignment corresponds to the alignment in Figure 4.9. The reordering is performed by numbering the alignment links and the corresponding target words in the source word order. The reordered target sentence is:

me would very the beginning of May suit .

From the monotonic alignment between the reordered target sentence and the original source sentence, the bilingual tuples are constructed using the GIATI method as described in Section 4.3.2.1:

mir|me wuerde|would sehr|very gut|\$ Anfang|the_beginning
Mai|of_May passen|suit .|.

Note that the resulting tuples are much smaller than the ones resulting from the alignment in Figure 4.9 and better reflect the translation equivalence. Thus, the tuple LM can be better estimated.

Optionally, after reordering all target training sentences as described above, we can retrain the local alignment cost matrices by repeating the EM training of the state occupation probabilities with GIZA++ using the original source corpus and the reordered target corpus. Since the IBM alignment models and the HMM models can not be directly constrained to estimate monotonic alignments, the alignment computed from the re-estimated cost matrices as in Equation 4.26 may not necessarily be monotonic. Therefore, we make use of the cost matrix representation and compute a monotonic minimum-cost alignment with a dynamic programming algorithm similar to the Levenshtein string edit distance algorithm. As costs of each "edit" operation we consider the local alignment costs. The resulting alignment $\breve{B}$ represents a minimum-cost monotonic "path" through the cost matrix. To make $\breve{B}$ a function of target words we forbid "deletions" (corresponding to "many-to-one" source word alignments) in the dynamic programming search.

4.3 Tuple-based context-dependent speech translation model

By computing the alignments B (and, optionally, $\check{B}$) using the cost matrices we obtain a consistent reordering and monotonization framework which is always aiming at a minimum-cost alignment. Thus, we are able to avoid different heuristics for handling the non-aligned words as well as general alignments which are not functions. The proposed approach reduces the number of distinct tuples. This leads to a larger number of observations for the training of the m-gram tuple LM and thus to an improved learning of the correspondences between source and target tuple sequences.

4.3.4.3 Target language reordering after search

After reordering the target sentences in training, we can only produce translations in the search which have the structure of the source sentence, e.g. `me would very the beginning of May suit` in Example 4.10. The word order of such sentences can be corrected in a post-processing step. Unfortunately, such a correction can not change the produced words, but only their order. This means that we only have a chance to improve error measures such as word error rate and BLEU, whereas the position-independent error rate will remain unchanged. A better solution would be to perform the reordering of source sentences both in training and coupled with translation [Kanthak & Vilar+ 05]:

$$\hat{e}_1^I = \text{project-output}(\text{best}(\text{permute}(L) \circ T)). \qquad (4.27)$$

Here, $\text{permute}(L)$ is the acceptor representing multiple permutation of the input source sentence computed under some reordering constraints such as the IBM constraints or local constraints. These permutation automata can be computed efficiently on-demand using coverage vectors if L is a linear acceptor for the first-best ASR output. However, no efficient computation is feasible if L is an ASR word lattice. Nevertheless, the constraints on the permutations of the source sentences which are applied in the search that implements Equation 4.27 are also applicable for permutations of the target language translation hypotheses in the postprocessing phase. For example, we can apply the local constraints or the inverse IBM constraints [Kanthak & Vilar+ 05]. All constraints have a "window" size parameter which controls the extent of the reordering, e.g. by limiting the number of word positions which can be skipped or the maximum distance of the new word's position to its original position. Examples of such constraints applied to a sequence of 4 words are given in Figure 4.11.

We score the different permutations of the target translation using an n-gram target LM estimated on the original target training sentences. Similar to the WFST-based search, the

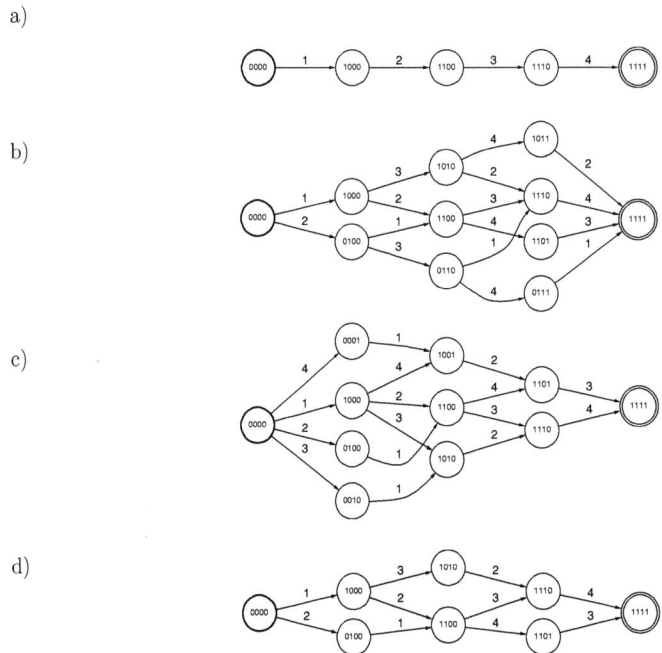

Figure 4.11: Permutations of a) positions $i = 1, 2, 3, 4$ of a target translation $e_1 e_2 e_3 e_4$ using a window size of 2 for b) IBM constraints, c) inverse IBM constraints and d) local constraints.

LM scoring is implemented via the composition operation with the LM acceptor G:

$$\bar{e}_1^I = \text{best}(\text{permute}(\hat{e}_1^I) \circ G). \tag{4.28}$$

Here, $\text{permute}(\hat{e}_1^I)$ is the permutation automaton for the initial translation found in the MT search (see Equation 4.24), and $\bar{e}_1^I$ is the best permutation of that translation. In addition to the LM probabilities, we can use reordering probabilities to score the permutations. Especially for the case of nearly monotonic translation it is beneficial to restrict the degree of non-monotonicity that we allow when translating a sentence. We propose a simple approach which gives a higher probability to the monotonic transitions in the permutation automaton and penalizes the non-monotonic ones. We assign the probability α to each arc that is on a monotonic path and distribute the remaining probability mass $1 - \alpha$ uniformly among the remaining arcs. The experiments which show the benefit of such weighting were presented in [Kanthak & Vilar+ 05].

4.4 Phrase-based speech translation using a log-linear model

In this section, we will present an extension of the phrase-based log-linear translation model described in Chapter 1. This extension will allow us to apply this strong model for translation of ASR word lattices, both with and without reordering. First, we will give a motivation why the phrase-based log-linear model should be preferred over the tuple-based joint probability model for speech translation. Then, we will describe the model extensions, and the enhanced monotonic and non-monotonic search algorithms. Finally, we will show how to combine the tuple-based and phrase-based translation paradigms in a single model.

4.4.1 Advantages over the tuple-based model

Tuple-based speech translation models similar to the one presented in Section 4.3 are convenient from the implementation point of view, especially if WFSTs are used to implement them. However, WFST implementations are not as flexible as dedicated dynamic programming implementations and in most cases can not be extended with additional features. Furthermore, the tuple-based models have some disadvantages with respect to the phrase-based model from the modeling point of view. The main differences between the two models which show that the phrase-based model is superior are summarized below:

Model smoothing: The WFST implementation of the tuple-based model described in this thesis does not include single-word based bilingual lexicon probabilities $p(f|e)$ and $p(e|f)$. Experiments of [Mariño & Banchs+ 06] have shown that these probabilities are important for smoothing the model. The smoothing of the tuple m-gram model with LM backing-off is not a good replacement for the word-based lexicon smoothing, because for unseen m-grams the model often backs off to unigrams $p(t)$ where t is of the form $f|e$. This unigram probability is estimated with the relative frequency $N(t)/N$ where N is the number of tuples in the transformed bilingual corpus. For rarely observed tuples, this probability is very low and does not reflect the possibly strong dependency of f and e on each other. Thus, the tuple LM does not discriminate well between different translations of the same word if the context of this word has not been observed in training. In contrast, the conditional probabilities for single-word phrases used in the phrase-based model can more reliably predict the translations for the words not memorized in phrasal context.

4 Coupling of speech recognition and machine translation

Deletion errors: Another disadvantage of the tuple-based models is the presence of a high number of "deletion" tuples of the type $f|\$$, especially in the case of non-monotonic translation. Due to the backing-off mechanism, the presence of these tuples may cause, in the worst case, a deletion of a source word without context. In contrast, a "deletion" of a word in the phrase-based approach is only possible in the context of neighboring source words in a phrasal translation. Experimental results in fact show that the translations produced with the tuple-based model are on average shorter than those produced using the phrase-based model due to additional deletion errors.

Reordering: The important advantage of the phrase-based model is its cardinality-synchronous search implementation that allows for exhaustive reordering *on the phrase level*. In addition, most local reorderings are already saved in the phrase pairs, so that reordering in training is not necessary nor helps MT quality. Using the tuple-based model for non-monotonic translation is effective only with reordering in training. However, reordering in training implies reordering in or after the search using some *word-level* permutations. Experiments show that the current reordering models are too weak to provide good reordering alternatives with probabilities; at the same time, the tuple-based model is often too weak to differentiate between the "good" and "bad" reordering alternatives.

4.4.2 Model features and training

Speech translation using log-linear model combination is performed in accordance with the decision criterion 4.7. As features of the log-linear model we use the features used in text translation (see Equations 1.15, 1.16, 1.17, and 1.18), namely the phrase-based and word-based translation probabilities in source-to-target- and target-to-source directions, word and phrase penalty, and target language model. In the case of non-monotonic translation, also the distortion model is included.

For translation of word lattices, the following two features can be added to the log-linear model, namely the acoustic probability of the hypothesized source word sequence:

$$h_{Ac}(f_1^J, x_1^T) = \log \prod_{j=1}^{J} p(x_{\tau_{j-1}}^{\tau_j} | f_j) \tag{4.29}$$

and the source m-gram language model probability for this sequence:

$$h_{SLM}(f_1^J, x_1^T) = \log \prod_{j=1}^{J} p(f_j | f_{j-m+1}^{j-1}) \,. \tag{4.30}$$

4.4 Phrase-based speech translation using a log-linear model

The likelihood of a particular word hypothesis in a word lattice or confusion network can also be modeled using word posterior probabilities as defined by Equations 4.10 and 4.11:

$$h_{Post}(f_1^J, x_1^T) = \log \prod_{j=1}^{J} p_j(f_j | x_1^T) \tag{4.31}$$

The word posterior probabilities are most commonly computed based on a transformation of a lattice into a confusion network. For a confusion network slot $\bar{S}$ and word f we calculate the slot-wise word posterior as:

$$p_{\bar{S}}(f | x_1^T) = \sum_{\mathbf{a} \in \bar{S}, \text{word}(\mathbf{a}) = f} \text{FB}(\mathbf{a}), \tag{4.32}$$

where $\mathbf{a}$ are the lattice arcs assigned to the CN slot $\bar{S}$ and $\text{FB}(\mathbf{a})$ is the forward-backward probability of arc $\mathbf{a}$. Translation experiments with CNs as input cannot use the acoustic scores anymore, because they would be incorrect for the extra paths introduced by the CN. Instead, the slot-wise word posteriors are used. In the proposed lattice translation approach, no extra paths are introduced and we can measure the impact of using word posteriors instead of the acoustic scores in our experiments. To this end, we set the score of each lattice arc to the negated logarithm of the slot-wise word posterior. Thus, in practice, either the acoustic feature h_{Ac} or the posterior probability feature h_{Post} is used.

When the two features from Equations 4.29 and 4.30 are used in the log-linear model combination together with the 7 MT features described by Equations 1.15 to 1.18[e], we can explicitly rewrite the decision criterion in Equation 4.7 using all 9 features:

$$\hat{e}_1^{\hat{I}} = \underset{I, e_1^I}{\text{argmax}} \max_{J, f_1^J} \max_{K, (j_k, i_k)_{k=1}^K} \left\{ \prod_{k=1}^{K} \left(c_1 \cdot p(f_{j_{k-1}+1}^{j_k} | e_{i_{k-1}+1}^{i_k})^{\lambda_1} \cdot p(e_{i_{k-1}+1}^{i_k} | f_{j_{k-1}+1}^{j_k})^{\lambda_2} \cdot \right. \right.$$
$$\prod_{i=i_{k-1}+1}^{i_k} \left[c_2 \cdot p(e_i | e_{i-n+1}^{i-1})^{\lambda_3} \cdot p(e_i | f_{j_{k-1}+1}^{j_k})^{\lambda_4} \right] \cdot \tag{4.33}$$
$$\left. \left. \prod_{j=j_{k-1}+1}^{j_k} \left[p(f_j | e_{i_{k-1}+1}^{i_k})^{\lambda_5} \cdot p(f_j | f_{j-m+1}^{j-1})^{\lambda_6} \cdot p(x_{\tau_{j-1}}^{\tau_j} | f_j)^{\lambda_7} \right] \right) \right\}$$

In Equation 4.33, the optimization is performed over all possible source word sequences f_1^J (contained in the word lattice), all possible target translations of a source word sequence e_1^I, as well as over the best segmentation of the two sequences into bilingual phrase pairs with boundaries $(j_k, i_k), k = 1, \ldots, K$. For each phrase pair, Equation 4.33 includes the conditional phrase translation probabilities in source-to-target and target-to-source direction, scaled by factors λ_1 and λ_2, respectively, a phrase penalty c_1, word lexicon probabilities in

---
[e]and their formulation for the inverse translation direction

both translation directions scaled by factors λ_4 and λ_5, the target LM probabilty scaled with factor λ_3, and a word penalty c_2 for each produced target word. For each considered source word hypothesis, the source LM and the acoustic probabilities are included, scaled by factors λ_6 and λ_7, respectively. To simplify the presentation, Equation 4.33 contains the decision criterion for monotonic translation. In case of a non-monotonic search, the distortion penalty model from Equation 1.19 can be added as another feature. Note that by setting $\lambda_6 = \lambda_7 = 0$ and omitting the optimization over the source sentence hypotheses we obtain the optimization criterion for translation of the fixed single best ASR output f_1^J.

The translation model features, source and target LM features, and the acoustic feature in Equation 4.33 are scaled with a set of exponents $\lambda = \{\lambda_1, \ldots \lambda_7\}$. Together with c_1 and c_2, their values are optimized in a single log-linear model simultaneously. As described in Section 1.3.1.4, the optimization is performed under the minimum error training framework [Och 03] iteratively with the Downhill Simplex algorithm. In each iteration, the ASR word lattices for a development set are translated using the search procedure described in Section 4.4.3 below. The criterion for optimization is an objective machine translation error measure like the translation edit rate or the BLEU score.

4.4.3 Search

The phrase-based search using word lattices as input consists of two more or less independent algorithms:

- matching of phrases along each path of the input lattice and loading of translation candidates for each matched phrase;
- the search using the matched phrases, organized by successive lattice nodes or by positions or slots corresponding to certain arcs in the lattice.

The novel approach for labeling lattice arcs with slot information will be described in Section 4.4.3.1. An efficient algorithm for phrase matching will be described in Section 4.4.3.2. Following that, two types of search will be presented: monotonic search with an extension that allows for very limited phrase reordering and the cardinality-synchronous search as described in Chapter 1 extended to work on word lattices.

4.4.3.1 Preparing word lattices

In previous work, the lattice-based search using phrase-based models was either monotonic or performed a very limited word or phrase reordering, e.g. by allowing the search

4.4 Phrase-based speech translation using a log-linear model

algorithm to skip one word or phrase and translate it at a later stage [Zens & Bender[+] 05, Mathias & Byrne 06]. The reason for this is the high computational complexity of reordering.

In order to solve the reordering problem, translation of confusion networks has been proposed [Bertoldi & Zens[+] 07]. As described in Section 1.3.2, the recognized word hypotheses in a CN are aligned to specific positions, or *slots*. At each slot, there are several word alternatives, including the empty word. The structure of a CN allows for an MT search that is similar to the established search for text input, where translation hypotheses with the same cardinality are expanded under certain reordering constraints. Long-range reordering becomes possible. Given a clear definition of the slots in a CN, other, more sophisticated types of decoding e. g. using hierarchical phrases (CYK-style search) can also be performed [Dyer & Muresan[+] 08].

However, the CN representation has its drawbacks. When a lattice is collapsed into a CN, extra paths may be introduced which were not part of the original search space. Current MT models are often not strong enough to differentiate between "good" and "bad" paths in the confusion network, especially if reordering is involved. Because of this, and to reduce the search complexity, the CNs are pruned so that only a few word alternatives remain at each position. Pruning may remove some promising hypotheses. Also, in a CN the original acoustic and LM scores can not be used.

In [Matusov & Hoffmeister[+] 08], we proposed to combine the advantages of a cardinality-based search with the advantages of using the original word lattice. We introduced an approach for labeling a general lattice with slot information from a CN and then used this information in MT search.

To associate a slot label with each arc in the lattice, we collapse the lattice into a confusion network and enumerate the CN slots. Each original lattice arc is now associated with a CN slot and gets the slot number as its label. An example lattice in which arcs are labeled with slot positions is shown in Figure 4.12.

The translation runtime of the search depends on the number of slots in the CN. In order to reduce the number of slots, we remove slots containing only ε-arcs, i. e. arcs having the empty word as word label. Empty words from the lattice are not considered in translation and hence ε-arcs do not need a slot label. Because of this, there can be gaps in the slot enumeration so that one word hypothesis can cover two or more slots for which other, shorter words are hypothesized in the lattice.

Before the slot-labeled lattices can be translated, there is another lattice processing step involved. Lattices produced by ASR systems are usually highly redundant w.r.t. the information required by an MT system. They include symbols representing non-word events

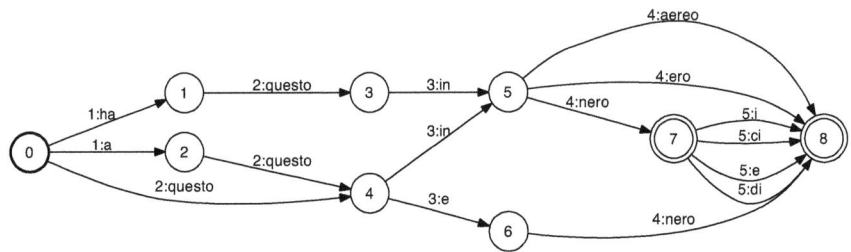

Figure 4.12: An example word lattice in which arcs are labeled with slot information.

like noise, and they store time information for each word. By omitting all the information not relevant for MT and applying standard graph algorithms (minimization, ε-removal), the lattice size can be drastically reduced as described in Section 4.3.3. The compression of the lattices significantly reduces MT runtime without changing the result.

The confusion network algorithm used for the slot labeling is based on the algorithm proposed by [Mangu & Brill[+] 00], where the clustering is guided by a pivot path, see [Hakkani-Tür & Riccardi 03]. The algorithm requires time information for each lattice arc and thus has to be performed on the original ASR lattice. This contradicts the lattice preprocessing described above, which changes the lattice structure and thus destroys the mapping between CN slots and lattice arcs. Even worse, the lattice preprocessing includes minimization, which might collapse two lattice arcs assigned to different CN slots. These problems can be elegantly solved by prefixing the word label of each arc by its slot label. This coerces the minimization into keeping arcs separated which are associated with different slots and preserves the correct slot label for each word.

After all of the above transformations, the paths of the modified lattice have slot information and can be efficiently explored for matching source phrases, as described in the following section.

4.4.3.2 Phrase matching for lattice input

As pointed out in [Dyer & Muresan[+] 08], the number of source phrases which can be extracted from a word lattice is exponential in the number of lattice nodes. However, there exists an efficient phrase matching procedure for matching the possible translations of every span in a lattice as described e. g. in [Zens & Ney 07]. This implementation is based on a prefix-tree representation for the source phrases in the phrase table. From every lattice state, the translation alternatives are generated incrementally over the span length, until a leaf of the prefix tree is reached, or the source phrase of the span is not found in the prefix tree. The intermediate expansions are stored on a stack. In practice, the phrase matching procedure is computationally inexpensive since translation options exist only for very few spans of length ≥ 2.

For each lattice span with an existing translation, we extract *phrase translation candidates* with the following information: source and target word sequence, the set of covered slots, as well as the IDs of the beginning and the end state of the span. In case of gaps in the slot enumeration, we assume that one word covers two or more slots and add the right number of slots to the coverage set. By saving the span state boundaries we separate translation candidates which have the same coverage sets and target phrases, but which arise from different lattice spans. For example, given the lattice in Figure 4.12 we differentiate between two candidates translating **questo in**, one starting at state 1 and ending at state 5, and the other one starting at state 2 and ending at state 5. This separation will be of value in the cardinality-synchronous search, as described in Section 4.4.3.5.

Before we describe the lattice-based cardinality synchronous search, for which the span state boundaries are needed, we will review the monotonic lattice-based search and its extension presented e.g. in [Zens 08]. This type of search will be used in contrastive experiments for this thesis.

4.4.3.3 Monotonic lattice-based search

Monotonic search for lattice input using the log-linear phrase-based translation model is implemented in analogy to the monotonic search for single best ASR output [Zens 08]. Instead of traversing the source positions, the nodes of the input lattice are visited in topological order. For a node j, the topological order guarantees that all nodes on the paths from the initial node to j have already been visited. The dynamic programming recursion 1.25 is modified. The auxiliary quantity $Q(j, \tilde{e})$ is defined as the maximum score of a phrase sequence ending with LM history $\tilde{e}$ and translating a path from the initial node 1 to node j. For this quantity, the following holds:

$$Q(j, \tilde{e}) = \max_{j' < j, \tilde{e}', \tilde{e}'': \tilde{e} = \tilde{e}' \oplus \tilde{e}''} \left\{ Q(j', \tilde{e}') + q_{TM}(\tilde{e}'', j', j) + q_{LM}(\tilde{e}'' | \tilde{e}') \right\} \quad (4.34)$$

Here, $q_{TM}(\tilde{e}'', j', j)$ is the function that computes the translation score for translating a path from node j' to node j with the target phrase $\tilde{e}''$. This function is similar to the $q_{TM}(\cdot)$ function for single best input as defined by Equation 1.20, except that nodes play the role of positions, and the acoustic and source LM costs of the partial path in the input lattice are included.

4 Coupling of speech recognition and machine translation

Note that there may be multiple paths from node j' to node j. Thus, there may be multiple (distinct) source phrases along those paths. If the same target phrase can be generated from multiple source phrases, we choose the one with the best translation model score. This can be done during the efficient phrase matching along all paths between nodes j' and j as described in Section 4.4.3.2.

4.4.3.4 Extension to allow limited reordering

Without the slot information for word hypotheses in the ASR lattice, performing reordering on word or phrase level in the search would require explicit memorization of all the paths being reordered. This is very computationally expensive, because any algorithm that considers the permutations of even a single lattice path potentially has exponential complexity. Nevertheless, to allow at least for some limited reordering, [Zens 08] suggests rather strict reordering constraints for lattice-based search which follow the IBM or 'skip' reordering constraints as described in [Berger & Brown$^+$ 96, Tillmann & Ney 00] for single-word based models. The idea is that the lattice is processed in an almost monotonic way, but a source phrase can be skipped and its translation can be inserted later. As we have to memorize which phrase has been skipped, the search space is increased considerably. Therefore, only one phrase is allowed to be skipped at a time.

To implement these constraints, the dynamic programming recursion and the auxiliary quantity have to be changed. Let $\mathcal{S} \subset \{(j,j')|1 \leq j < j' \leq J\}$ denote the set of skipped phrases. We define the auxiliary quantity $Q(j,\tilde{e},\mathcal{S})$ as the maximum score of a hypothesis which ends in node j, has language model history $\tilde{e}$ and has skipped the blocks in $\mathcal{S}$.

$$Q(j,\tilde{e},\mathcal{S}) = \max\left\{\max_{\substack{j'<j \\ \tilde{e}',\tilde{e}'':\tilde{e}=\tilde{e}'\oplus\tilde{e}''}}\left\{Q(j',\tilde{e}',\mathcal{S})+q_{TM}(\tilde{e}'',j',j)+q_{LM}(\tilde{e}''|\tilde{e}')\right\},\right. \quad (4.35)$$

$$\left.\max_{\substack{(j',j''):(j',j'')\notin\mathcal{S} \\ \tilde{e}',\tilde{e}'':\tilde{e}=\tilde{e}'\oplus\tilde{e}''}}\left\{Q(j,\tilde{e}',\mathcal{S}\cup\{(j',j'')\})+q_{TM}(\tilde{e}'',j',j'')+q_{LM}(\tilde{e}''|\tilde{e}')\right\}\right\}$$

$$Q(j,\tilde{e},\mathcal{S}\cup\{(j',j)\}) = Q(j',\tilde{e},\mathcal{S}) \quad (4.36)$$

The first one of the two inner max operations in Equation 4.35 is the monotonic expansion. In the second max operation, a block (j',j'') that has been skipped at an earlier stage is translated. In Equation 4.36, a block (j',j) is skipped.

The experimental results will show that the monotonic search with this extension can improve the translation quality significantly. However, for language pairs with strong differences in word order, the more flexible cardinality-synchronous search obtains the same or better translation results and requires much less computation time.

4.4.3.5 Source cardinality-synchronous search

The source cardinality-synchronous search (SCSS) for word lattice input is performed in analogy to the same type of search for text input (see Section 1.3). The search proceeds synchronously with the cardinality of the already translated source slots c, and partial target translations are created from left to right. With each hypothesis a coverage set $C \subseteq \{1, \ldots, \hat{J}\}$ is associated, it holds $c = |C|$. $\hat{J}$ is the last slot in the lattice: the longest path in it has length $\hat{J}$. Given a hypothesis with cardinality c, the decoder selects a range of source slots $j', \ldots, j''$ for which a target phrase translation exists and extends the current hypothesis with this phrase. The extension is valid in terms of coverage if there is no overlap with the already translated slots, i.e. $C \cap \{j', \ldots, j''\} = \emptyset$. For lattice-based input, the slots are defined in the process of constructing a confusion network and then are assigned to the arcs of the original lattice, as described in Section 4.4.3.1. An example lattice in which arcs are labeled with slot information is shown in Figure 4.12.

In the search, when extending a hypothesis with a phrase translation candidate, besides checking that the extension is valid, we also have to ensure that only valid lattice paths are followed. Considering a hypothesis with cardinality c and coverage vector C, and a possible extension covering slots $j', \ldots, j''$ with start and end states n' and n'', we say that *node accessibility constraints* are fulfilled if the following holds:

- n' is reachable from the lattice state $\hat{l}$ which corresponds to the nearest already covered slot to the left of j', as given by the current hypothesis. In case no slot has been covered to the left of j', the condition is fulfilled by definition and does not have to be checked.

- From n'' we can reach the lattice state $\hat{r}$ from which the nearest covered slot to the right of j'' has been translated. In case no slot has yet been covered to the right of j'', the condition is also already fulfilled, since there is always a path to a final state of the lattice.

The constraints are explained on the example lattice in Figure 4.12. Here, given a possible translation candidate translating "`aereo`" at slot 4 from state 5 to 8, we can use this candidate only if there is a path to state 5 from the nearest covered slot to the left of slot 4 (e.g. the arc with the source word "`in`" ending in state 5 has been already translated). This condition is not fulfilled for a hypothesis translating "`e`" and ending at state 6, since there is no path from state 6 to state 5. Indeed, the translation of "`aereo`" should not follow the translation of "`e`"

4 Coupling of speech recognition and machine translation

since the two words are not on the same path. Similarly, if e.g. due to reordering the word "di" between states 7 and 8 has already been translated, the translation can not continue with "e" at slot 3 since there is no path from state 6 to state 7.

The procedure that checks the state accessibility constraints can be efficiently implemented. The test whether a path exists between two arbitrary lattice states is performed once in advance for all state pairs using the all-pairs shortest path algorithm (APSP). ASR lattices are acyclic by definition which allows us to compute the APSP adjacency list in time $\mathcal{O}(|S|^2|E|)$, where $|S|$ is the number of states in the lattice and $|E|$ the number of arcs. For the minimized lattices the number of states rarely exceeds several thousands. This makes it possible to compute the complete APSP adjacency lists.

If the state accessibility constraints are fulfilled, the hypothesis is expanded. As in the case of monotonic lattice-based search described in Section 4.4.3.3, The costs $q_{TM}(\cdot)$ of the phrase translation extension include the source LM and acoustic model costs for the words in the span covered by the extension, with corresponding scaling factors. These costs are added to the total costs of the currently considered hypothesis.

The whole algorithm is formulated in pseudo-code in Figure 4.13. The difference to the algorithm for text input in Figure 1.5 is in the lines 7 and 8 printed in bold and line 14. In line 7, the loop is over all source phrases which match a lattice subpath between slots j' and $j' + l$. Each of such subpaths begins in node n' and ends in node n''. The node accessibility constraints informally described above are checked in the Path_OK function in line 8. The backpointer $B(C, \tilde{e}, j)$ is a parameter of this function, because it is used to retrieve the lattice states $\hat{l}$ and $\hat{r}$ of the previous expansions; then, the accessibility of n' from $\hat{l}$ and $\hat{r}$ from n'' is checked. If the constraints are not fulfilled, the source phrase is discarded; otherwise the translation options for the source phrase are considered. In line 14, the saved backpointer information now includes also the first and last state of the lattice subpath with the best translation.

The presented algorithm is a generalization of the CN translation algorithm presented e.g. in [Bertoldi & Zens+ 07]. As already mentioned, a CN is a special case of a lattice, in which each path from the start state to the end state goes through all the other states. Therefore, the state accessibility constraints are automatically fulfilled for a CN. A word lattice can be collapsed into a CN by placing all arcs with the same slot id between two adjacent nodes and inserting ε arcs in case of gaps in the slot enumeration. As a consequence, a CN derived from a lattice contains all the paths of the lattice and – normally many – extra paths which have to be searched in the MT process. As our experiments show, this can make CN translation slower than translation of a general lattice from which this CN was generated. Moreover,

4.4 Phrase-based speech translation using a log-linear model

INPUT: lattice L, translation options $E(j', j'', n', n'')$ for each lattice slot range (j', j'') between lattice states n' and n'', models $q_{TM}(\cdot)$, $q_{LM}(\cdot)$ and $q_{DM}(\cdot)$.

0   $Q(\emptyset, \$, 0) = 0$; all other $Q(\cdot, \cdot, \cdot)$ entries are initialized to $-\infty$.
1   FOR cardinality $c = 1$ TO $\hat{J}$ DO
2   FOR source phrase length $l = 1$ TO $\min\{L_s, c\}$ DO
3   FOR ALL coverages $C \subset \{1, ..., \hat{J}\} : |C| = c - l$ DO
4   FOR ALL start positions $j' \in \{1, ..., \hat{J}\} : C \cap \{j', ..., j' + l\} = \emptyset$ DO
5   coverage $C' = C \cup \{j', ..., j' + l\}$
6   FOR ALL states $\tilde{e}, j \in Q(C', \cdot, \cdot)$ DO
7   **FOR ALL lattice node pairs** (n', n'') **in** $E(j', j' + l, \cdot, \cdot)$ **DO**
8   **IF NOT** Path_OK$(n', n'', B(C, \tilde{e}, j))$ **CONTINUE;**
9   FOR ALL phrase translations $\tilde{e}' \in E(j', j' + l, n', n'')$ DO
10   score $= Q(C, \tilde{e}, j) + q_{TM}(\tilde{e}', j', j' + l) + q_{LM}(\tilde{e}'|\tilde{e}) + q_{DM}(j, j')$
11   language model state $\tilde{e}'' = \tilde{e} \oplus \tilde{e}'$
12   IF score $> Q(C', \tilde{e}'', j' + l)$
13   THEN $Q(C', \tilde{e}'', j' + l) = $ score
14                 $B(C', \tilde{e}'', j' + l) = (C, \tilde{e}, j, n', n'')$
15                 $A(C', \tilde{e}'', j' + l) = \tilde{e}'$

Figure 4.13: Non-monotonic source cardinality-synchronous search algorithm for word lattice input (without pruning).

translating the original lattices is usually a better option in terms of translation quality, since the translation model is in most cases not strong enough to differentiate between correct and incorrect extra paths added to the search space in the process of CN construction. Experiments in Section 4.5.3 support this consideration.

The main advantage of SCSS for word lattices is that the same reordering constraints can be used as in case of single best input. For instance, word-based or phrase-based IBM or local constraints can be applied. The reordering window (i. e. the number of word positions or gaps which can be skipped for later processing) is defined in terms of slots. The constraints are computed from the coverage vector C, the last covered slot, and the first candidate slot j'. The jump-based or the lexicalized maximum-entropy based distortion model can also be used in the log-linear model combination. All of this is possible because the reordering is defined in terms of source/target phrase pairs and their positions as given by the slot enumeration, and is completely separated from the lattice topology. The only limitation on the reordering is the computational complexity of the search which is higher for lattice than for single best input. For large lattices, it may be necessary to perform reordering using only a small window size. Another option is to prune the original lattice, or to adjust the pruning thresholds used in the search.

4.4.4 Combination with the tuple-based model

In an effort to improve the overall translation quality, a novel combination of the phrase-based and tuple based translation models has been proposed in [Matusov & Zens[+] 06]. The idea was to perform the monotonic lattice-based beam search or the cardinality-synchronous search using bilingual phrase pairs, but additionally score the sequences of these phrases with a tuple-based m-gram LM when they are created in the search. To this end, we had to first obtain the word alignment between the words within each phrase pair as learned in training. Then, based on this word alignment, the phrase pair was transformed into a sequence of bilingual tuples.

To keep the size of the additional LM minimal, we chose to use the bilingual pair transformation as described in Section 4.3.2.1, including reordering of the source words within the source phrase for monotonization of the alignment (see Section 4.3.4.2). To this end, we first determined full-coverage alignments for all the source words within a phrase pair, reordered the source words to make the alignment monotonic, and, finally, obtained one-to-one alignments by leaving out all but the minimum-cost link in a many-to-one alignment link group.

Generally, a within-phrase alignment was available as a cut-out from the alignment of the training sentence pair from which the phrase pair in question had been extracted. However, these alignments are optimized for phrase extraction and are usually more general than one-to-one alignments, i.e. contain many-to-many links and many empty word connections. To obtain the alignments needed for the transformation to bilingual pairs, we performed the following. If a source word was unaligned we aligned such a word with the word in the other language that had the smallest word-based lexicon costs. After reordering of the source words, in case of a many-to-one alignment link group we kept only one alignment connection which again had the lowest word-based lexicon costs.

The transformation of the bilingual training corpus for the estimation of the tuple m-gram LM was similar to the transformation of the phrase pairs in the sense that full-coverage one-to-one alignments were used[f], resulting in sequences of bilingual pairs for each sentence pair. However, here the cost matrices computed from the state occupation probabilities were used to determine the alignments as described in Section 4.3.2.2, instead of the Viterbi alignment connections and lexicon costs. The resulting small mismatch between sequences of the bilingual pairs used for training of the LM and those scored by this LM in the search had to be accepted, because the word alignment for training sentence pairs computed using alignment cost matrices may not be the optimal alignment for phrase extraction. Computing such alignment for each instance of a phrase pair as extracted based on some (combination of) Viterbi alignments would have been too inefficient.

The joint m-gram LM probability was included in the log-linear translation model in the following way. Given a transformation (with source sentence reordering) of the source sentence f_1^J and its possible translation e_1^I into K bilingual pairs t_1^K of the form $f|e$, $f|\$$, $\$|e$, the joint translation probability feature is given by:

$$h_{tuple}(f_1^J, e_1^I) = \log \prod_{k=1}^{K} p(t_k | t_{k-m+1}^{k-1}). \qquad (4.37)$$

In the search, the translation is built by concatenating bilingual phrases. Similar to the LM score, the bilingual m-gram LM score is computed based on previous phrase translation decisions. Thus, we extend the algorithm in Figure 4.13 by adding another score in Line 10:

$$q_{tuple}(\tilde{e}, \tilde{e}', \tilde{f}, \tilde{f}') = \sum_{k=1}^{K(\tilde{f},\tilde{e})} \log p(t_k | t_{k-1}, \ldots, t_1, \bar{t}(\tilde{f}', \tilde{e}')) \qquad (4.38)$$

In Equation 4.38, the index k runs over the bilingual pair sequence for the phrase pair $(\tilde{f}, \tilde{e})$. The value $K(\tilde{f}, \tilde{e})$ is the total length of this sequence. The term $\bar{t}(\tilde{f}', \tilde{e}')$ denotes the tuple sequence for the previously translated phrase pair. It represents the context across phrase boundaries. In practice, the context is limited to $m-1$ words so that tuples from $\bar{t}(\tilde{f}', \tilde{e}')$ are used as LM history in the computation of the m-gram probability only for the first couple of tuples of the current phrase pair. Each state in the search space $(C, \tilde{e}, j)$ (see Section 1.3) has to be extended to save the history of the bilingual tuple-based LM in addition to the target LM history.

Experimental results show that the introduction of the tuple LM feature can slightly improve translation quality. The reason for this is that across-phrase context is considered not only through the n-gram target LM dependency, but also through the dependency on up to $m-1$ source words in the tuple LM. The model is especially useful for translation of ASR lattices since it provides an additional knowledge source for selecting well-formed source word

---

[f] including possible reordering of the words in the source sentence

sequences. When the model is added, such sequences are selected based not only on the source language model information, but also based on the coherence of the source word sequences with their possible target language translations, as modelled by the joint probability tuple-based translation model. In fact, experiments prove that the tuple-based model can to some extent replace the source LM for lattice translation (see Section 4.5.2).

Combination of phrase-based and tuple-based models was later also proposed in [R. Costa-jussà & Crego[+] 07]. However, they performed the combination in a re-ranking framework. The N-best list produced by the phrase-based translation system was scored using the tuple-based system and re-ranked based on combination of both systems' scores.

4.5 Experimental results

The goals of the experiments in this chapter are

- to show that, under specific conditions, alternative paths in ASR word lattices can be used by an MT system to avoid some recognition errors and therefore improve translation quality;
- to explore the potential of the lattice-based translation and find out what types of ASR and MT errors are usually corrected;
- to compare the performance of two different speech translation models and test their combination;
- to test the role that different representations of ASR output and different ASR scores play in the improvements obtained through translation of multiple ASR hypotheses;
- to show that a translation algorithm that allows for exhaustive reordering can be effectively used for lattice input.

In Section 4.5.1, we first describe the four small and large vocabulary speech translation tasks on which the experiments were performed. Section 4.5.2 shows under which conditions one should expect translation quality improvements using word lattices with ASR scores. There we show how two translation systems deal with lattices of different quality on several small and large vocabulary tasks. The first system is the joint probability system realized with WFSTs, as described in Section 4.3; we denote it with the acronym FSA. The second system is the implementation of the phrase-based log-linear model presented in Section 4.4, which we denote with PBT (phrase-based translation). We compare the performance of the two models and investigate their combination.

Table 4.1: Corpus statistics of the development and test data for the BTEC Italian-to-English and Chinese-to-English translation tasks.

		Italian	Chinese
Dev:	Sentences	253	506
	Running Words/Characters	1 472	4 158
	Out-Of-Vocabulary rate [%]	3.1	0.2
	ASR WER/CER [%]	23.3	19.3
	avg. lattice density	49	14.6
	ASR graph error rate [%]	15.6	4.1
Test:	Sentences	253	506
	Running Words/Characters	1 459	4 540
	Out-Of-Vocabulary rate [%]	2.5	0.3
	ASR WER/CER [%]	21.4	20.6
	avg. lattice density	59	18.3
	ASR graph error rate [%]	15.4	4.7

Section 4.5.3 compares different search strategies and helps to find out which representation of multiple ASR hypotheses – lattices or confusion networks – leads to better translation results. We also explore the potential of the approach by conducting "oracle" experiments.

Finally, in Section 4.5.5 we investigate the importance of word and phrase reordering for translation of word lattices and show that significant improvements can be obtained using the PBT system with phrase-based reordering on a task with significant differences in word order between the source and the target language.

4.5.1 Corpus statistics

The experiments are performed on the following three small and medium vocabulary tasks and one large vocabulary task. The corpus statistics for the MT training data for these tasks are provided in Appendix A.

- *BTEC Italian-to-English task:* the *Basic Travel Expression Corpus* (BTEC) consists of tourism-related sentences usually found in phrase books for tourists going abroad. We were kindly provided with this corpus by FBK (Trento, Italy). The training corpus statistics are shown in Appendix in Table A.2. The development and test corpus statistics for this task are given in Table 4.1. Word lattices of a 506 sentence CSTAR'03

Table 4.2: Corpus statistics of the LC-STAR Spanish development and test corpora used for translation to English and Catalan.

		Spanish
Dev	Sentences	518
	Running Words	12030
	Out-Of-Vocabulary rate [%]	2.2
	ASR WER [%]	27.3
Test	Sentences	519
	Running Words	13365
	Out-Of-Vocabulary rate [%]	2.2
	ASR WER [%]	31.9

test corpus have been provided. The corpus was divided in two equal parts, one of which was used as a development set to tune the model scaling factors. The lattice density in Table 4.1 is defined as the number of arcs in a lattice divided by the segment reference length, averaged over all segments. It is measured after determinization and minimization of the original lattices. The ASR graph error rate is the minimum WER among all paths through the lattice. For the evaluation, 16 reference translations of the correct transcriptions were made available. The evaluation was performed using the established measures BLEU, TER, WER and PER which are described in Chapter 3. The evaluation was case-insensitive, without using punctuation marks.

- *BTEC Chinese-to-English task*: Another BTEC corpus was available to us for Chinese-to-English translation through participation in the evaluation campaign of the International Workshop on Spoken Language Translation (IWSLT, [Eck & Hori 05]). The CSTAR'03 set was the development set, and the IWSLT'05 set was the test set. The corpus statistics for the training corpora can be found in Appendix in Table A.2. The translation system was trained on the character level to alleviate the large mismatch between the Chinese vocabulary used in ASR lattice generation and the vocabulary used for the MT training corpus. Therefore, Table 4.1 lists the number of Chinese characters for the used development and test corpora. The ASR word lattices were also converted from representing word hypotheses to representing character hypotheses. To this end, a lattice arc representing a word with multiple characters was converted into a sequence of character arcs, and the hypothesized duration of the word was divided uniformly among its characters as described in [Hoffmeister & Plahl[+] 07]. On this task, the evaluation conditions were the same as for the Italian-to-English translation, except that punctuation marks were included.

Table 4.3: Corpus statistics of the development and test data for the TC-STAR Spanish-to-English speech translation task.

	2006 EPPS	2007 EPPS	2007 Spanish Parliament
Sentences	792	746	596
Running Words	22 474	25 829	29 498
Out-Of-Vocabulary rate [%]	0.2	0.4	0.6
ASR WER/CER [%]	7.2	8.2	12.9
avg. lattice density	57	62	148
ASR graph error rate [%]	2.01	2.7	4.2

- *LC-STAR Spanish-to-Catalan and Spanish-to-English tasks*: the third task is based on bilingual corpora which had been prepared within the European LC-STAR project [Arranz & Castell+ 03] and contain spontaneous utterances from travel and appointment scheduling domains. The original LC-STAR training corpus contained a high percentage of singletons, especially for Spanish. Therefore, some Spanish singletons were mapped to their morphological baseforms for training of word alignments and phrase extraction. When translating from word lattices, we also mapped the singletons in the word lattice by composing it with an appropriate transducer. The utterances in the LC-STAR test data are complete telephone dialog turns and significantly longer (about 23 words on average) than the utterances in the BTEC corpus. They were recognized with the RWTH ASR system in 2005. The development and test corpus statistics for this task are given in Table 4.2. The training corpus statistics are provided in Appendix in Table A.1.

- *TC-STAR Spanish-to-English large vocabulary task*: we also tested lattice translation on a large vocabulary task, namely machine translation of parliamentary speeches given in the European Parliament Plenary Sessions (EPPS) and in the Parliament of Spain. The training corpus for this task has been collected in the framework of the European research project TC-STAR. It contains over 30 million words of bilingual Spanish-English data. In addition, about 40 hours of speech data has been transcribed. Here, we present experimental results for translation from Spanish to English. We use the same test corpora as in the 2006 and 2007 TC-STAR evaluations, for which two reference translations were available. However, we use the ASR output of the RWTH ASR system [Lööf & Gollan+ 07] (single best and word lattices) instead of the official evaluation data for the ASR condition. The training corpus statistics for this task are given in Appendix in Table A.7. The translation vocabulary sizes are as large as 125 thousand words. The vocabulary used for Spanish speech recognition is smaller – about

50 thousand words. The development and test data statistics are shown in Table 4.3. The 2006 EPPS test set was used as a held-out development corpus for translation results on both 2007 test sets. For experiments on the 2006 EPPS test set, the 2007 EPPS test set played the role of the development data.

4.5.2 Translation of word lattices

The goal of the experiments in this section is to show how and under which conditions speech translation quality can be improved using multiple ASR hypotheses represented in word lattices. We investigate the influence of acoustic and source LM scores in the lattice on the translation results. We also compare the performance of two different translation systems: the WFST implementation of the joint probability MT system described in Section 4.3 (FSA) and the phrase-based MT system that uses a log-linear model, see Section 4.4 (PBT). Finally, we estimate the benefits and risks of using ASR word lattices as input to statistical MT systems in dependency on the general quality of these MT systems and on the general quality of the ASR systems that produced those lattices.

4.5.2.1 BTEC Italian-to-English task

We begin with the experiments on the BTEC Italian-to-English task. For the FSA system, a 4-gram tuple translation model was estimated on the bilingual representation of the training corpus for this task. To train this model, we performed reordering of the target language training sentences based on the word alignment (see Section 4.3.4.2). Therefore, the hypotheses produced by the system had to be permuted and scored using a target language model. The reordering constraints were selected based on the translation quality on the development set. The best results were achieved using IBM constraints with a window size of 2. To score the reordering graph, we used a 4-gram English LM.

The same 4-gram English LM was used in the search by the PBT system. In order to include the source language model feature in this system, we extended each word lattice by the scores of a trigram language model. Moderate pruning of coverage hypotheses was applied in the PBT system, whereas the experiments with the FSA system were performed without any pruning.

In this section, we present the experiments with the PBT system using only the monotonic beam search and its reordering extension described in Sections 4.4.3.3 and 4.4.3.4. This is done to enable a fair comparison with the FSA system which also performs monotonic translation with a very limited local word reordering as a postprocessing step. To make the two systems

Table 4.4: Translation results on the BTEC Italian-to-English task. Comparison of the log-linear model approach (PBT, see Section 4.4) with the joint probability approach (FSA, see Section 4.3).

System:	Input:	BLEU [%]	TER [%]	WER [%]	PER [%]
FSA	correct transcript	61.5	27.8	29.3	22.9
	single best	53.2	37.3	38.2	32.7
	lattice without scores	55.0	35.6	36.2	31.1
	lattice + ac. scores	55.7	34.3	35.0	29.8
PBT	correct transcript	66.2	26.0	26.6	22.9
	single best	53.4	37.3	38.2	32.0
	+ re-optimization on ASR output	55.5	36.2	37.2	31.2
	lattice without scores	54.8	37.2	37.8	33.3
	+ ac. + LM scores	56.2	35.8	36.5	31.7
	+ optimize all factors	57.7	34.2	34.8	30.5
	+ reordering (skip 1 phrase)	58.4	35.0	35.9	30.4

even more comparable, we limit the source phrase length used in the PBT system to 4, and do not use any extra features such as the phrase count features described in [Mauser & Zens[+] 06]. We also optimize the PBT model scaling factors with respect to WER/TER, since this was the criterion for selecting the best translation model scaling factor for the FSA system (see the experiments below). The experiments using the cardinality-synchronous search for lattice input and the comparison of this more advanced search with the monotonic beam search will be presented in Section 4.5.3.

The automatic error measures for the two systems on the BTEC Italian-to-English task are summarized in Table 4.4. In the table, we differentiate between the following conditions:

- *Correct transcript:* translation of the manually transcribed test data.
- *Single best:* translation of the single best speech recognition result for the same data. The ASR word error rate for this result is given in Table 4.1.
- *Lattice:* translation of ASR word lattices. Here, we first consider the case "*without scores*" when the acoustic/source LM scores are not used (their scaling factors are set to 0). Then, we either add the acoustic model feature "*+ ac. scores*" for the FSA system or both the acoustic and source LM features as given by Equations 4.29 and 4.30 for the PBT system. The scaling factors for these features are optimized on the development set.

4 Coupling of speech recognition and machine translation

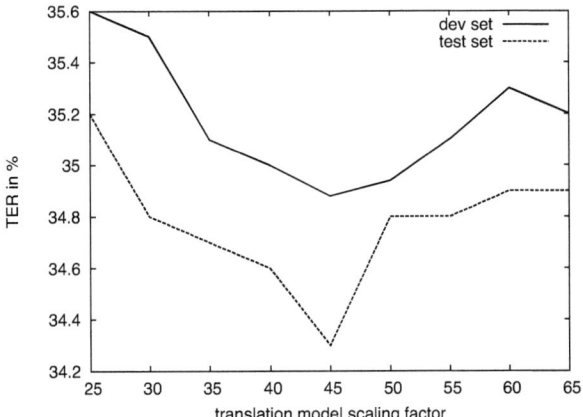

Figure 4.14: Dependency of the translation edit rate for WFST-based ASR translation on the scaling factor for the translation model (BTEC Italian-to-English task, development and test sets).

In case of the PBT system, we also optimized the MT features and the ASR features of the log-linear translation model together ("*opt all factors*"). Finally, the line "*reordering (skip 1 phrase)*" refers to the one-phrase "skip" reordering of the PBT system described in Section 4.4.3.4.

For the FSA system, it can be observed in Table 4.4 that exploring the alternative ASR hypotheses from the word lattices without using their scores can somewhat improve the MT error measures (e. g. TER from 37.3 to 35.6%). The improvements become statistically significant when we combine the acoustic model from the speech recognition with the tuple-based LM. To this end, we include a scaling factor for one of the two models: the translation model. It is important to optimize this scaling factor on a development set. Figure 4.14 shows the TER results in dependency on the translation model scaling factor on the development and test sets. As mentioned in Section 4.2.1, replacing the translation model in the decision criterion for the joint probability approach with the source language model would result in the standard (source-channel) decision criterion for speech recognition. Therefore, one could assume that the scaling factor for the translation model should be the same as the usual scaling factor for the LM in ASR, e. g. not higher than 20. However, our experiments show that an optimal translation model factor is generally higher. On this task, the optimal scaling factor is 45. This can be explained by the nature of the translation model. Since the tuple LM was trained by counting the joint events of a source word sequence and its target translation, it gives high probabilities to the source n-grams with frequently observed translations, but can

Table 4.5: Examples of improvements with the integrated speech translation approach (BTEC Italian-to-English task, PBT system).

Input	Translation
single best	I'm very sick lost
lattice	I feel much better now
reference	I feel much better now
single best	when should I take it ma'am
lattice	when should I take it sir
reference	when should I bring it sir

strongly penalize the n-grams which are frequent in the source language, but the translations of which are very ambiguous or were rarely seen in training. To partially counteract this effect and balance the influence of the translation model with the power of the acoustic model, the scaling factor for the translation model has to be this large.

The second part of Table 4.4 presents the speech translation results for the PBT system (monotonic beam search). First, it is notable that using the PBT system as a "black box" to translate single best ASR output (without re-optimization of the 7 log-linear translation model parameters on the ASR output) results in worse translation quality than when the translation model parameters are re-optimized on the single best ASR output for the development set. Since the ASR scores in the lattice are to be optimized together with the translation scores also on the ASR output (in this case, using ASR lattices), it is clear that a comparison of lattice translations to this second result would be more fair. Using lattices without scores as input to the PBT system does not improve the translation quality if compared to this fair baseline. This means that in some cases the system is confused by hypotheses which are easy to translate but have little in common with the spoken words.

In the next experiment we added both the acoustic model score and the source language model score with corresponding scaling factors to the log-linear model of the PBT system. As already stated, the language model score is used to model the context dependency for the source language. Without this model, such dependency is only captured within the source phrases of the phrasal lexicon. The scaling factors for the two recognition features only or for translation and recognition features simultaneously (a total of 9 features) were optimized in the log-linear model on a development set. Using the Downhill Simplex algorithm, we iteratively improved word error rate. Table 4.4 shows the improvements in translation quality on the test set when using optimized scaling factors. When all 9 features are optimized jointly,

4 Coupling of speech recognition and machine translation

the improvements are significant. The largest improvement as compared to the more fair baseline reaches 2.1% in BLEU and 2.0% in TER absolute. Examples of translation quality improvements with the PBT system are given in Table 4.5.

In summary, the improvements in translation quality on the BTEC Italian-to-English task due to processing of ASR lattices are significant for both FSA and PBT systems, provided that the ASR scores are included in the decision criterion for speech translation with appropriate scaling factors. In addition, we explain these positive results by the following qualities of the ASR and MT systems which were combined on this task:

- The ASR system with more than 20% first-best error rate is not very robust. However, the graph error rate of 15.4% (see Table 4.1) shows that many of the correct ASR hypotheses are contained in the word lattices produced by this system and can be explored by the subsequent speech translation algorithms.

- On the given task with a limited vocabulary size and short sentences with only local word order differences between source and target language, both statistical MT systems produce good-quality translations (e.g. having only around 23% word choice errors (PER) on correct transcripts) with strong translation models. These models are therefore often able to discriminate between correct and erroneous ASR hypotheses.

If we compare the performance of the FSA system and the PBT system on this task, we can observe that the PBT system generally performs significantly better than the FSA system in terms of measures like BLEU, TER, and WER for which the correct word order in the translations is important. In terms of the position-independent error rate PER, the performance of the two systems is similar. We attribute the better performance of the PBT system to the fact that many local reorderings of the "noun-adjective" pair common to translations from Italian to English are already captured in the phrase pairs extracted for the PBT system. For the FSA system, the reordering in such cases has to be performed as a postprocessing step. Also, the log-linear model of the PBT system has the advantage that several phrase-based and word-based translation features in this model supplement each other. In the FSA system, only a single tuple-based translation model is used.

In the FSA system, the reordering as a postprocessing step is performed under the IBM constraints so that a few long-range reorderings become possible. Therefore, it may be useful to compare the performance of the FSA system not only with the monotonic beam search in the PBT system, but also to its extension that allows to skip a phrase in the style of IBM constraints as described in Section 4.4.3.4. The corresponding experimental result is included in the last line of Table 4.4. We observe that the additional reordering only improves the BLEU score, whereas TER and WER show a negative impact of the "skip". Thus, this type of reordering is not very effective on this task. In Section 4.5.5, it will be shown that a higher improvement in both BLEU and TER can be obtained using reordering in the cardinality-synchronous search.

4.5.2.2 TC-STAR Spanish-to-English task

Next, we present speech translation results on the TC-STAR Spanish-to-English task. This is a large vocabulary task with about 1.2 million parallel sentence pairs for training (see Table A.7 in Appendix A). The development and test data consists of speeches made by several speakers in the European and Spanish Parliament. The ASR output provides only a rough acoustic segmentation of these speeches into long utterances. To obtain sentence-like units suitable for translation, we developed and applied a sentence segmentation algorithm. This algorithm will be described in detail in Chapter 5. The algorithm was applied to the single best ASR output. Based on the new segment boundaries, the ASR word lattices were generated in another recognition pass. The word hypotheses in the ASR lattices included the acoustic model score and a 4-gram source LM score.

Due to the complexity of this task, we only trained the PBT system with the monotonic beam search. Reordering was performed as a postprocessing step on the translation hypotheses. For this purpose, the MT output was automatically tagged with part-of-speech tags, and manual reordering rules for noun-adjective and noun-adverb pairs were applied. The details of this procedure are described in [Popović & Ney 06].

In translation, we used a 4-gram target LM. We also performed model combination as described in Section 4.4.4. The extracted phrase pairs were scored with a trigram tuple-based LM.

The evaluation was case-insensitive, using punctuation marks. The ASR output did not contain punctuation marks; therefore, they had to be predicted in the translation process as described in Chapter 5. The produced translations were based on this automatic sentence segmentation. Thus, the translation output had to be re-segmented for the evaluation so that it matches the segmentation of the manual reference translations using the algorithm proposed in Chapter 3.

Table 4.6 presents the results of speech translation experiments on three different corpora: the 2006 and 2007 TC-STAR evaluation sets with speeches from the European Parliament and the 2007 TC-STAR evaluation set with speeches from the Spanish parliament. Here, we compare the following experimental conditions:

- *correct transcript:* translation of the correctly transcribed speeches;

Table 4.6: Speech translation results on the TC-STAR Spanish-to-English task.

Test set	Input	BLEU [%]	TER [%]	WER [%]	PER [%]
2006 EPPS	correct transcript	46.9	39.9	43.1	29.7
	single best	42.9	44.3	47.7	32.5
	word lattice	43.3	43.9	47.4	32.2
2007 EPPS	correct transcript	46.6	39.3	42.4	28.7
	single best	42.4	43.5	46.6	32.0
	word lattice	42.7	43.3	46.3	31.8
2007 Spanish Parliament	correct transcript	40.1	45.3	48.9	31.8
	single best	34.3	51.1	54.8	36.2
	word lattice	34.6	50.8	54.4	36.1

- *single best:* translation of the single best ASR output;

- *word lattice:* translation of ASR word lattices. For these experiments, the acoustic and source LM scores of the lattices were optimized together with the 7 translation features in the log-linear model on a development set. The optimization criterion was the BLEU score.

The results in Table 4.6 show that consistent improvements in all error measures and on all three test sets can be obtained by exploring multiple ASR hypotheses in the word lattices and using the power of the translation model features to avoid some recognition errors still present in the single best ASR output. However, the improvements are rather small - not more than 0.4 absolute in BLEU or TER. We attribute this to the fact that the ASR WER of the single best ASR output is already rather low - e.g. only 7.2% for the 2006 test set. Thus, the translation model may not be trained well enough to correct the few remaining errors.

This argument is supported by the following experiment. We modified the RWTH ASR system in such a way that some of its features are not used. This allowed us to produce two additional sets of ASR word lattices which correspond to single best ASR output of an inferior quality to the one used for experiments in Table 4.6. Thus, in total we could compare the translations of the output from the following 3 ASR systems:

1. The first system is the official RWTH ASR system that participated in 2007 evaluation and obtained a 7.2% WER on the 2006 test set. It used an acoustic front end consisting of Mel Frequency Cepstral Coefficient (MFCC) features, augmented with a voicedness feature. Vocal Tract Length Normalization (VTLN) was applied to the filterbank within the MFCC extraction both in training and testing. In recognition, a fast one pass VTLN

Table 4.7: Improvements in BLEU due to word lattice translation using lattices produced by ASR systems of different quality (TC-STAR Spanish-to-English task, 2006 EPPS test set). Comparison with the approach of [Bertoldi & Zens[+] 07] who translate confusion networks for another EPPS test set.

	ASR system 1	ASR system 2	ASR system 3	[Bertoldi & Zens[+] 07]
ASR single best WER [%]	7.2	10.0	16.2	22.4
avg. lattice density	57	180	472	?
ASR graph error rate [%]	2.01	2.55	4.68	8.45
BLEU single best ASR [%]	42.88	41.83	38.58	37.6
BLEU word lattice [%]	43.26	42.69	39.63	39.2
absolute BLEU improvement [%]	0.38	0.86	1.05	1.6
relative BLEU improvement [%]	0.89	2.06	2.72	4.26

method was used, where the warping factor was estimated using a Gaussian mixture classifier, trained on the acoustic training corpus. The recognition system also includes constrained maximum likelihood linear regression (CMLLR) including speaker adaptive training (SAT), maximum likelihood linear regression (MLLR), and discriminative minimum phone error (MPE) training. Details are described in [Lööf & Gollan[+] 07].

2. The second system is the same as the evaluation system, but we only take the results of the first search pass, skipping the speaker adaptation in the second pass. The single best ASR word error rate on the 2006 test set deteriorates to 10.0%.

3. the difference of the third system to the first one is that it uses a single Gaussian for the HMM emission probabilities instead of the full Gaussian mixture model; here, we also performed only the first search pass. Thus, we obtain the WER of 16.2% on the 2006 test set.

Table 4.7 shows the BLEU scores for translations of single best and lattice output of these three ASR systems. It can be observed that both absolute and relative improvement due to word lattice translation increases if we use less and less sophisticated ASR systems. The improvement in BLEU for system 3 is more than 1% absolute. Thus, translating word lattices can result in significant improvements of MT quality even on a large vocabulary task. It is worth noting that the lattice density for systems 2 and 3 is much larger[g], so that the graph error rate does not degrade significantly, and good-quality paths are thus still available for selection by the MT system.

---

[g]The same pruning settings were used to create all three sets of lattices.

Table 4.8: Improvements due to lattice-based translation: comparison of the error rates for those segments, for which the lattice-based translation produced results different from the translations of the single best output (TC-STAR 2007 EPPS test set).

Input	BLEU [%]	TER [%]	WER [%]	PER [%]
single best	40.3	45.6	49.0	33.1
lattice	41.0	45.1	48.3	32.8

The improvements of around 3% relative in BLEU when using system 3 are comparable to those of [Bertoldi & Zens+ 07], who translated confusion networks on the same TC-STAR Spanish-to-English task, but with a different MT system and on a different, but similar EPPS test set (see the last column of Table 4.7). The single best ASR WER in their experiments is 22.4%, which is even worse than the WER of system 3. This makes it easier to achieve improvements by considering better ASR hypotheses in the confusion networks or lattices. Based on this comparison, the lattice translation system proposed in this thesis can compete with a state-of-the-art speech translation approach that also considers multiple ASR hypotheses.

The ASR systems 2 and 3 have a smaller real-time factor than system 1 and therefore are better suited for coupling with an MT system if the whole architecture is to be used for on-line translation. Therefore, it may be reasonable to pursue lattice-based translation in such cases to improve the final output quality of an on-line system.

Even if we use the best available ASR system, the phrase-based MT system can effectively avoid some recognition errors by assigning them a bad score. In Table 4.8, we only show the results on the 315 out of 746 (reference) sentences of the 2007 EPPS test set for which the result of the lattice-based translation was different from the result of the single best ASR output translation. The ASR system 1 was used. It can be observed that all error measures improve; the BLEU score improves by 0.7% absolute. Examples of these improvements are given in Table 4.9. Whereas in the first three examples in the table the translation quality is clearly improved by avoiding recognition errors, the last example is more difficult to explain. Here, the single best ASR output is correct, but the lattice-based MT still selects a better translation for "investigadores ni fiscales", most probably due to a differently translated context in the following part of the sentence not shown here. Additional examples of lattice-based translations from the 2007 EPPS test set can be found in Appendix B.

In the results for the TC-STAR task presented above, we always combined the phrase-based model with the joint probability tuple-based model by scoring each phrase pair with a trigram tuple LM (see Section 4.4.4). The tuple LM score was used as an additional feature in the

Table 4.9: Examples of translation quality improvements due to the lattice-based translation (TC-STAR Spanish-to-English task). The recognition errors are marked in bold.

Condition	Transcription/translation
single best ASR	Europa **nos** ha hundido en el mar
correct transcript	Europa no se ha hundido en el mar
MT of single best	Europe has sunk into the sea
MT of lattice	Europe has not sunk in the sea
reference	Europe has not sunk in the ocean
single best ASR	este Parlamento que ha sido **par** pionero en muchas otras ocasiones ...
correct transcript	este Parlamento que ha sido pionero en muchas otras ocasiones ...
MT of single best	this Parliament , which has been couple pioneering on many other occasions ...
MT of lattice	this Parliament , which has been a pioneer in many other occasions ...
reference	this Parliament , which has been a pioneer on many other occasions ...
single best ASR	... pero también por **las ong se** han alegado aquí
correct transcript	... pero también por unas razones que se han alegado aquí
MT of single best	... but also by the NGOs have been mentioned here
MT of lattice	... but also for the reasons which have been mentioned here
reference	... but also for some reasons that have been alleged here
single best ASR	cierto es que no somos investigadores ni fiscales ...
correct transcript	cierto es que no somos investigadores ni fiscales ...
MT of single best	it is true that we are not researchers or tax ...
MT of lattice	it is true that we are not investigators and prosecutors ...
reference	it is truth that we are not investigators or prosecutors ...

log-linear model combination. In [Matusov & Zens[+] 06], it was mentioned that this feature results in some translation quality improvements for translation of the correct transcripts. The tuple LM feature may be important for word lattice translation because it contains context dependency on the previous bilingual tuples (e.g. on the last two tuples in case of a trigram tuple LM) and, therefore, the dependency on previous source words. Thus, this feature can either play the role of the source LM to better evaluate the quality of the alternative ASR

4 Coupling of speech recognition and machine translation

Table 4.10: ASR lattice translation: the role of translation model combination for the case when the source LM feature is not used in the log-linear model (TC-STAR Spanish-to-English task).

Test set	Features include:	BLEU [%]	TER [%]	WER [%]	PER [%]
2007 EPPS test set	source LM, tuple LM	42.7	43.3	46.3	31.8
	source LM, no tuple LM	42.7	43.2	46.2	31.8
	no source LM, tuple LM	41.0	45.6	48.7	33.6
	no source LM, no tuple LM	39.8	46.4	49.4	34.3

hypotheses in the MT search, or it can supplement the source LM.

Table 4.10 shows the results for lattice translation on the 2007 EPPS test set including a source LM and/or tuple LM feature, or without one or both of these features. For each of the four experiments, the scaling factors for the translation and ASR features were re-optimized on the development set. We can observe that, unfortunately, the tuple LM provides almost no gain in translation quality when used together with the source LM. However, when the source LM is not used, the tuple LM feature can significantly improve the error measures. Thus, we can observe in practice that the context dependency on the previous source words as modelled in the joint probability translation approach at least partially can help to select well-formed source word sequences in translation of word lattices. This result justifies the use of only the acoustic model score for translation of ASR word lattices with the joint probability model and therefore experimentally supports the use of decision rule derived in Equation 4.17. In case of the phrase-based log-linear model, however, the source LM feature has a better power to discriminate between well-formed and erroneous recognition hypotheses than the tuple LM feature.

4.5.2.3 LC-STAR Spanish-to-English and Spanish-to-Catalan task

The LC-STAR Spanish-to-English and Spanish-to-Catalan task is a small vocabulary task. The development and test data was the same Spanish speech, which had to be translated either to English or to Catalan. On this task, the RWTH Spanish speech recognition system had a word error rate of more than 30 % (see Table 4.2) due to limited training data, low sampling rate and large speaker variability. On the other hand, the test utterances were rather long, thus the corresponding ASR word lattices were very dense. The experimental results for the LC-STAR task can be found in Table 4.11. On this task, we used the joint probability tuple-based model for translation (FSA system). Similarly to the BTEC Italian-

Table 4.11: Translation results for the LC-STAR Spanish-to-English and Spanish-to-Catalan tasks (FSA system, see Section 4.3).

	Input:	BLEU[%]	TER[%]	WER[%]	PER[%]
Spanish	correct text	37.5	41.9	44.4	32.5
to	single best	26.1	58.4	61.1	45.6
English	word lattice	25.8	57.7	60.3	45.4
Spanish	correct text	80.8	11.8	12.2	10.5
to	single best	47.7	38.4	39.7	32.1
Catalan	word lattice	53.9	33.9	34.8	28.6

to-English task, here we also applied reordering of the target part of the training corpus as described in Section 4.3.4.2. We then trained a language model on the level of bilingual tuples for translation, and a second language model on the monolingual corpus in order to score and select different reorderings of the produced translations in a postprocessing step. Optimal results were achieved using a 3-gram for the translation model and a 4-gram for the monolingual language model.

In Table 4.11, we again consider the conditions "correct text", "single best", and "word lattice". In the "word lattice" condition, the acoustic model score was used together with the translation model score, and a scaling factor for the latter model was optimized on the development data. The optimal scaling factor λ for the translation model scores was determined to be 60 in both of the experiments in Table 4.11. When the highly erroneous single best recognition hypotheses are translated into *English*, the TER is as high as 58.4 %. The translation quality can be improved only slightly when we translate high-density word lattices with acoustic scores. We attribute this to the undertrained translation model (the error rates are already rather high for the correct Spanish input). This translation model can not discriminate well between correct and erroneous hypotheses in the word lattice. This is supported by the following observation. When we use exactly the same Spanish word lattices and translate to *Catalan*, we reach an enormous improvement of over 12 % relative in e.g. WER over the translation of the single best input (see the last lines of Table 4.11). Here, the translation model is more robust since the difference in structure and word order between Spanish and Catalan is much smaller than between Spanish and English. Thus, we can observe that the potential for improvement due to lattice translation strongly depends not only on the ASR performance, but also on the overall quality of the MT system translating the lattices.

Table 4.12: Estimation of the potential for translation quality improvement due to considering multiple ASR hypotheses based on experimental results on different ASR and speech translation tasks. The ASR system quality is estimated using WER, and the MT quality is estimated using PER on translations of correct transcripts. The estimations range from ⋆ (very small or no potential) to ⋆ ⋆ ⋆⋆ (very high potential).

ASR WER MT quality	low (< 10%)	medium (10 − 25%)	high (> 25%)
high (PER < 20%)	?	⋆ ⋆ ⋆	⋆ ⋆ ⋆⋆ LC-STAR Es-Ca + 13% BLEU rel.
medium (PER 20 − 30%)	⋆⋆ TC-STAR Es-En + 0.9% BLEU rel.	⋆ ⋆ ⋆ BTEC It-En + 4% BLEU rel.	⋆ ⋆ ⋆ BTEC Ch-En + 5% BLEU rel.
low (PER > 30%)	⋆	⋆ GALE Ch-En −	⋆⋆ LC-STAR Es-En + 1.2% BLEU rel.

4.5.2.4 Discussion

In the above experiments, we used multiple ASR hypotheses in the form of word lattices for translation of speech on three different tasks. The experimental results show that improvements by considering alternative ASR lattice paths and possibly avoiding some recognition errors can be either very small or very high depending on the quality of the involved ASR and MT systems.

Based on these and other experimental results, Table 4.12 gives an overview of the potential for improvements due to word lattice translation in dependency on the recognition quality of the ASR system that produces the word lattices and the translation quality of the MT system that is used to translate these lattices. We can roughly classify the ASR systems into 3 classes: good-quality systems with WER less than 10%, medium-quality systems with WER in the range from 10 to 25% and low-quality systems with WER higher than 25%. To classify the MT systems (or, also, the translation tasks, since the quality of the same system may be different depending on the languages and data involved), we use the position-independent word error rate. This error rate does not take reordering into account and allows for a more fair comparison of different tasks. We roughly estimate a speech translation system to have high quality if its PER on a manual speech transcript is less than 20%. A medium-quality

MT system is usually the one with a PER of 20 to 30%, and a low-quality system usually produces translations with PER scores of more than 30%.

The highest potential for improvement due to word lattice translation is for tasks where the MT quality is high, but the speech recognition quality is low. An example of such task is the translation from Spanish to Catalan where highly significant improvements can be reached. A possible application scenario where it would be of advantage to translate word lattices is a speech translation task with similar source and target languages, limited domain and/or vocabulary, but adverse acoustic conditions or speaker accent which cause many recognition errors. An example of such scenario is translation of tourism-related questions and answers on specific, limited topics, when spoken into a hand-held device on a noisy street.

A significant improvement through word lattice translation can also be reached for the case of high MT quality and medium ASR quality, or low ASR quality and medium MT quality, or for medium MT quality and an ASR system with medium word error rates. Examples include the BTEC Italian-to-English and Chinese-to-English tasks. Experiments for the Chinese-to-English translation on the BTEC task will be presented in the following sections.

Only a small improvement can be reached when the MT quality is medium, but the ASR quality is good. An example of such conditions is the TC-STAR Spanish-to-English task (with the best ASR system) where the relative improvement in e.g. BLEU does not exceed 1%. The LC-STAR Spanish-to-Catalan task shows that even with low quality of the single best ASR output an improvement with word lattices is small if the MT quality is also low.

In some cases, it is highly unlikely that the MT system will be able to discriminate between correct and erroneous hypotheses in the ASR lattices. These are the cases where the MT quality is poor, but the ASR quality is medium or good. An example of a speech translation task which fulfills these criteria is the translation of broadcast news from Chinese into English using a large vocabulary system. Such translations were performed by RWTH within the GALE research project. The quality of the unlimited domain MT from Chinese to English on this task still leaves to be desired (e.g. PER with 4 reference translations is as high as 50%), whereas the RWTH ASR system could reach character error rates of as low as 10% [Plahl & Hoffmeister[+] 08]. Preliminary experiments with word lattices produced by this system have shown that no improvement of translation quality can be expected on this task.

Finally, it is not clear if considering multiple ASR hypotheses in speech translation would be helpful if both the ASR and MT system are of good quality. So far, there have been no tasks where this was the case. Given all of the considerations above, it becomes clear that the baseline MT systems involved in word lattice translation first have to be significantly improved before it would be worth the effort to implement word lattice translation in most practical speech translation applications.

4.5.3 Comparison of input types and search strategies for speech translation

In this section, we present experiments with the phrase-based log-linear model and cardinality-synchronous search with word lattice input. This search that allows for exhaustive reordering is compared with the monotonic beam search and its limited reordering extension. We also compare experimentally the translation of ASR word lattice with translations of confusion networks constructed from these lattices. We investigate if speech translation quality can be improved by using word posterior probabilities to score word hypotheses in word lattices and CNs instead of acoustic and source LM probabilities.

4.5.3.1 BTEC Chinese-to-English task

First, we present experiments on the BTEC Chinese-to-English task. This is a medium vocabulary task with the same domain as the BTEC Italian-to-English task (see Table A.2 in Appendix). For Chinese-to-English translation, punctuation marks were kept in the target phrases so that MT system could insert them in the translation process (more details of this procedure are presented in Chapter 5). In translation with the log-linear phrase-based model, we used the features described in Section 1.3.1.4, with an addition of phrase count features [Mauser & Zens[+] 06]. When the cardinality-synchronous search was used, we also included the distance-based distortion model. The reordering was constrained with IBM constraints with the maximum number of gaps 3 and maximum jump of 7 word positions/slots. As the target language model, we used a 6-gram English LM. The BLEU score was used as the optimization criterion for tuning the log-linear model scaling factors on the development set.

The word lattices for this corpus were available to us through participation in the evaluation campaign of the 2005 International Workshop on Spoken Language Translation ([Eck & Hori 05]). They include acoustic and source LM scores. To create the confusion networks from these lattices, we used an algorithm based on the one proposed in [Mangu & Brill[+] 00] (see Section 4.4.3.1).

Table 4.13 presents the results for the BTEC Chinese-to-English task on the test set. In the experiments, we considered the following settings:

Table 4.13: Lattice vs. confusion network translation on the BTEC Chinese-to-English task.

System	Input:	BLEU[%]	TER[%]	WER[%]	PER[%]
beam search	single best	45.1	44.8	45.9	39.5
+ skip	lattice with ASR scores	48.3	42.2	43.2	36.8
cardinality-	single best	46.1	44.7	46.0	38.9
synchronous	word lattice	47.0	43.6	45.1	38.8
search	with ASR scores	48.4	42.6	43.9	37.4
with	with posterior score	47.3	43.7	45.1	38.9
exhaustive	confusion network	45.3	45.4	46.5	39.7
reordering	with posterior score	48.1	42.7	44.3	36.6
	correct transcript	56.7	35.5	37.6	30.3

- *correct transcript*: translation of correct speech transcript using source cardinality-synchronous search (SCSS) with reordering as described in Chapter 1;

- *single best*: translation of single best ASR output either using the monotonic beam search with the "skip-a-phrase" extension described in Section 4.4.3.4 (*"beam search + skip"*) or using SCSS.

- *word lattice*: translation of ASR word lattices with one of the two search strategies used for the "single best" condition. In case of the SCSS, we can either include the original ASR scores (acoustic + source LM) or the logarithm of the word posterior probability as given in Equation 4.31. In all cases, the weights for these scores are re-optimized together with translation model weights.

- *confusion network*: translation of confusion networks for the same test data using the SCSS and, optionally, the word posterior probabilities.

For the "single best" condition, using the monotonic beam search is inferior to using cardinality-synchronous search on this task. However, when the ASR word lattices are translated, both search methods result in similar translation quality. Nevertheless, the cardinality-synchronous search is up to 7 times faster and requires significantly less memory (cf. the results in Table 4.19).

Translation of single best ASR output with the CER of 20.6% has a 10% lower BLEU score than the translation of the correct transcript. Using a word lattice without ASR features in the log-linear MT model improves both BLEU and TER by about 1% absolute. In contrast, translating confusion networks[h] without scores results in a degradation of translation quality.

---
[h] created from the same lattices

Table 4.14: Comparison of the proposed lattice-based translation approach (RWTH) with the CN-based translation approach of [Shen & Delaney[+] 08] on the same test set (BTEC Chinese-to-English translation task, BLEU scores in %).

Input	RWTH	[Shen & Delaney[+] 08]
single best	46.1	42.9
word lattice/CN	48.4	45.0

We attribute this to the fact that the translation and the target language model alone can not differentiate between correct and erroneous paths, especially since reordering takes place. Translations of incorrect word hypotheses may become well-formed word sequences after a permutation; yet these sequences may have nothing to do with the spoken utterance. Including the word posteriors in the log-linear model improves the CN translations dramatically. We observe a 2.0% absolute improvement in BLEU over the single best baseline. Similarly, translating word lattices using acoustic and source LM probabilities with optimal scaling factors results in an even larger improvement of 2.3% in BLEU. Using the word posterior probabilities in lattice-based translation is inferior to using the ASR scores on this task.

For the 2008 IWSLT evaluation, the authors of [Shen & Delaney[+] 08] tested their CN-based translation approach on the same BTEC test set, for which we report results in Table 4.13. To the best of our knowledge, the original lattices which they converted to CNs are the same as the ones used in our experiments (see Table 4.1 for the lattice statistics). The main difference between the approach proposed here and the work of [Shen & Delaney[+] 08] is that they use a parallel corpus of 20K training sentences plus some additional development sets instead of the 40K corpus for training the MT systems. This makes the results hard to compare directly. Nevertheless, in Table 4.14 we report the BLEU scores for the translations of single best ASR output and word lattices or confusion networks using the two systems. The improvements in BLEU due to considering multiple ASR hypotheses are of similar magnitude for both systems, with a slightly better result for the approach presented in this thesis. Thus, the comparison in Table 4.14 again proves the competitiveness of the proposed lattice translation method.

4.5.3.2 BTEC Italian-to-English task

The main goal of the additional experiments on the BTEC Italian-to-English task was to obtain the best possible translation quality using source cardinality-synchronous search and advanced translation model features. In contrast to the PBT system presented in Section 4.5.2.1 that had been trained to be similar to the tuple-based FSA system, here we placed no restriction on the maximum phrase length and included the phrase count features. In addition, the SCSS

Table 4.15: Comparison of the word lattice and confusion network input for the phrase-based source cardinality-synchronous search (BTEC Italian-to-English task).

System:	Input:	BLEU [%]	TER [%]	WER [%]	PER [%]
cardinality-	single best	58.9	34.2	35.0	29.5
synchronous	lattice with ASR scores	61.6	33.6	34.1	30.1
search	with posterior score	63.6	32.0	32.2	27.9
with	+ LM score	62.6	31.9	32.1	28.0
exhaustive	confusion network				
reordering	with posterior score	61.1	32.3	33.0	27.9
	correct transcript	68.7	24.8	25.8	20.7

used a distortion model feature and IBM reordering constraints on the word level with the window size (maximum number of slots allowed to be skipped) of 4. The improvements in the translation model make the PBT beam search results from Section 4.5.2.1 incomparable to the SCSS results presented below; therefore, those results are not reported here again.

Table 4.15 presents the error measures on the test set for the Italian-to-English translations using the phrase-based SCSS. The conditions "single best", "lattice with ASR scores", etc. are the same as for the Chinese-to-English task. The improvement in BLEU over the translation of single best ASR output using lattices with ASR scores is about as large as when using the CNs scored with the logarithms of the word posterior probabilities (the condition "confusion network with posterior score"). At the same time, taking advantage of the alternative paths in the CNs improves all other error measures even by a larger margin (e. g. from 29.5 to 27.9% in PER). However, the largest improvement of e. g. 4.7% absolute in BLEU and 2.2% in TER is obtained by using lattices with posterior scores. This contradicts the results on the Chinese-to-English task where the best result was achieved using the theoretically motivated acoustic and source LM scores. The reason for this may be parameter overfitting. The 9 parameters from Equation 4.33 plus the scaling factors for the 3 phrase count features and the distortion model had to be optimized on the development corpus of only 253 utterances. Another reason may be the difference in lattice structure and quality between the two tasks.

4.5.4 Oracle experiments

The goal of the experiments in this section is to find out the boundaries for the potential improvement through word lattice translation, as well as to investigate, what kind of errors in the single best ASR output are usually avoided by the MT system by selecting alternative recognition hypotheses. We also propose an interesting idea for sharing the benefits of lattice-

Table 4.16: Word error rates for some hypotheses extracted from the ASR word lattices on the BTEC Italian-to-English task (development + test set).

ASR hypothesis:	WER [%]	DEL [%]	INS [%]	SUB [%]	Num. words
lattice oracle	15.4	2.8	1.5	11.1	2893
CN oracle	14.2	4.1	0.7	9.4	2831
single best	23.5	3.6	4.5	15.4	2956
selection of PBT SCSS	23.0	7.4	2.7	12.9	2795

based translation with MT systems which are not able to process multiple ASR hypotheses.

In Table 4.16, we present the ASR word error rates for some of the hypotheses which can be extracted from ASR word lattices and confusion networks on the BTEC Italian-to-English task. These hypotheses are:

- *single best*: the single best ASR output according to ASR model scores;
- *lattice oracle*: the path in the lattice which has the lowest edit distance to the correct transcript (averaged over the whole test corpus);
- *CN oracle*: the path in the CN which has the lowest edit distance to the correct transcript;
- *selection of PBT SCSS*: the path in the lattice which was selected for translation based on the decision of the phrase-based log-linear model in the process of the cardinality-synchronous search with reordering. This path can be traced back using the backpointers of the dynamic programming algorithm.

From the WER results in Table 4.16 and their decomposition into deletion, insertion, and substitution errors we can conclude that the single best ASR output has a high number of substitution errors and a balanced number of deletions and insertions. Computing the "oracle" path in the lattices reduces the number of insertions and substitutions dramatically, whereas deletion errors remain a problem. The WER of this path is 2/3 of the single best WER. Thus, the lattices do contain enough good-quality paths which can be chosen by the MT system to improve translation quality. The "oracle" path in the confusion networks created from these lattices further reduces the "oracle" WER to 14.2%. However, this further reduction is again due to fewer insertion and substitution errors.

The lattice path that the MT system chooses for translation has a WER which is only 0.5% absolute lower than the single best ASR output. However, the distribution of the errors changes dramatically: the number of substitution and insertion errors decreases, whereas the number of deletion errors is twice as high as in the single best ASR hypothesis. This suggests that insertion and substitution errors have the highest impact on speech translation quality.

Table 4.17: Oracle experiments on the test set of the BTEC Italian-to-English task.

System:	Input:	BLEU [%]	TER [%]	WER [%]	PER [%]
PBT	single best	58.9	34.2	35.0	29.5
SCSS	* lattice + posterior score	63.6	32.0	32.2	27.9
	lattice oracle	63.2	29.5	30.3	25.2
	CN oracle	63.8	30.0	30.7	25.7
	correct transcript	68.7	24.8	25.8	20.7
FSA	single best	53.2	37.3	38.2	32.7
	lattice with ac. score	55.7	34.3	35.0	29.8
	translation of the path selected by *	58.3	34.2	34.9	29.6

If a word or word sequence is erroneously inserted, it has to be translated into an erroneous phrase; content word substitution errors also lead to incorrect translations. However, the analysis of the deletion errors frequently made by the ASR system shows that most of these errors involve short function words. These words (e. g. articles) are not always necessary for a more or less correct translation into another language, so that the "deletion" of these words does not have a significant effect on MT quality. Moreover, the lattice-based translation system sometimes avoids substitution and insertion errors just by skipping the corresponding words in translation, which explains the increased deletion error rate. This leaves some parts of the spoken utterance untranslated, but the overall translation quality of the utterance would have been much worse if a wrong translation would have been produced instead. Such behavior of the system is reasonable, because in most application scenarios (and especially in translation of dialog speech) it is better to provide no translation than to provide a misleading translation.

Table 4.17 shows the translation results for the lattice/CN paths, for which the WER was given in Table 4.16. For comparison, the results of the best lattice-based translation and the correct transcript translation with the PBT system from Table 4.15 are also shown. Interestingly, translating lattice and CN "oracle" paths does not further improve the BLEU score in comparison with the lattice translation itself. However, all other measures still improve significantly, e. g. TER from 32.0 to 29.5%. This discrepancy can be attributed to the estimation of model weights which has been done for the lattice-based translation on a development set to improve the BLEU score. Another interesting fact is that translating CN "oracle" versus lattice "oracle" only slightly improves the BLEU score, but the other measures deteriorate. Thus, the CN "oracle" seems to contain already too many deletion errors which were not part of the original ASR search space.

The "gap" in the error measures for single best and correct transcript translation (e. g. in

4 Coupling of speech recognition and machine translation

TER from 34.2 to 24.8%) can be reduced by about 23% through lattice-based translation. The maximum improvement which theoretically could be achieved is approximated by the TER of the lattice "oracle" path which reduces the "gap" by exactly 50%. Note that the lattice "oracle" has a 34% relative lower WER than the single best ASR output, but its translation has the MT WER of only 14% relative lower than the translation of the single best ASR hypothesis. Also, the remaining ASR WER of 15.4% for the lattice "oracle" path accounts only for 4.4% absolute increase in the MT WER from the MT WER of the correct transcript translation. Similar effects of ASR errors on MT measures were observed on other speech translation tasks.

Table 4.17 includes the results of a novel and interesting experiment. In this experiment, for each sentence we first extract the lattice path which was selected in the process of lattice-based translation with the PBT system. Then, we translate the resulting corpus using the FSA system. The results in the last line of Table 4.17 show that this experiment results in significantly better translation quality than the FSA translation of the single best ASR output, but is even better than the lattice-based translation of the FSA system. The improvement is especially notable for the BLEU score which is 58.3 vs. 55.7% for the FSA lattice-based translation. Thus, the lattice path selected by a statistical phrase-based MT system improves the translation quality not only of this system, but also of another system which uses a different model for translation. The results of this experiment open a new research direction, when complicated MT systems designed to only handle text input (e. g. syntax-based systems which rely on parses of the source sentence) can benefit from using the ASR output preferred by another (simpler) MT system that is capable of translating word lattices. The novel experiment therefore proposes a method for combining MT systems with different types of input. Another method which has a similar goal, but works on the target language side, will be presented in Chapter 6.

4.5.5 Reordering in the context of lattice translation

In this section, we investigate the importance of word and phrase reordering for lattice-based translation in experiments on the BTEC Italian-to-English and Chinese-to-English speech translation tasks.

First, we show that reordering of the target hypotheses is important for translation quality when the joint probability FSA system is used. Then, we perform the experiments with the log-linear phrase-based model (PBT system) and compare the "skip-a-phrase" reordering extension of the lattice-based monotonic beam search with the reordering capabilities of the cardinality-synchronous search. We also test how the extensive reordering improves MT error

Table 4.18: The role of target language reordering as postprocessing (lattice-based translations with the FSA system, BTEC Italian-to-English task).

Corpus transformation	BLEU [%]	TER [%]	WER [%]	PER [%]
GIATI	54.6	35.9	36.2	31.8
reordering in training	51.8	36.0	37.6	29.8
+ reordering as postprocessing	55.7	34.3	35.0	29.8

measures when word lattices or the corresponding confusion networks are translated.

FSA system:

As mentioned in Section 4.3.4, the reordering in the FSA system for the case of lattice-based speech translation is only effectively possible on the target side as a postprocessing step. This reordering can be combined with a reordering of target sentences in training that makes the word alignment monotonic. Alternatively, we can use the GIATI monotonization technique in training and save reordering in the target side of the tuples used in the tuple-based translation model. Table 4.18 presents the FSA translation results on the BTEC Italian-to-English task using the following setups:

- *GIATI*: the monotonic lattice translation with reordering memorized in the tuples;

- *reordering in training*: the monotonic lattice translation using the model which had been trained with reordered target sentences. Without additional *reordering as postprocessing*, this setup results in target language sentences with the structure of the source sentence.

In terms of position-independent error rate, the translations based on reordering in training clearly outperform the GIATI monotonization technique: the PER is 29.8% vs. 31.8%. This PER can not be further improved through reordering after translation, because only the best MT hypothesis is reordered using IBM constraints with a window size of 2 and probability of the monotonic path of 0.6. However, all the other measures improve significantly, because even these quite tight constraints allow for the restoration of the English word order (e.g. by reordering noun-adjective groups). The overall improvement in other measures is thus also significant (e.g. 1.1% absolute in BLEU). From these experiments, we can conclude that the proposed consistent scheme for reordering in training and after translation is a good-quality alternative to the GIATI monotonization technique for joint-probability tuple-based speech translation models.

Table 4.19: Comparison of reordering approaches for lattice- and CN-based search (BTEC Chinese-to-English task).

Input/algorithm:	BLEU [%]	TER [%]	WER [%]	PER [%]	words/sec
lattice PBT beam search no reordering	45.0	44.4	46.1	38.0	6.6
lattice PBT beam search + skip	48.3	42.2	43.2	36.8	0.25
lattice PBT SCSS no reordering	45.3	44.6	46.0	38.7	18.9
lattice PBT SCSS exhaustive	48.4	42.6	43.9	37.4	1.7
CN PBT SCSS no reordering	45.1	45.0	46.4	38.4	10.6
CN PBT SCSS exhaustive	48.1	42.7	44.3	36.6	1.1

PBT system:

Next, we show how reordering on phrase level can improve word lattice translation quality for the PBT system. Here, we present the results on two tasks: BTEC Chinese-to-English (Table 4.19) and Italian-to-English (Table 4.20). Chinese is a language which has a substantially different structure and word order than English and requires long-range phrase reordering for good translation quality. In contrast, the differences between the word order in Italian and English are mostly local. On the two tasks, we apply either the monotonic *beam search* with or without the *skip* reordering extension described in Section 4.4.3.4 or the cardinality-synchronous search with or without *exhaustive reordering* under phrase- or word-level IBM constraints. For the latter search algorithm, we also compare the effect of reordering on lattice and confusion network input.

On the Chinese-to-English task (Table 4.19), both the extended beam search and the SCSS with reordering improve MT error measures in comparison with monotonic translation. However, the SCSS algorithm is much faster (1.7 vs. 0.25 words/second) and requires less memory. The speed improvements are achieved in part due to a better organized pruning in the SCSS search [Zens 08]. Histogram pruning is applied separately to lexical hypotheses for each coverage and coverage hypotheses for each cardinality. However, the main reason for a faster search is that the lattice paths do not have to be considered explicitly, but only via the phrases that match their CN slots (see Section 4.4.3.5). The improvements due to SCSS-based reordering are also significant for the translation of confusion networks.

On the Italian-to-English task (Table 4.20), the improvements due to word and phrase reordering are smaller than on the Chinese-to-English task. This is reasonable since only local reorderings of 1 or 2 positions are usually sufficient to overcome the word order differences between English and Italian. In contrast to the beam search with the "skip" reordering,

Table 4.20: Comparison of reordering approaches for lattice- and CN-based search (BTEC Italian-to-English task).

Input/algorithm:	BLEU [%]	TER [%]	WER [%]	PER [%]	words/sec
lattice PBT beam search no reordering	57.7	34.2	34.8	30.5	7.8
lattice PBT beam search + skip	58.4	35.0	35.9	30.4	5.5
lattice PBT SCSS no reordering	62.7	32.1	32.5	28.3	16.2
lattice PBT SCSS exhaustive	63.6	32.0	32.2	27.9	8.1
CN PBT SCSS no reordering	60.2	32.7	33.5	28.1	1.2
CN PBT SCSS exhaustive	61.1	32.3	33.0	27.9	0.8

the reordering in SCSS improves all error measures. These improvements are of the same magnitude when word lattices or confusion networks are used as input. However, on this task the lattice-based SCSS algorithm has to search through fewer paths and is at 8 words/sec about 10 times faster than the CN-based system under the same pruning settings. This illustrates the efficiency of the proposed lattice-based cardinality-synchronous search.

The reordering experiments presented above clearly show that word and phrase reordering can be effectively performed even when high-density ASR word lattices are taken as input to the speech translation system. The reordering can be performed efficiently, and the translation quality improvement due to reordering is significant for MT tasks with significant structural differences between the source and the target language.

4.6 Other applications of lattice-based search

The lattice translation algorithms described and evaluated in this chapter were developed with the goal of improving speech translation quality by considering the ambiguity contained in ASR word lattices. However, the same methods can be used to represent other types of ambiguity or alternative entity representations as input to machine translation.

Reordering for text translation. In Section 4.3.4.3, it was mentioned that lattice-based monotonic beam search can be used to translate lattices explicitly representing alternative reorderings of the source sentence. Such an approach is especially efficient and effective if the reorderings were determined using syntax-based automatically or manually derived rules instead of permutations which are not dependent on the identity of a particular word. In [Zhang & Zens[+] 07], the lattice-based software framework developed for this thesis was used to represent alternative rule-based reorderings to improve text translation quality for Chinese-to-English. The rules were extracted based on word alignments and were assigned reordering probabilities which were then included in the log-linear translation model in a way similar to the acoustic and source LM probabilities in speech translation. In [Popović & Ney 06], the same framework was used to encode reorderings of adjective-noun groups for Spanish-to-English translation and re-positioning of verbs for German-to-English translation. For each source sentence to be translated, the lattice always contained the monotonic path, as well as all paths which were obtained by applying manually created POS-based rules. In both cases, the authors reported an improvement of translation quality by using lattices instead of single best reordering of the source sentence.

Word segmentation and morphological processing. In some languages like Chinese, the words are not separated by whitespace and the segmentation of a character sequence into words is ambiguous. For the phrase-based MT, alternative word segmentations can be represented in a lattice, so that the segmentation that matches the phrasal translations best can be selected in the search. [Xu & Matusov[+] 05] used the lattice-based translation system proposed here and could show that it is of advantage for MT quality to translate lattices of alternative hypotheses for Chinese word segmentation. Similar experimental findings were made by [Dyer & Muresan[+] 08]. In their work, a similar approach was used not only for Chinese-to-English, but also for Arabic-to-English translation. In case of the Arabic language with its rich morphology and high number of compound words (e.g. prepositions are often attached to nouns), it is crucial for translation quality to split some longer compounds into corresponding parts. Since this splitting is ambiguous, alternative splittings can be represented in a lattice, so that in translation the splitting which matches the MT training conditions and thus has the potential to improve MT error measures can be selected based on translation model scores.

Named entity detection and translation. A number of methods for automatic detection of named entities (NEs) and other entities such as number and date expressions have been developed in recent years. The detected entities are usually translated by a dedicated module, e.g. rule-based translation for date expression, name transliteration, etc.. To pass these special translations through a phrase-based MT system, a category label for the detected entity is often used. This label is translated by itself, and the corresponding translation of the entity is inserted into the sentence translation after the main MT search. Since the detection of named entities is not perfect, it would be of advantage to allow for ambiguity of the input with or without the detected named entities. Such an ambiguity can be most suitably represented in form of word lattices. Then, the decision on whether or not to accept a special named entity translation can be left to the MT system. In addition, confidences of the NE detection and translation can be used as an additional feature when this decision is made.

Punctuation insertion. For translation of speech it is often necessary to predict punctuation marks. Some MT systems already require the punctuation marks to be present in the input. In [Cattoni & Bertoldi[+] 07], the following strategy is followed: sentence-internal punctuation marks like commas are optionally inserted at several positions. The resulting multiple input hypotheses are represented in the form of a CN, which is then translated by a phrase-based MT system with a search similar to the SCSS used in this chapter. It is also possible to enrich the CNs with multiple ASR hypotheses with additional hypotheses for punctuation marks. In this work, we followed a different approach in which the MT system itself is used to generate punctuation marks. The details of this procedure are described in Chapter 5.

Paraphrasing. Finally, word lattices can be used to represent other ambiguities. One of the reasons for such ambiguities in translation of text may be the "uncertain" original data. For example, incorrect spelling or some colloquial/dialect expressions can be corrected by an automatic module, or some disambiguation techniques can be applied to improve subsequent translation. In such cases, it is of advantage not to make hard decisions in advance and let the MT system decide whether or not to use the suggested input changes. In other cases, it is conceivable that some source words (e. g. function words or hesitations) are not necessary for a correct translation. Therefore, these words can be optionally omitted in a lattice or confusion network by using ε-arcs. An example of such optional word removal for frequently unaligned words in Chinese-to-English translation is presented in [Zhang & Matusov[+] 09].

On the other hand, the methods for tighter coupling of the ASR system with the subsequent processing module – machine translation – can also be applied to different areas of natural language processing, such as natural language understanding (NLU). In its simplest form, NLU can consist of concept tagging, where the automatically recognized word sequence is divided into a sequence of semantic tags. This task is similar to a MT task, since the semantic tag sequence plays the role of the target word sequence. However, the concept tagging task is easier because it is a monotonic problem, and the number of distinct tags is usually quite limited. Currently, the modeling framework for concept tagging which results in the lowest tagging error rates are the conditional random fields (CRFs, [Hahn & Lehnen[+] 08]). To overcome the impact of speech recognition errors on tagging quality, acoustic and source LM scores of the word hypotheses in the ASR lattice can be used as features in the CRF framework. At RWTH, the work on lattice-based CRFs for concept tagging is on-going.

4.7 Conclusions

In this chapter we proposed solutions for a tighter coupling between automatic speech recognition and machine translation. Based on a thorough statistical decision theory for speech translation, we justified the use of a joint probability tuple-based context-dependent translation model and a log-linear phrase-based translation model to translate multiple ASR hypotheses in the form of word lattices. We have proposed and implemented a consistent training procedure for the joint probability model that improves translation performance in comparison with the previously presented methods. We also have presented a way to combine the tuple-based model with the phrase-based model.

We have shown that in combination with the acoustic and source LM scores of the lattice word hypotheses, the translation model scores can be used as an additional knowledge source to further constrain the search space of the ASR system and, as a consequence, avoid passing recognition errors from the source language utterance to its target language translation. We have presented experimental results which prove that MT quality of automatically recognized speech can be significantly improved on both large and small vocabulary tasks by performing word lattice translation. We have investigated under which conditions such improvements are to be expected. Finally, we introduced a possibility for passing these improvements to MT systems which are not capable of translating word lattices.

We have shown that the phrase-based log-linear model can achieve better speech translation quality than the joint probability model especially when extensive reordering has to be performed in the search. To enable this reordering for the case of lattice input, we introduced a novel approach for efficient translation of ASR word lattices with cardinality-synchronous search. We have shown that using this search on word lattices can be more effective and efficient than using it on confusion networks as it had been proposed in previous research.

5 Sentence segmentation and punctuation prediction for speech translation

In this chapter, it will be described how automatic transcriptions of speech can be annotated with additional information such as segment boundaries and punctuation marks, with the goal of employing this information in MT. Section 5.1 will present an algorithm for sentence segmentation that explicitly takes the needs of an MT system into account. In Section 5.2, several strategies for predicting punctuation marks in the process of translating ASR output will be described and compared. Section 5.3 will present the experimental results in which the presented sentence segmentation and punctuation prediction algorithms will be evaluated on small and large vocabulary machine translation tasks. The chapter will be concluded by a summary in Section 5.4.

5.1 Sentence segmentation

Most state-of-the-art ASR systems recognize sequences of words, neither performing a proper segmentation of the output into sentences or *sentence-like units (SUs)*, nor predicting punctuation marks. Usually, only acoustic segmentation into utterances is performed. These utterances may be very long, containing several sentences. Most MT systems are not able to translate such long utterances with an acceptable level of quality because of the constraints of the involved algorithms. Examples of such constraints include reordering strategies, the complexity of which is exponential in the length of the input sequence, or parsing-based approaches which assume the input to be a more or less syntactically correct sentence. The user of an MT system usually expects to see readable sentences as the translation output, with reasonable length and proper punctuation inserted according to the conventions of the target language.

Given this situation, algorithms are needed for automatic segmentation of the ASR output into SUs and for punctuation prediction. Three methods for predicting punctuation will be described in Section 5.2. In this section, a novel approach to sentence segmentation is explained. It was developed to explicitly consider the constraints of a (statistical) MT system.

5.1.1 Related work

Previous research on sentence boundary detection mostly concentrated on annotating the ASR output as the end product delivered to the user. Most authors tried to combine lexical cues (e.g. language model probability) and prosodic cues (pause duration, pitch, etc.) in a single framework in order to improve the quality of sentence boundary prediction [Liu & Shriberg+ 04]. A maximum entropy model [Huang & Zweig 02] or CART-style decision trees [Kim & Woodland 01] are often used to combine the different features. Various levels of performance are achieved depending on the task; the evaluation is performed in terms of precision/recall w.r.t. the sentence boundaries inserted by human transcribers. The sentence segmentation algorithm presented here was first described in [Matusov & Mauser+ 06]. This was the first published work which experimentally measured the influence of automatic sentence segmentation on translation quality. Further experiments on other languages (e.g. Chinese) and using a slightly different set of features were described in [Matusov & Hillard+ 07], as well as in [Fügen & Kolss 07]. In [Rao & Lane+ 07], the dependency of translation quality on the translation unit length was thoroughly analyzed, with the result that the best BLEU score is obtained for the average segment length of 10 words. In [Paulik & Rao+ 08], sentence segmentation was performed using a decision tree, with the main features being LM context, pause duration, and the duration of the word preceding a candidate segment boundary. The authors of that paper also used a feature for phrase coverage which is an extension of the work presented in Section 5.1.6. However, in contrast to the results in this thesis, they could not obtain improvements in translation quality by using the information on whether or not the candidate segment boundary breaks up a phrase with high-probability translations.

5.1.2 Explicit sentence length modeling

As mentioned above, it is important to produce translations of sentences or sentence-like units to make the MT output human-readable. At the same time, sophisticated speech translation algorithms (e.g. ASR word lattice translation, rescoring and system combination algorithms for (N-best) output of one or several SMT systems) may require that the number of words in the input source language SUs is limited to about 30 or 40. Furthermore, too short segments

(e. g. less than 3 words) are also undesirable for MT because of the missing context information. Given these requirements, it is natural to follow the idea of explicitly limiting the predicted segment length to take a value between a specified minimum and maximum segment length of l and L words, respectively.

Hard constraints on the sentence length could not be set using the state-of-the-art algorithms for sentence segmentation. These approaches treat segment boundaries as hidden events. A posterior probability for a possible boundary after a word is determined for each word position. Then, the actual boundaries are determined by selecting only those positions, for which the posterior probability of a segment boundary exceeds a certain threshold. This means that although the segmentation granularity can be controlled, the length of a segment may take any value from 1 to several hundred words.

The approach to segmentation of ASR output described below originates from the work of [Stolcke & Shriberg[+] 98] and thus also uses the concept of hidden events to represent the segment boundaries. A decision regarding the placement of a segment boundary is made based on a log-linear combination of language model and prosodic features. However, in contrast to existing approaches, we optimize over the length of each segment (in words) and add an explicit segment length model. Thus, we use a *whole constituent* hidden Markov model (HMM) that considers both the beginning and the end time of a segment in determining boundary location (see [Ostendorf & Favre[+] 08] for more examples and a discussion of whole constituent models). In the search, we explicitly optimize over the position of the previous segment boundary which is equivalent to optimization over the length of the segment. A similar approach to topic segmentation was presented in [Matusov & Peters[+] 03]. Such an approach makes it possible to introduce restrictions on the minimum and maximum length of a segment, and nevertheless produce syntactically and semantically meaningful sentence units which pass all the relevant context information on to the phrase-based MT system.

In the following we present the decision rule for the proposed sentence segmentation approach, describe the features used, as well as the search algorithm.

5.1.3 Decision rule

Formally, we are given an (automatic) transcription of speech, denoted by the words $w_1^N := w_1, w_2, \ldots, w_N$. The goal is to find the optimal segmentation of this word sequence into K segments, denoted by $n_1^K := (n_1, n_2, \ldots, n_K = N)$. Thus, we would like to find an optimal assignment of the segment boundaries to a given word sequence:

$$w_1^N \to n_1^K(w_1^N). \tag{5.1}$$

Among all the possible segmentations, we will choose the one with the highest posterior probability:

$$(\hat{K}, \hat{n}_1^{\hat{K}}) = \underset{K, n_1^K}{\operatorname{argmax}} \left\{ Pr(n_1^K | w_1^N) \right\} \tag{5.2}$$

$$= \underset{K, n_1^K}{\operatorname{argmax}} \left\{ Pr(n_1^K) \cdot Pr(w_1^N | n_1^K) \right\} \tag{5.3}$$

Using the chain rule, the probability $Pr(n_1^K)$ is decomposed into the product of probabilities for individual segment boundaries, assuming a dependency only on the previous boundary:

$$Pr(n_1^K) = \prod_{k=1}^{K} p(n_k | n_{k-1}) \tag{5.4}$$

$$= \prod_{k=1}^{K} p(\Delta n_k), \text{ with } \Delta n_k = n_k - n_{k-1}.$$

In Equation 5.4 we also reduced the dependency on the previous boundary to modeling of the distance between the current boundary n_k and the previous boundary n_{k-1}, i.e. the length of the sentence Δn_k.

The probability $Pr(w_1^N | n_1^K)$ from Equation 5.2 is modeled as an m-gram LM probability, but with an additional dependency on the fact whether or not a word w_n is near a segment boundary or within a segment. The following equation describes the model we use. Here, the hidden event of an arbitrary segment boundary is denoted with the symbol [s]:

$$Pr(w_1^N | n_1^K) \cong \prod_{k=1}^{K} \left[p([\texttt{s}] | w_{n_k-m+2}^{n_k}) \cdot \prod_{n=n_{k-1}+1}^{n_{k-1}+m-1} p(w_n | w_{n_{k-1}+1}^{n-1}, [\texttt{s}]) \cdot \prod_{n=n_{k-1}+m}^{n_k} p(w_n | w_{n-m+1}^{n-1}) \right] \tag{5.5}$$

Thus, each hypothesized segment is scored with the product of three different LM probabilities:

- the probability $p([\texttt{s}] | w_{n_k-m+2}^{n_k})$ of the segment boundary [s] in dependency on the last $m-1$ words of a segment;

- the product of the probabilities $p(w_n | w_{n_{k-1}+1}^{n-1}, [\texttt{s}])$ for the first $m-1$ words of a segment using a LM history that includes the last segment boundary represented by a hidden event [s];

- the m-gram probability $p(w_n | w_{n-m+1}^{n-1})$ of the other words within a segment that is independent of a segment boundary.

To simplify the following formulas, we define the probability $p_{LM}(w_{n_{k-1}+1}^{n_k}, [\texttt{s}])$ to be the

5.1 Sentence segmentation

product of these three probabilities:

$$p_{LM}(w_{n_{k-1}+1}^{n_k}, \text{[s]}) := p(\text{[s]}|w_{n_k-m+2}^{n_k}) \cdot \prod_{n=n_{k-1}+1}^{n_{k-1}+m-1} p(w_n|w_{n_{k-1}+1}^{n-1}, \text{[s]}) \cdot \prod_{n=n_{k-1}+m}^{n_k} p(w_n|w_{n-m+1}^{n-1}) \quad (5.6)$$

Inserting the right sides of the Equations 5.4 and 5.5 into Equation 5.2, we arrive at the following decision rule:

$$(\hat{K}, \hat{n}_1^{\hat{K}}) = \underset{K, n_1^K}{\operatorname{argmax}} \left\{ \prod_{k=1}^{K} \left[p(\Delta n_k) \cdot p_{LM}(w_{n_{k-1}+1}^{n_k}, \text{[s]}) \right] \right\} \quad (5.7)$$

5.1.4 Additional features

In practice, the source language model is estimated using a training corpus in which all sentence-end punctuation marks are replaced with the hidden event [s], and all other punctuation marks are removed. We use Kneser-Ney smoothing to estimate the m-gram LM probabilities. A similar strategy for training hidden-event LMs is described in [Stolcke & Shriberg[+] 98].

The sentence length probability distribution $p(\Delta n_k)$ is estimated on the corpus that is used to estimate the source language model. We chose the log-normal distribution for sentence length modeling, because it reflects the actual length histogram of the training sentences most accurately. The parameters of this distribution were determined using maximum likelihood estimation.

Since the true distributions for the length model and the hidden-event LM are not known and we employ only their estimations, it is of advantage to introduce scaling factors for the probabilities in Equation 5.7. These scaling factors can be optimized either manually or automatically with the goal of improving segmentation quality on a development set (see Section 5.3 for details). Also, additional features with their own scaling factors can be added to the model such as prosodic features at a hypothesized segment boundary. Thus, in practice we perform a log-linear feature combination similarly to the combination of translation and ASR features in Chapter 4.

A prosodic feature that is highly characteristic of a possible segment boundary is pause duration. We use the feature $h(w_{n_k}, w_{n_k+1})$ which is the normalized *pause duration* between the words w_{n_k} and w_{n_k+1} located directly before and after the hypothesized boundary n_k:

$$h(w_{n_k}, w_{n_k+1}) = \min\left\{\frac{\Delta t_{n_k}}{t_{max}}, 1\right\} \quad (5.8)$$

Here, Δt_{n_k} is the pause duration (in seconds) between the end of the recognized word w_{n_k} and the next recognized word w_{n_k+1}, and t_{max} is set to 10 seconds.

We also include a *segment penalty* $h_{\text{SP}}(n_1^K, w_1^N) = K$ in the log-linear feature combination. This is a simple heuristic that helps to additionally control the segmentation granularity. If the scaling factor of this model λ_{SP} is negative, generally more segments are produced because more segments reduce the total cost of the segmentation. Similarly, in case of a positive scaling factor of this feature, generally fewer segments are produced by the presented algorithm.

With the addition of the pause duration feature and the segment penalty, the decision rule that we use in practice can be formulated as follows:

$$(\hat{K}, \hat{n}_1^{\hat{K}}) = \underset{K, n_1^K}{\operatorname{argmax}} \left\{ \prod_{k=1}^{K} \left[e^{\lambda_{\text{SP}}} \cdot h^{\lambda_1}(w_{n_k}, w_{n_k+1}) \cdot p^{\lambda_2}(\Delta n_k) \cdot p_{\text{LM}}^{\lambda_3}(w_{n_{k-1}+1}^{n_k}, \texttt{[s]}) \right] \right\} \quad (5.9)$$

Other features can also be used in the log-linear combination. Two features that were experimentally useful are described in Section 5.1.6.

5.1.5 Search algorithm

The search is performed using dynamic programming. To this end, we define the following auxiliary quantity:

$$Q(n) = \underset{n_1^{\hat{k}-1}}{\max} \left\{ \prod_{k=1}^{\hat{k}} e^{\lambda_{\text{SP}}} \cdot h^{\lambda_1}(w_{n_k}, w_{n_k+1}) \cdot p^{\lambda_2}(\Delta n_k) \cdot p_{\text{LM}}^{\lambda_3}(w_{n_{k-1}+1}^{n_k}, \texttt{[s]}) \right\} \quad (5.10)$$
$$\text{with } n = n_{\hat{k}}$$

$Q(n)$ is the probability of the best partial path that hypothesizes a sequence of segments denoted by boundary position indices n_k, the last of which ends directly after the word w_n. This definition of the auxiliary quantity allows for explicit segment length modeling based on the difference between the current boundary index n_k and the previous boundary index n_{k-1}.

The dynamic programming *recursion equation* is derived as follows. For every word position n, the optimization is performed over the position n' where the last assumed segment has ended (or, in other words, where the current segment has begun). This optimization strategy involves the following steps:

1. use the already calculated value $Q(n')$ ($n' < n$) that quantifies the probability of the best partial segmentation of the words $w_1^{n'}$.
2. evaluate the sentence length probability of the sentence length $n - n'$.

5.1 Sentence segmentation

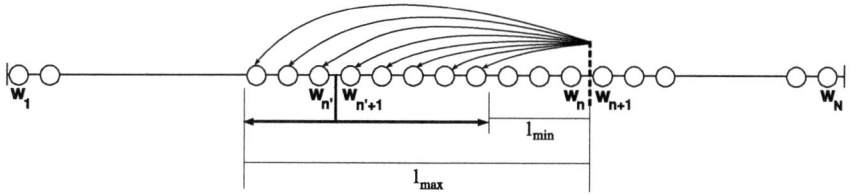

Figure 5.1: Illustration of the search algorithm for sentence segmentation with explicit optimization over segment length.

3. compute the pause duration feature at the segment boundary (pause duration between positions n and $n+1$).

4. evaluate the product of LM probabilities including the hidden event [s] as described in Section 5.1.4.

These probabilities are computed including their scaling factors, and all the knowledge sources are combined. All of this is expressed in Equation 5.11.

$$Q(n) = \max_{n-L \leq n' \leq n-l} \left\{ Q(n') \cdot e^{\lambda_{\text{SP}}} \cdot h^{\lambda_1}(w_n, w_{n+1}) \cdot p^{\lambda_2}(n-n') \cdot p^{\lambda_3}_{\text{LM}}(w^n_{n'+1}, \text{[s]}) \right\} \quad (5.11)$$

In the search, the word sequence w_1^N is processed from left to right, and the quantities $Q(n)$ are computed recursively (see Figure 5.1). The globally optimal sentence segmentation for the document is determined when the last word of the document is reached, i.e. with computing $Q(N)$. In practice, all the computation is performed using model scores which are negated logarithms of the original probabilities; in that case, in Equation 5.11 the product of the scaled probabilities is replaced by the sum of weighted scores. Backtracing the optimal segmentation decisions n_1^K can be performed in the usual fashion by saving the locally optimal segment boundary candidates in a backpointer array.

Note that the minimum and/or maximum sentence lengths l and L can be explicitly set by limiting the values of n' to $l \leq n - n' \leq L$ during optimization over n', as depicted in Figure 5.1. The complexity of the algorithm is in $O(N \cdot (L-l))$ since at each word position $(L-l)$ previous segment boundary candidates are considered. The costs of computing the LM probability for within-segment words can be kept constant if the running sums of the LM scores up to a certain word position n are precomputed before the main search. Since usually the maximum length L does not exceed 50 or 60 words, the algorithm is rather fast: e.g. 30 000 words are segmented in less than a second.

5.1.6 Phrase coverage feature

The log-linear feature combination described in Section 5.1.4 allows us to use additional feature functions beyond the LM probabilities for words and the hidden event of a segment boundary, segment length probability and segment penalty, and pause duration. In order to be compatible with the search algorithm, these additional features have to be local in the sense that they can depend on the currently hypothesized segment boundary and/or on the previous segment boundary (zero-order or first-order dependency).

In [Matusov & Hillard+ 07] a zero-order posterior feature $p_{\text{post}}(w_n, w_{n+1})$ was used. This posterior probability estimates the likelihood of a hidden boundary event between the words w_n and w_{n+1}. It was computed using the sentence segmentation system of [Zimmerman & Hakkani-Tur+ 06] based on hidden-event language models and combination of speaker, prosodic, and lexical cues. The prosodic features include various measures of pause duration, phone duration, fundamental frequency and energy, and their normalized versions. The experimental results show that a slight improvement can be achieved by using the posterior feature, but the pause duration feature was shown to be by far more important than other prosodic cues.

A more powerful feature is motivated by the phrase-based machine translation algorithm that will be applied to the segmented speech in the next processing step. The idea is to make sure that word sequences for which good phrasal translations exist will not be broken into subsequences by a sentence boundary. To this end, we extract all bilingual phrases from the training data of the MT system which match any source language word sequence in the evaluation data. Then, we train a bigram language model on the source language parts of these bilingual phrases. The phrases are treated as sentences, so words within the phrase (but not across phrases) are used to estimate the bigram LM probabilities. When training the language model, we consider each phrase as a separate sentence and count it as many times as it appears in the MT training data.

The phrase coverage feature for each word w_n in the input is then the bigram language model probability $p(w_{n+1}|w_n)$. If this probability is high, the word sequence $w_n w_{n+1}$ most probably has a good phrasal translation, and a sentence boundary directly after w_n is undesirable. If this probability is low, the MT system will probably translate each of the two words by backing off to single-word translations. In this case, the phrasal context will be lost anyway, so that an (incorrect) boundary between w_n and w_{n+1} will probably not have a significant negative influence on translation quality.

Note that by introducing the phrase coverage feature we may improve the MT quality, but not necessarily improve the segmentation results with respect to precision and recall.

5.1.7 Sentence segmentation for word lattices

In cases when a tighter integration between ASR and MT is desired (see Chapter 4), the task of sentence segmentation becomes more complicated, since the input to MT is not the single best sequence, but a word lattice or a confusion network.

Theoretically, the sentence segmentation algorithm can be extended to work with word lattices. However, the method would become much more complex and inefficient. The main reason for this is the unclear definition of word boundaries in a lattice: many hypothesized word boundaries overlap. In case of a confusion network or a lattice with clearly defined slots as described in Chapter 4 the problem can be simplified. First, the segment boundaries are found using the first-best hypothesis. Then, the CN/lattice is cut at those slots which were labeled as boundaries.

In practice, another possibility can be effective. This is a two-pass approach, in which first the ASR system generates its single best output. This output is divided into segments, for which the ASR system performs another recognition pass, generating word lattices. Experiments of the ASR research group at the Lehrstuhl für Informatik 6 showed that not only the sentence segmentation quality is high, but also the recognition WER can be slightly improved by using better segment boundaries in the second pass than just the acoustically motivated boundaries. Examples of automatic segment boundaries which were used for generation of word lattices and subsequent lattice-based MT are provided in Appendix B.

5.2 Punctuation prediction

The task of punctuation prediction is considered here from the MT perspective. This means that the final goal is to have proper punctuation marks (commas, question and exclamation marks, periods) in the target language translations; the quality or even the presence of punctuation in the source language transcriptions is not important. Another objective of this section is to investigate if automatically predicted sentence-internal punctuation marks like commas can improve the baseline translation quality by introducing constraints on word and phrase reordering.

Related work: Related work on punctuation restoration focused mostly on enriching source language transcriptions with punctuation marks [Beeferman & Berger[+] 98]. Recently,

5 Sentence segmentation and punctuation prediction for speech translation

[Lee & Roukos[+] 06] performed automatic punctuation restoration in order to translate ASR output for the TC-STAR 2006 evaluation. In this approach, the segments are already known and each segment is assumed to end with a period so that only commas are predicted. A comma is restored only if the bigram or trigram probability of a comma given the context exceeds a certain threshold. In the work of [Cattoni & Bertoldi[+] 07], the punctuation marks are predicted using hidden event language models, but are inserted into a confusion network with ε-arcs as alternatives, so that they can be skipped by a CN-based MT search algorithm. A similar approach was followed by [Shen & Delaney[+] 07]. A method for automatic prediction of commas in Chinese speech is described in [Hillard 08]; it will be used in some experiments for this chapter. The authors of [Paulik & Rao[+] 08] follow the approach presented below and let the machine translation system predict the sentence-internal punctuation marks. They claim that this approach achieves the best results in terms of automatic MT error measures.

5.2.1 Alternative punctuation prediction strategies

Figure 5.2 depicts three alternative strategies for predicting punctuation marks in the process of machine translation of automatically recognized speech. We have investigated each strategy in our experiments. In all three cases, we begin by taking the raw output of an ASR system, which is a long sequence of words. The sentence segmentation algorithm as described in Section 5.1 is applied to produce sentence-like units of the length acceptable both to humans and as input to an MT system.

Although it is possible to predict punctuation marks in an unsegmented text and then use the automatically inserted periods, question marks, and exclamation marks as segment boundaries, our preliminary experiments showed that this approach leads to poor segmentation results. It is much easier to predict a segment boundary (considering lexical and also prosodic features like the pause length) than to predict whether a specific punctuation mark has to be inserted or not at a given word position in the transcript. In the context of machine translation, separating sentence segmentation and punctuation prediction also allows for more flexible processing of the determined segments. Here, we are interested in having proper punctuation in the target language translation and thus may want to predict punctuation marks not directly in the source, but in the target language, where the rules and conventions for punctuation may be different from the source language.

Starting by performing sentence segmentation of the ASR output in the source language, one can follow three different approaches with the goal of having punctuation in the target language translations (Figure 5.2). For each of the approaches, three different types of bilingual phrase pairs are extracted based on the same word alignment between the bilingual sentence

5.2 Punctuation prediction

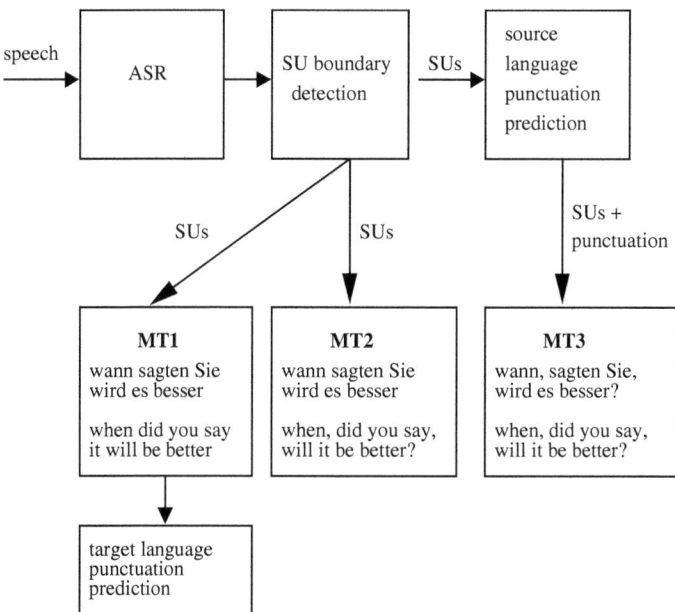

Figure 5.2: Three different strategies for predicting punctuation in the process of speech recognition and machine translation.

pairs in the training data. Thus, three MT systems are created.

5.2.1.1 Target-side punctuation prediction

In the first system $MT1$ punctuation marks are removed from the source language and the target language training corpus together with their alignment links. The alignment indices are adjusted accordingly. Thus, the phrases extracted using the modified training corpora and alignment do not contain punctuation marks. With this system, the target language translation of the ASR output also does not contain punctuation marks. Punctuation marks have to be inserted based on the lexical context in the automatically produced translation, e. g. using a hidden-event target language model and the method of [Stolcke & Shriberg[+] 98].

The advantage of this method is the possibility to optimize the parameters of the MT system with the goal of improving the lexical choice independent of any punctuation marks. Also, the absence of punctuation marks allows for better generalization and longer matches of bilingual phrase pairs.

125

One drawback of the approach is that the punctuation marks have to be predicted using only language model information. Moreover, this prediction is performed on the translation hypotheses which may contain errors with respect to both word choice and word order. In the current state of technology, these errors are much more numerous than the speech recognition errors. The presence of these errors may result in poor quality of the automatically predicted punctuation. Another drawback is that any prosodic features which are characteristic to a certain punctuation type (e. g. the pitch at the end of a question) cannot be directly used in the target language punctuation prediction. Transferring these features as the annotation of the translation hypothesis may be possible, but is complicated due to the reordering performed in MT search.

5.2.1.2 Source-side punctuation prediction

To train the system $MT3$, the phrase pairs are extracted including punctuation marks both in the source and the target training corpus. Generally, a system like $MT3$ can be a standard system for translating written text input with correctly placed punctuation marks. In order to use this system for the ASR output, the punctuation has to be predicted in the source language. This is a good strategy if prosodic features are used to improve the performance of the punctuation prediction algorithm. However, if the punctuation prediction algorithm is not robust enough and makes many errors, this may have a significant negative effect on the machine translation quality. For instance, long source phrases with good translations may not match the input due to an extra or missing comma, so that shorter phrases will have to be used, with a negative influence on the fluency and adequacy of the produced translation.

If the MT system $MT3$ is capable of translating ASR word lattices, it would mean that punctuation will have to be predicted within a lattice. This is a non-trivial problem, for which an efficient and robust solution is hard to find. Thus, the system $MT3$ is probably not suitable for processing ASR word lattices. For introducing punctuation marks into a confusion network, a method has been developed by [Cattoni & Bertoldi[+] 07]. Here, optional punctuation marks are introduced after each slot in the CN. The method can be used for single best ASR output, too, alleviating the phrase matching problem mentioned above.

Another disadvantage of this system originates in the differences in punctuation rules and conventions between languages, which make the task of translating punctuation marks from the source to the target language a very ambiguous one. For example, some commas in Chinese are not translated into English. Also, Chinese has two types of commas which have to be either omitted in translation or translated to a comma in English, etc. Due to this ambiguity, the translation of punctuation marks is not error-free. Thus, we cannot expect much better performance of *MT*3 which translates punctuation marks than of the system *MT*2 which inserts punctuation marks in the translation process.

5.2.1.3 Punctuation prediction by the MT system

The system *MT*2 is created by removing punctuation marks only from each source language training sentence, together with their alignment connections to the words in the corresponding target sentence. Thus, the punctuation marks in the target sentence which had been aligned with punctuation marks in the source sentence become non-aligned. Next, in the phrase extraction phase, for the same sequence of words followed or preceded by a punctuation mark, two different phrase pairs are extracted, one containing the target phrase with the punctuation mark, and one with the punctuation mark omitted from the target phrase. In the example in Figure 5.2, this would mean that e. g. for the phrase **sagten Sie** the MT system would memorize four translations:

```
          did you say
        , did you say
          did you say ,
        , did you say ,
```

With this heuristic, target phrases with punctuation marks compete with phrases without punctuation marks in the search, and the language model and other features of the phrase-based system described in Chapter 1 help to select the best hypothesis. It is also possible to optimize the scaling factors of the models involved in the MT system to obtain the best translation performance as measured using reference translations with punctuation marks. This aspect makes the approach more flexible than the one where punctuation marks are predicted using only the target language model, in a postprocessing step. In practical terms, this implicit approach is easy to use, since it requires neither preprocessing nor postprocessing with respect to punctuation. This is especially of advantage when taking ASR word lattices as input for MT.

A similar technique of implicit punctuation prediction by using the phrase-based MT system was tested independently by [Lee 06] for Arabic-to-English translation and showed promising results.

5.2.2 Using sentence-internal punctuation as reordering constraints

Sentence-internal punctuation marks like commas are not only necessary for better readability and understanding of an automatic speech transcript or translation. They can also be used to place constraints on the MT process. For example, it can be observed that a comma in most cases separates two clauses, which can be translated well independently of each other. Based on this observation, [Fügen & Kolss 07] translate sub-sentence units identified by commas and other punctuation and show improved translation quality. Moreover, they argue that good splitting points are those positions where the first-pass MT system continues the translation monotonically after some reordering (the so called reordering boundaries).

In [Matusov & Hillard[+] 07], a related idea is followed. However, in that work commas are first predicted in the source language transcript and then used as soft boundaries. The MT system still translates the whole sentence, possibly making use of the phrase context at a soft boundary, but word and phrase reordering across such a boundary is penalized. This approach was motivated by analyzing a small corpus of human-made word alignments where it was found that very little reordering occurs across commas.

The commas which are used as soft boundaries are predicted using lexical and prosodic features as described in [Hillard 08]. While comma and sentence boundary prediction could be treated jointly as a multi-class problem, here the predicted sentence boundaries are assumed to be given, and then the commas are predicted within each sentence.

The constraints on the reordering across a soft boundary are introduced by modifying the reordering model, which is one of the features in the log-linear translation model as described in Chapter 1. The reordering model of the baseline system is a distance-based model. It assigns costs based on the distance from the end position of a phrase to the start position of the next phrase; "jumps" over a long distance are penalized. This simple reordering model is widely used (e. g. in [Koehn 04]). This model can be also combined with a lexicalized maximum entropy model predicting the probability of a phrase orientation class [Zens & Ney 06]. When we use the latter model in our experiments, we discriminate between two classes, based on the new position of the first word in a phrase after reordering w.r.t. its original position. The first class is for phrase movements to the right, and the second class is for movements to the left.

In this work, the reordering model is extended by an additional penalty, the *soft boundary penalty*. Reordering across a soft boundary is assumed to be highly unlikely and is penalized. The soft boundaries implicitly divide a source sentence into several parts (see Figure 5.3). Each word f_j at position j in a sentence is labeled with an integer label $c(j)$ which encodes

j	1	2	3	4	5	6	7	8	9	10	11
	Despite	the	criticism	they	continued	working	and	people	finally	liked	it
c(j)	0	0	0	1	1	1	2	2	2	2	2
r(j)	0	0	0	1.39	1.39	1.39	3.69	3.69	3.69	3.69	3.69

Figure 5.3: Example of reordering penalties computed using automatically predicted commas.

the (soft boundary separated) section of the sentence that the word is from. We penalize the movement of a phrase from the position j to a position j' by a weight $w(j, j')$ proportional to a parameter α if the two positions have different section labels:

$$w(j, j') = \alpha \cdot |c(j') - c(j)| \quad (5.12)$$

The reason for introducing such a penalty is the assumption that the words between two soft boundaries usually represent a sentence clause. Nevertheless, the phrasal translation and language model context beyond the soft boundary can be taken into account. This context is lost if we translate each sentence part as if it were a separate sentence. Note that the penalty in Equation 5.12 naturally increases by a factor of α in case the hypothesized phrase movement is across two, three, etc. boundaries, making reordering from the beginning to the end of a long sentence highly unlikely.

Given a text or a speech transcript with sub-sentence punctuation, we can consider commas to be soft boundaries and define the labels $c(j)$ accordingly. In case of automatically predicted soft boundaries we can use the posterior probability of a boundary to make the penalty dependent on the confidence with which the soft boundary was predicted. Thus, for boundaries with low confidence the penalty is small, since phrase reordering across this boundary may still be rather probable. Incorporating soft boundary confidence scores is straightforward: the integer labels $c(j)$ in Equation 5.12 are replaced by real values $r(j)$ (see Figure 5.3), which are computed recursively as follows:

$$r(j) = \begin{cases} 0, & \text{if } j = 0 \\ r(j-1), & \text{if } c(j) = c(j-1) \\ r(j-1) - \log p_{nb}(j) & \text{if } c(j) \neq c(j-1) \end{cases} \quad (5.13)$$

Here, $p_{nb}(j)$ is the posterior probability that the soft boundary *does not* appear between the words f_{j-1} and f_j. If the new position j' and the old position j of the first word in a phrase are in the same sentence part, no penalty will be added, since $r(j) - r(j') = 0$.

Another option for constraining the reordering with soft boundaries is to include the comma predictions as features in the maximum entropy reordering model of [Zens & Ney 06]. In addition to the baseline features which include source and target words that end or start a phrase, we introduce three additional binary features that encode if the first source word of the next phrase is from the previous, same, or the next boundary section as the last word of the current phrase. The sections are defined based on the labels $c(j)$ as described above. When training the model, these labels can be obtained either by using the reference commas in the MT source training sentence, or automatically predicted commas. The experiments on using a soft boundary feature in the maximum entropy reordering model were performed by D. Hillard in a joint effort with the author of this thesis. Details can be found in [Hillard 08].

5.3 Experimental results

5.3.1 Sentence segmentation

The quality of the proposed sentence segmentation algorithm was evaluated in two ways. First, the precision and recall in comparison to manually defined sentence boundaries was computed. These boundaries are inserted by humans into the correct transcript of the document that has to be translated. To evaluate the quality of the automatic segmentation of ASR output, the reference boundaries are inserted into the automatically produced transcript by aligning it with the correct transcript using the minimum edit distance (Levenshtein) algorithm.

We also measured the influence of the presented segmentation algorithm on the translation quality. To this end, different automatic segmentations of a spoken document were translated, and their MT error rates and scores (BLEU, TER, WER, PER) were compared.

When translating ASR output with automatic sentence segmentation, the number of automatically determined segments may be different from the number of segments in the human reference translations. In this case, we use the algorithm described in Chapter 3 to obtain the alignment with the multiple reference translations based on the word error rate and, using this alignment, to re-segment the translation output to match the number of reference segments. Then, the usual MT evaluation measures can be computed.

The experiments for automatic sentence segmentation were performed on the IWSLT Chinese-to-English task, the TC-STAR English-to-Spanish task, and GALE Chinese-to-English and Arabic-to-English tasks. Detailed corpus statistics for the training and test data used are given in Appendix A.

Table 5.1: Quality of sentence segmentation measured with Precision (P) and Recall (R) on the IWSLT Chinese-English task (minimum sentence length set to 3, maximum to 30 words). Comparison of the RWTH approach with the approach of SRI [Stolcke & Shriberg[+] 98] (`hidden-ngram` tool). No prosodic features were used.

Corpus	RWTH		hidden-ngram	
	P [%]	R [%]	P [%]	R [%]
IWSLT test 2005	84.2	84.1	84.1	85.5
IWSLT dev 2006	59.5	64.6	57.0	62.4
IWSLT test 2006	56.4	61.0	54.9	57.6
IWSLT test 2006 (ASR)	56.0	55.2	55.4	52.6

5.3.1.1 IWSLT Chinese-to-English task

The first experiments were performed on the IWSLT Chinese-to-English small vocabulary task (2006 IWSLT evaluation). This task consisted of translating manually and automatically transcribed utterances related to tourism. The corpus statistics for the task are provided in Appendix in Table A.3. For this task, the segmentation algorithm employed a 4-gram hidden-event LM trained on 300K Chinese words and a parametric length model. The pause duration feature could not be used, since all of the utterances had been recorded separately. On this task, we compared the performance of the algorithm across different types of data. The 2005 test set with 3208 words and 506 reference segments is very similar to the training data on which the 4-gram LM was trained, whereas the 2006 test set with 5550 words and 500 segments contains more spontaneous utterances. We were also interested in the effect of speech recognition errors on sentence segmentation. The Chinese character error rate was 12.8% for the development set and 15.2% for the 2006 test set.

Table 5.1 gives an overview of the segmentation results for this task. In columns denoted with *RWTH*, we evaluate the performance of the sentence segmentation algorithm presented in Section 5.1. In the last two columns, the performance of the *hidden-ngram* tool is evaluated. This tool is part of the SRI LM toolkit [Stolcke 02] and implements the well-established approach of [Stolcke & Shriberg[+] 98].

The RWTH system performs very well on the 2005 test data, but not as well on the more spontaneous data. The ASR errors mostly affect recall, presumably because some of the words which are typical for the beginning or the end of a sentence had not been recognized correctly.

The results of the algorithm presented in Section 5.1 are better than or comparable to the approach of [Stolcke & Shriberg[+] 98] using the same language model. For the experiments

Table 5.2: Quality of sentence segmentation measured with Precision (P) and Recall (R) in % on the TC-STAR English ASR output (minimum sentence length set to 3, maximum to 50 words).

	Development		Test	
	P[%]	R [%]	P [%]	R [%]
baseline	54.2	52.1	54.0	50.4
+ length model	54.7	52.5	55.3	51.7
+ pause model	68.8	68.4	70.5	69.7
baseline + pause model	68.1	68.3	69.9	70.3

with the SRI's hidden-ngram tool, the threshold for the SU posterior probability was optimized for precision/recall on the same development set.

5.3.1.2 TC-STAR English-to-Spanish task

The experiments for the TC-STAR task reported below concern the prediction of sentence boundaries in the English ASR output on the 2006 English-to-Spanish EPPS evaluation data. The ASR word error rate was 6.9%. The corpus statistics for the training, development and test data on this task are given in Appendix in Table A.6. The scaling factors of the segmentation model features, as well as the minimum and maximum segment length parameters were tuned manually on the development set (with about 28K words and 1194 segments in the verbatim (correct) transcription) with the goal of increasing and balancing precision and recall. Then, these scaling factors were used for detecting segment boundaries in the evaluation set (with about 28K words and 1155 segments in the verbatim transcription).

The precision and recall percentages for the development and test set are given in Table 5.2. In this table, we compare the following experiments:

- *baseline*: sentence segmentation using the algorithm described in Section 5.1, but only with language model probabilities and segment penalty as features;
- *+ length model*: the baseline setup plus the parametric sentence length model;
- *+ pause model*: the baseline setup plus both the sentence length model and the pause duration feature;
- *baseline + pause model*: the baseline setup plus only the pause duration feature.

The baseline system for sentence segmentation makes use of a 4-gram language model trained on the English part of the European Parliament corpus (over 31 million words). The

5.3 Experimental results

Table 5.3: Translation quality on the TC-STAR English-to-Spanish task using various sentence segmentation and punctuation prediction settings.

transcription	segmentation	punctuation prediction	BLEU [%]	TER [%]	WER [%]	PER [%]
correct	correct	correct	45.5	40.5	42.8	31.9
automatic	correct (aligned)	correct (aligned)	40.2	45.1	47.5	35.7
	automatic	correct (aligned)	39.9	45.4	47.8	36.1
	correct (aligned)	automatic	37.8	46.9	49.6	36.8
	automatic	automatic	36.4	48.3	50.9	37.8

parametric sentence length model was also estimated on this data, but the improvement in sentence segmentation quality with this model was not statistically significant. The largest and significant gains in performance came from using the pause duration feature, which indicates that in many cases the speakers do make pauses to mark the start of a new sentence. The best segmentation results reach 70% precision and recall.

To measure how automatic segmentation affects the quality of machine translation output we evaluated the segmentation algorithm in a machine translation setup. The results in Table 5.3 show the effect of the various types of segmentation on the quality of machine translation from English to Spanish. We compare combinations of the following conditions:

- correct vs. automatic speech transcription;
- correct sentence segmentation vs. automatic sentence segmentation with the algorithm presented in Section 5.1 using all of the main features (i. e. hidden-event language model, pause duration, length model and segment penalty). In order to separate the effects of ASR errors and segmentation, we aligned the ASR output with the correct transcription using the edit distance algorithm and inserted human reference boundaries into the automatic transcription.
- correct vs. automatic punctuation prediction: here, we either insert the reference punctuation parks into the ASR output based on the edit distance alignment or predict punctuation marks automatically using one of the strategies described in Section 5.2.

The results in Table 5.3 show that recognition errors account for the largest share of the loss in translation quality as compared to the translation of the correct transcription (e. g. from 45.5 to 40.2% in BLEU). In contrast, the MT evaluation measures only degrade slightly (e. g. from 45.1 to 45.4% in TER) when automatic segmentation is used (with reference punctuation marks). This shows that the presented approach to SU boundary detection is robust enough to be used in a machine translation framework. The restriction on the maximum sentence length (50 words) allows for efficient translation. On the other hand, the restriction on the minimum sentence length of 3 words helps to avoid breaking apart word groups, for which a good phrasal translation exists. Sentences shorter than 3 words are usually standard expressions like "yes" and "thank you", which are translated accurately even if they become part of a longer segment.

The last two lines of Table 5.3 indicate that automatic punctuation prediction methods do not perform as well as the presented automatic segmentation algorithm. The reasons for this will be discussed in Section 5.3.2, where the experiments with different punctuation prediction strategies will be presented.

5.3.1.3 GALE Chinese-to-English and Arabic-to-English tasks

In this section, we tested the segmentation and translation quality on the GALE Chinese-to-English and Arabic-to-English large vocabulary tasks. The MT systems for the two tasks were created at RWTH for participation in the international research project GALE [GALE 07] and its evaluation campaigns. The performance of the sentence segmentation algorithm presented in this chapter was evaluated on the automatically recognized broadcast news portion of the GALE 2006 MT evaluation data.

To perform automatic segmentation with the presented algorithm, we use m-gram hidden-event language models with modified Kneser-Ney smoothing as implemented in the SRILM toolkit [Stolcke 02]. The LMs for sentence boundary prediction were trained with the same data sources as for training the Chinese ASR language models, including broadcast news speech transcripts, TDT2 and TDT3 text data, the Chinese Gigaword corpus, the Chinese portion of various news translation corpora, and web news data collections. For tuning the parameters of the sentence segmentation system, we used a held-out part of TDT4 as a development set for Chinese and the BBN 2006 tune set for Arabic (automatically recognized broadcast news speech data). The ASR output was generated by the SRI 2006 Mandarin and Arabic evaluation systems. The reference transcriptions of the Chinese evaluation data contain about 19K characters and 633 sentence units. The Arabic reference transcriptions contain about 12K words and 661 sentence units. The Mandarin ASR system has a character error rate (CER) of 5.6% on the development, and 17.8% on the evaluation set. The Arabic system has a WER of 17.1% on the development set, and 33.7% on the evaluation set.

The MT systems for the two tasks were trained using the bilingual training corpora from LDC. The statistics of the training corpora are shown in Appendix in Table A.9. The baseline translation model scaling factors were optimized w.r.t. the BLEU measure, using the NIST 2004 evaluation set as the development set. Additional tuning of parameters was performed on

Table 5.4: Segmentation and translation results for different sentence segmentation settings on the GALE Chinese-to-English task. Comparison of the approach presented in this chapter (RWTH) with the ICSI+ approach of [Zimmerman & Hakkani-Tur[+] 06] using different thresholds for selecting the sentence boundaries, as well as combination of both approaches.

algorithm	P [%]	R [%]	F-score [%]	BLEU [%]	TER [%]
ICSI+ 0.8	93.1	38.6	54.6	19.2	68.5
ICSI+ 0.5	81.8	64.8	72.3	20.2	67.5
ICSI+ 0.2	69.6	83.2	75.8	20.7	67.3
RWTH	72.2	74.3	73.2	20.7	67.4
+ phrase coverage	57.2	82.2	67.5	21.2	67.0
RWTH+ICSI	75.0	77.5	76.2	20.8	67.1
boundary after every 30 words				18.1	69.7
reference sentence units				20.7	66.9

the automatically recognized broadcast news development data described above. The factor for the reordering model, the target language model and the phrase penalty were affected by this tuning. For the evaluation data, the MT error measures were calculated using three reference translations manually created by LDC. For the speech development data, only single reference translations were available. The MT evaluation was case-insensitive, with punctuation marks. The punctuation marks were predicted using the MT system as described in Section 5.2.1.3. The segmentation results for this task are reported not only in terms of precision and recall, but also in terms of their combination known as the F-score.

Table 5.4 summarizes the segmentation and translation results on the Chinese-to-English task. Here, we compare the presented algorithm with the approach developed at ICSI (see [Zimmerman & Hakkani-Tur[+] 06]). We consider the following conditions:

- *ICSI+*: under this condition, we directly use the algorithm of [Zimmerman & Hakkani-Tur[+] 06]. The boundaries are inserted if the sentence end posterior probability exceeds a certain threshold. Here, we tried the thresholds 0.2, 0.5, and 0.8.

- *RWTH*: the sentence segmentation algorithm presented in Section 5.1 with all major features included (language model, pause duration, segment length model, etc.).

- *RWTH + phrase coverage*: here, the RWTH system was extended with the phrase coverage feature described in Section 5.1.6.

- *RWTH+ICSI*: the sentence end posterior probability from the ICSI+ approach was included as an additional feature in the RWTH approach (without using the phrase coverage feature).

Table 5.4 also includes translation results for the case when a segment boundary was inserted after every 30 words and when the reference sentence units were used, inserted into the ASR output based on the edit distance alignment.

When the ICSI+ approach is used directly, the posterior probability thresholds 0.2, 0.5, and 0.8 lead to average segment lengths of 16, 24, and 45 words, respectively. The best threshold determined on a development set is 0.2. This means that shorter segments are better for translation, i. e. recall is more important than precision. For this algorithm, the setting with the highest F-score also results in the best translation quality.

The RWTH approach described in this chapter has a lower F-score than the ICSI+ system, but performs similarly in terms of BLEU and TER. One advantage of this algorithm is that extreme sentence lengths cannot occur in its output. Here, the minimum and maximum SU length was set to 4 and 60 words, respectively. In contrast, even using a small posterior probability threshold of 0.2 that favors short SUs, the ICSI+ system produced 5 sentences that were 100 or more words long. 40 sentences contained only 1 word. Most probably, the translations of these "sentences" were not adequate. This is proved by the system where the ICSI+ posteriors are used as an additional feature in the log-linear model combination as mentioned in Section 5.1.6. The segmentation and translation error measures improve, e. g. F-measure from 75.8 to 76.2%, and TER from 67.4 to 67.1%.

The best translation quality (BLEU score of 21.2%) is achieved by adding the phrase coverage feature described in Section 5.1.6. It is notable that the F-score for this setup is low, but the recall is high. The phrase coverage feature results in additional SU boundaries that may not correspond to manually defined boundaries, but have less impact on the translation because phrasal context at these extra boundaries was not captured during MT training.

For comparison, we also report the translation results for two baseline setups. In the first setup, a boundary is inserted after every 30 words in a document. This is clearly not a good idea, since the BLEU score is low. In the second setup, the manual reference boundaries are inserted into the ASR output based on the edit distance alignment with the correct transcriptions. We see that the automatic SU boundary prediction results in translations of the same or even somewhat better quality than when reference boundaries are used.

In Table 5.5, we report the results for the same experiments on the Arabic-to-English task. Here, the F-measures for the SU boundaries are lower than for Chinese. The main difference relative to Chinese-to-English translations is that it is advantageous to produce

Table 5.5: Segmentation and translation results for different sentence segmentation settings on the GALE Arabic-to-English task.

algorithm	P [%]	R [%]	F-score [%]	BLEU [%]	TER [%]
ICSI+ 0.8	76.9	43.3	55.4	21.8	62.2
ICSI+ 0.2	40.1	84.9	54.4	21.6	62.8
RWTH	52.6	54.4	53.5	22.0	62.3
+ phrase coverage	49.7	60.3	54.5	22.1	61.9
RWTH+ICSI	61.3	68.8	64.8	21.9	62.4
boundary after every 30 words				20.6	63.7
reference sentence units				21.5	62.4

longer segments. We attribute this to the fact that reordering is mostly local when translating from Arabic to English. If two sentences are translated as one, their words are usually not swapped. In general, the Arabic-to-English MT is less sensitive to the quality of sentence segmentation than the Chinese-to-English MT. The combination of the RWTH and ICSI+ approaches improved the F-score, but did not yield the expected gain in MT quality on this task. It is worth noting that all automatic segmentation approaches are as good in terms of MT quality as when the reference SU boundaries are inserted into the ASR output.

5.3.2 Punctuation prediction

5.3.2.1 Translation quality in the context of punctuation prediction

The three alternative punctuation prediction methods described in Section 5.2 were tested experimentally on the IWSLT and TC-STAR tasks. The goal was to obtain the most accurate punctuation in the automatic translations without degrading the general MT quality. Therefore, the evaluation was performed by computing the standard MT error measures using multiple references with punctuation marks.

For punctuation prediction either in the source or in the target language the `hidden-ngram` tool from the SRI toolkit [Stolcke 02] was used. The 4-gram hidden event language model was trained, the hidden events were comma, period and question mark.

Each of the three MT systems corresponding to the three punctuation prediction strategies was optimized on the development set. The scaling factors for the log-linear translation model features were automatically tuned to increase the BLEU score. The system which translates punctuation marks predicted in the source language and the system which generates them in

Table 5.6: Translation quality for the IWSLT 2006 Chinese-to-English task (evaluation set).

transcription	segmentation	punctuation prediction	BLEU [%]	TER [%]	WER [%]	PER [%]
correct	correct	source	18.9	67.7	70.3	55.9
		in translation	**21.2**	**64.3**	66.7	54.0
		target	18.8	67.3	69.9	55.6
	automatic	source	19.7	67.6	69.8	57.4
		in translation	**21.1**	**64.8**	66.9	55.2
		target	20.0	67.4	69.8	56.8
automatic	correct	source	16.2	70.5	72.8	59.2
		in translation	**18.2**	**67.6**	69.8	57.5
		target	16.3	70.8	73.3	59.7
	automatic	source	15.8	71.1	73.1	60.9
		in translation	**18.9**	**67.7**	69.6	58.4
		target	16.8	70.9	72.7	60.9

the translation process were optimized using references with punctuation marks. The system that had been trained without punctuation marks was optimized using references without punctuation marks; then, punctuation was added as a postprocessing step.

Table 5.6 shows the results for the IWSLT 2006 experiments. Here, we distinguish between:

- correct and automatic transcription of the IWSLT 2006 evaluation set;
- correct or automatic sentence segmentation, with the latter produced by the algorithm proposed in Section 5.1;
- three types of punctuation prediction strategies: "source", "target", and "in translation", corresponding to their descriptions in Section 5.2.

The best quality of translations with punctuation marks is achieved by predicting them using the translation model. The BLEU and TER scores for this strategy are highlighted in bold. When the punctuation marks are predicted in translation, the improvements in BLEU, TER, and other error measures in comparison with the source-side and target-side prediction are very large: for e. g. the correct text and segmentation condition, the improvement from 67.3 to 65.8% in TER would have been already statistically significant, but the obtained result of 64.3% is even better. This method has the advantage that the translation quality of the phrase-based translation system is not negatively influenced by falsely inserted punctuation marks on the source side. This is especially important for the IWSLT task, since the corpus is

5.3 Experimental results

small and data sparseness problems may have a negative effect on the quality of the source-side punctuation prediction. Furthermore, the translation quality of the overall system including punctuation prediction is optimized as a whole. On the small task, using the translation model and the target language model in combination to generate punctuation on the target side improves system performance. With the presence of recognition errors and using automatically determined sentence boundaries, the advantage of predicting punctuation marks using the translation model is even more clear.

Table 5.7 gives an overview of the English-to-Spanish MT quality when punctuation marks are predicted for the TC-STAR task on the ASR output. The following conditions are compared:

- *correct (aligned)* segmentation: the manually defined SU boundaries are inserted into the ASR output; then, either the same is done with the reference punctuation marks, or the punctuation marks are predicted automatically on the source side using the `hidden-ngram` tool.

- *automatic* segmentation: here, given the automatic sentence segmentation produced by the algorithm described in Section 5.1, we test the three punctuation prediction strategies "source", "in translation", and "target" as described in Section 5.2. In addition, we test the translation without sentence-internal punctuation marks using the MT system which was trained using punctuation marks both on source and target side (the condition "full stop only (source)"). Finally, we include the result from Table 5.3 for the experiment in which reference punctuation marks are inserted into the automatically segmented ASR output.

On this task, all strategies for predicting punctuation marks work similarly well. The best translation results are obtained by inserting punctuation marks in the source language. This can be explained by the low recognition error rate on this corpus, which makes punctuation prediction in the source language sufficiently reliable.

Note that predicting all punctuation marks works significantly better than predicting only periods for this task (cf. the conditions "source" and "full stop only" in Table 5.7). This means that a significant number of commas is present in the reference translations and can be matched to the commas in the system output. However, the experiments comparing translations of the ASR output with reference vs. automatically predicted punctuation marks (using either correct or automatic sentence segmentation) show that the quality of automatic punctuation prediction still leaves much to be desired. The reason for this is that, on this task, the translation is mostly monotonic, and rules for comma placement in English and Spanish are similar. Thus, the reference commas inserted on the source side are almost always correctly

5 Sentence segmentation and punctuation prediction for speech translation

Table 5.7: Translation quality on the TC-STAR English-to-Spanish task (ASR output) using different punctuation prediction strategies.

segmentation	punctuation prediction	BLEU [%]	TER [%]	WER [%]	PER [%]
automatic	source	36.4	48.3	50.9	37.8
	in translation	35.7	48.7	50.9	38.5
	target	35.3	48.8	51.3	38.4
	full stop only (source)	34.0	50.2	53.0	38.3
	correct (aligned)	39.9	45.4	47.8	36.1
correct (aligned)	source	37.8	46.9	49.6	36.8
correct (aligned)		40.2	45.1	47.5	35.7

transferred to the target side and match the commas in the reference translations, which increases e.g. the BLEU score. On the other hand, the analysis of the English training data has shown that commas are often placed by humans inconsistently, which makes it hard for any automatic approach to predict them correctly.

5.3.2.2 Sentence-internal punctuation marks in reordering for MT

The sentence segmentation results for the GALE task presented in Section 5.3.1.3 show that shorter segments can be better translated by the Chinese-to-English system than long segments. One reason for this is that erroneous reordering across a missed SU boundary can cause translation errors. However, the context information may be lost when short segments split sentences because each piece is then translated individually. So, especially for Chinese, the prediction of soft boundaries as described in Section 5.2.2 could constrain and thus correct MT reordering without the negative effect of cutting the context.

We used the system of [Hillard 08] to predict commas and caesuras in Chinese to be used as boundaries. This is a more elaborate system than the one used in punctuation prediction experiments on the IWSLT and TC-STAR tasks. The hidden-event LM for comma prediction is trained on the Chinese Gigaword corpus, where the training text has been stripped of all punctuation but comma and caesura. The positions of the predicted commas and caesuras were then used to divide each test source sentence into several parts and to compute the soft boundary penalties $c(j)$ and $r(j)$ as described in Section 5.2.2.

Table 5.8 presents the comma prediction and translation results for three settings. In the first setting "reference SUs", we used the integer penalties $c(j)$ as in Equation 5.12. The penalties

Table 5.8: Comma prediction and translation results for the different SU and soft boundary settings on the GALE Chinese-to-English task.

SU algorithm	P [%]	R [%]	F-score [%]	BLEU [%]	TER [%]
reference SUs	100	100	100	20.7	66.9
RWTH+ICSI	73.8	35.6	48.0	20.8	67.1
ICSI+ 0.5	77.0	40.1	52.7	20.2	67.5

Table 5.9: Examples of improved MT quality by using automatically predicted commas as soft boundaries (GALE Chinese-to-English task).

baseline	according to statistics , in 2005 , the china national tourism administration ...
+ commas	according to the china national tourism administration statistics in 2005 ...
reference	the statistics from the national tourism administration shows that in 2005 ...
baseline	the protesters , chanting slogans green belt ...
+ commas	protesters circumspect green belt , shouted slogans ...
reference	the protesters , wearing green turbans , shouted slogans ...
baseline	after rapid reaction , the government mud-rock flows ...
+commas	mud-rock flows , the government has reacted ...
reference	after the mudslide broke out , the government responded ...

were computed relative to the reference commas and SU boundaries that had been inserted into the ASR output. The second setting "RWTH+ICSI" uses automatically predicted commas and their posterior probabilities as in Equation 5.13, which were inserted given the SU boundaries predicted by the RWTH+ICSI sentence segmentation system. Here, we considered only the commas with probability > 0.2. In the third setting, we used the commas predicted given the somewhat longer SUs of the ICSI+ system at a threshold of 0.5, which resulted in using more automatically predicted commas (with higher comma recall). Comma recall increases for less frequent sentence boundaries because inserted SUs can often occur at reference comma locations. In all cases, the BLEU and TER improvements were not significant with respect to the translation results without using the soft boundaries. Nevertheless, in some translated sentences, word order and cause-effect relations were subjectively more correct when the soft boundary penalty was used. Several examples of this are shown in Table 5.9.

One of the reasons why the soft boundary penalty has little effect on translation quality is that it is not integrated into the maximum entropy reordering model that already restricts unnecessary long-range phrase reordering. Since in some syntactic contexts the reordering may occur across sub-sentence boundaries, it would be useful to make the boundary a feature rather than a constraint. Several experiments in which the soft boundary constraint is added to the maximum entropy model as another feature are reported in [Hillard 08]. The machine translation tests with the extended reordering model were performed by the author of this thesis in cooperation with D. Hillard. Unfortunately, no improvement in translation error measures could be observed, but some qualitative improvements were found by comparing the translations manually. The results of these experiments are presented in detail in [Hillard 08].

5.4 Conclusions

In this chapter, an algorithm for automatic sentence segmentation was presented that had been specifically designed for machine translation needs. The approach uses a constituent-based HMM, in which an explicit sentence length model is included. The method is at least as strong as the state-of-the-art approaches in terms of precision and recall, but has the advantage that the length of the produced segments can be explicitly controlled and adjusted to the needs of machine translation algorithms. The method utilizes language model and pause duration cues, as well as additional features. One important novel feature characterizes phrase coverage in the MT system of the words that span the candidate boundaries, so that a boundary that brakes a phrase with a good translation can be avoided. The robustness of the proposed method was confirmed when it was evaluated in terms of the resulting machine translation quality. It was shown on two large vocabulary tasks that translations of automatically segmented speech transcript can achieve the same quality as the translations of the same transcript with manually inserted segment boundaries.

Also in this chapter, three different strategies for target language punctuation generation were compared. It was shown that punctuation prediction using a phrase-based MT system can be the most effective solution for generating good-quality translations with punctuation marks. On the other hand, sentence-internal punctuation marks like commas which were predicted in the source speech transcript were utilized as additional soft boundary constraints on the phrase-based reordering in MT search.

The proposed sentence segmentation and punctuation prediction methods have shown their usefulness in experiments on several small and large vocabulary MT tasks. It is worth noting that a preliminary version of the described sentence segmentation algorithm was used by all participants to segment the raw ASR output during the 2006 TC-STAR speech translation evaluation [Matusov & Zens+ 06].

6 Combination of multiple machine translation systems

An improvement of translation quality for both text and speech can be achieved by combining the outputs of multiple translation systems. In this chapter, we propose a novel algorithm for computing a *consensus* translation from the output of multiple MT engines. The algorithm works under the assumption that different MT systems tend to make different errors, and that ideally at each word or phrase position the majority of the individual systems agree on a correct translation. Therefore, the consensus translation is computed by weighted majority voting on a confusion network, similarly to the well-established ROVER approach of Fiscus [Fiscus 97] for combining speech recognition hypotheses. To create the CN, pairwise word alignments of the original MT hypotheses are learned using an enhanced statistical alignment algorithm that explicitly models word reordering. The context of a whole corpus of automatic translations rather than a single sentence is taken into account in order to achieve high alignment quality. The confusion network is scored with a target language model and other features, and the consensus translation is extracted as the best path.

The proposed system combination approach was evaluated in the framework of two major international projects: the TC-STAR speech translation project [TC-STAR 07] and the GALE project [GALE 07]. In the experiments, up to eight state-of-the-art statistical translation systems from different project partners were combined. Significant improvements in translation quality from Spanish to English and vice versa, as well as from Chinese to English and Arabic to English were achieved in comparison with the best of the individual MT systems. Significant improvements were also obtained on other tasks.

A useful application of MT system combination for translation of speech is to combine systems which translate different type of input (single best ASR hypothesis, word lattice). It will be shown that through such a combination the translation quality can be improved beyond the advantages of performing word lattice translation with a single MT system.

6 Combination of multiple machine translation systems

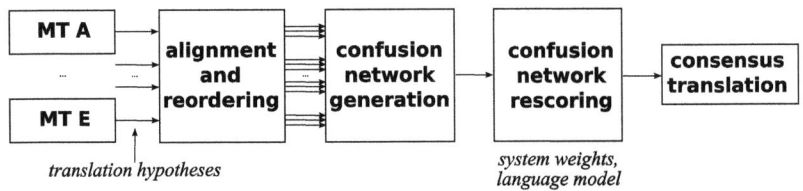

Figure 6.1: The system combination architecture.

6.1 Introduction

Combining outputs from different systems was shown to be quite successful in automatic speech recognition (ASR). Voting schemes like the ROVER approach of Fiscus [Fiscus 97] use edit distance alignment and time information to create confusion networks from the output of different ASR systems for the same audio input. The consensus recognition hypothesis is generated by weighted majority voting.

In comparison to ASR, the biggest challenge in the application of system combination algorithms in MT is the need for word reordering. Different translation hypotheses from different systems may have different word order. In many cases these are all correct translations. In other cases the differences in the word order arise from the fact that some systems are not able to produce a syntactically correct target language sentence due to weak models and/or restrictions on reordering in the MT process. Nevertheless, the hypotheses of these systems contain valuable information which can be used to improve the word choice in the consensus translation. Therefore, some hypotheses have to be reordered so that corresponding words can be aligned with each other in the confusion network.

In this work we show how the reordering problem in system combination for MT can be solved. Our approach to computing a consensus translation includes an enhanced alignment and reordering framework. In contrast to existing approaches, ([Jayaraman & Lavie 05, Rosti & Ayan[+] 07]), the context of the whole corpus rather than a single sentence is considered in this iterative, unsupervised procedure, yielding a more reliable alignment. The basics of the alignment procedure and some first system combination results have been previously described in [Matusov & Ueffing[+] 06]. In this chapter, we present a more thorough theoretical motivation for the approach. We also give an exhaustive set of experimental results on several important tasks, successfully combining state-of-the-art speech translation systems.

Figure 6.1 gives an overview of the basic system combination architecture described in this section. The outputs of several MT systems are first aligned at the word level, and all but one of the hypotheses are reordered based on this alignment. Then, a confusion network is constructed from the aligned and reordered hypotheses. Finally, the best path in the CN is selected based on combination of system weights and language model score.

All of these steps will be described in detail in the following sections. Following the review of the related work for MT system combination in Section 6.2, we will present the details of the enhanced alignment that is used to find correspondences between words in the multiple MT system hypotheses in Section 6.3. Section 6.4 will describe how the confusion network is constructed based on the word alignments and how subsequently the consensus translation is extracted from the CN. In Section 6.5 we will explain additional features which further improve the system combination algorithm. The experimental results are given in Section 6.6. The chapter is concluded with a summary.

6.2 Related work

The related work on MT system combination can be divided in two main categories. The first set of methods are *selection* methods, i.e. for each sentence, one of the provided hypotheses is selected. Thus, the resulting translation comes from a set of already produced translations. The hypothesis selection is made based on the combination of different scores from n-gram language models [Callison-Burch & Flournoy 01, Nomoto 04], but also from translation models and other features [Paul & Doi[+] 05]. The best translation can also be selected from the combined N-best list of the different MT systems. Such approaches often require comparable sentence translation scores. However, the scores produced by most statistical machine translation (SMT) systems are not normalized and therefore not directly comparable. For some other MT systems (e.g. knowledge-based systems), the scores of hypotheses may not be even available. If scores are available, they have to be rescaled. Some suggestions how this can be done are presented in [Nomoto 04, Tidhar & Küssner 00]. If scores are not available or completely incomparable, some other features such as lexicon model probability and n-gram agreement between the hypotheses in the combined N-best list can be used [Rosti & Ayan[+] 07, Hildebrand & Vogel 08].

The second set of approaches generates the system combination translation from sub-sentence parts (words or phrases) of the original system translations. The advantage of these approaches is that a possibly new translation can be produced that includes "good" partial translations from each of the involved systems. Some authors determine word alignments between the system translations, which then are used to build confusion networks so that a consensus translation can be computed in the style of [Fiscus 97]. Bangalore et al. [Bangalore & Bordel[+] 01] use multiple sequence alignments (a generalization of the edit distance alignments) to construct a CN from several translation hypotheses. This algorithm produces monotonic alignments only; hence, it is not able to align translation hypotheses with significantly different word order. Jayaraman and Lavie [Jayaraman & Lavie 05] try to overcome this problem. They introduce a method that allows for non-monotonic alignments of words in different translation hypotheses for the same sentence. However, this approach uses many heuristics and is based on the alignment that is performed to calculate a specific MT error measure; performance improvements have been reported only in terms of this measure. Recently, [Rosti & Ayan[+] 07] also followed a confusion network combination approach. They used the alignment based on translation edit rate (TER, [Snover & Dorr[+] 06], as described in Chapter 3). This alignment procedure computes the edit distance extended by allowing shifts of word blocks. Only exactly matching phrases can be shifted, and the shifts are selected greedily. The costs of aligning synonyms to each other are the same as those of aligning completely unrelated words. In many cases, the synonyms will not be matched to each other, but will be considered as insertions or deletions in their original positions. This is suboptimal for CN voting, for which it is important to align as many corresponding words as possible, considering reasonable reorderings of words and phrases. Extending their previous work, the authors of [Rosti & Zhang[+] 08] experiment with an incremental alignment approach in which subsequent system hypotheses are aligned to a partially constructed CN; however, the alignment is still based on the translation edit rate. Another extension in which the TER alignment algorithm is modified to match synonyms derived from WordNet is presented in [Ayan & Zheng[+] 08].

Previous approaches for aligning multiple translations only exploited the alternative system hypotheses available for a particular sentence. In contrast, the enhanced Hidden Markov Model (HMM) alignment algorithm presented in [Matusov & Ueffing[+] 06] and explained in detail in Section 6.3 makes the alignment decisions depend on probabilities iteratively trained on a whole corpus translated by the participating multiple MT systems. Thus, the alignment of synonyms and other related words can be learned automatically. Examples in Figure 6.2 indicate that the alignments produced using this method (as well as the word reordering based on these alignments) compare favorably with the TER alignment used by Rosti et al. [Rosti & Ayan[+] 07].

Finally, a few other system combination approaches do not perform the alignment between the hypotheses, but rather rely on the alignment with the source sentence. In one of the first publications on system combination in MT, [Nirenburg & Frederking 94] create a chart structure where target language phrases from each system are placed according to their

6.2 Related work

TER Alignment	HMM Alignment
I think that you know # you will be aware , I believe	
$ $ I think that you know $ $ know	I think that you $ $ know
will be aware , I you believe	I believe , you will be aware
a huge fall in average prices # a decline strong in the prices means	
a huge fall in average prices $	a huge fall in $ average prices
a decline strong in the prices means	a strong decline in the means prices

Figure 6.2: Examples of the TER-based alignment in comparison with the alignment produced by the enhanced alignment and reordering algorithm of [Matusov & Ueffing+ 06] (HMM Alignment). In each example, the second translation is reordered to match the word order of the first one, given the alignment. The $ symbol denotes deletions/insertions in the alignment. The examples are from the evaluation data of the TC-STAR Spanish-to-English speech translation task.

corresponding source phrases, together with their confidence scores. A chart-walk algorithm is used to select the best translation from the chart. More recently, [Huang & Papineni 07] and [Rosti & Ayan+ 07] show that a system combination translation can be produced by performing a new search with one of the involved phrase-based MT systems, but using only the phrases from the translation hypotheses provided by the participating systems. Syntactical phrases have to be flattened in order to pursue this approach. Although this method is superior to a selection approach, it is limited by the fact that all of the systems have to provide phrasal alignments with word sequences in the source sentence. In particular, this means that all the systems are required to work with the same preprocessing of the source sentence, which may reduce the diversity in their translations. Another limitation is that the final translation is generated by the "simple" phrase-based decoder, so that the system combination translation is bound to its structural restrictions.

In the latest work by [He & Yang+ 08], the alignment between the translation hypotheses is computed using an indirect HMM whose parameters are estimated from a variety of sources including word surface similarity, distance-based distortion penalty and semantic similarity. The latter is a novel concept in MT system combination. It is computed using the source sentence as a hidden layer: two target words are considered similar if there is a high bilingual lexicon probability that they are translated by the same source word(s). However, the authors show experimentally that semantic similarity is less important for the quality of the system combination translation than the surface similarity. In the HMM alignment approach proposed in the next section, the surface similarity (e.g. alignment of identical words or words with identical prefixes) also plays an important role. However, it is learned implicitly, since each sentence is present both in the "source" and in the "target" training corpus for the alignment.

6.3 Word alignment algorithm

In this section the details of the proposed word alignment and reordering strategy for system combination are explained.

Given a single source sentence F in the test corpus, we combine M translation hypotheses $E_1, \ldots, E_m, \ldots, E_M$ originating from M MT engines. Each hypothesis E_m consists of I_m target language words:

$$E_m := e_{m,1}, e_{m,2}, \ldots, e_{m,i}, \ldots, e_{m,I_m}$$

In the following, we will consider an *alignment* between two hypotheses E_n and E_m translating the same source sentence, $m, n \in \{1, ..., M\}; m \neq n$. In general, an alignment $A \subseteq I_n \times I_m$ is a relation between the words of the two hypotheses. Here, we will only consider alignments which are functions of the words in hypothesis E_m, i.e. $A : \{1, \ldots, I_m\} \to \{1, \ldots, I_n\}$.

The proposed alignment approach is a statistical one. It takes advantage of multiple translations for a whole corpus to compute the pairwise alignments of the MT outputs for each sentence in this corpus.

For each source sentence F in the test corpus, we select one of its translations $E_n, n = 1, \ldots, M$ as the *primary* hypothesis. Then we align the *secondary* hypotheses E_m ($m = 1, ..., M; n \neq m$) with E_n to match the word order in E_n. Since it is not clear which hypothesis should be primary, i.e. has the "best" word order, we let every hypothesis play the role of the primary translation, and align all pairs of hypotheses (E_n, E_m); $n \neq m$ (see Section 6.4).

The word alignment is *trained* in analogy to the alignment training procedure in statistical MT (see Section 1.3.1.2). The difference is that the two sentences that have to be aligned are in the same language. We consider the conditional probability $Pr(E_m|E_n)$ of the event that, given the hypothesis E_n, another hypothesis E_m is generated from the E_n. Then, the alignment between the two hypotheses is introduced as a hidden variable $\mathcal{A}$:

$$Pr(E_m|E_n) = \sum_{\mathcal{A}} Pr(E_m, \mathcal{A}|E_n) \qquad (6.1)$$

This probability is then decomposed into the alignment probability $Pr(\mathcal{A}|E_n)$ and the lexicon probability $Pr(E_m|\mathcal{A}, E_n)$:

$$Pr(E_m, \mathcal{A}|E_n) = Pr(\mathcal{A}|E_n) \cdot Pr(E_m|\mathcal{A}, E_n) \qquad (6.2)$$

6.3 Word alignment algorithm

As in statistical machine translation, we make modeling assumptions. We use the IBM Model 1 [Brown & Della Pietra+ 93] and the Hidden Markov Model (HMM, [Vogel & Ney+ 96]) to estimate the alignment model.

The lexicon probability of a sentence pair is modelled as the product of the single-word based probabilities of the aligned words:

$$Pr(E_m|\mathcal{A}, E_n) = \prod_{j=1}^{I_m} p(e_{m,j}|e_{n,a_j}) \qquad (6.3)$$

Here, the alignment $A = a_1^J$ is a function of the words in the secondary translation E_m, so that each word $e_{m,j}$ in E_m is aligned to the word $e_{n,i}$ in E_n on position $i = a_j$.

The alignment training corpus is created from a test corpus[a] of N sentences (e.g. a few hundred) translated by the involved MT engines. However, the effective size of the training corpus is larger than N, since all pairs of different hypotheses have to be aligned. Thus, the effective size of the training corpus is $M \cdot (M-1) \cdot N/2$.

The model parameters – the lexicon model $p(e|e')$ and the alignment model – are trained iteratively with the EM algorithm using the GIZA++ toolkit [Och & Ney 03]. The training is performed in the directions $E_m \rightarrow E_n$ and $E_n \rightarrow E_m$. The updated lexicon tables from the two directions are interpolated after each iteration using the method presented in [Zens & Matusov+ 04].

The final alignments are determined using a cost matrix C for each sentence pair (E_m, E_n). The elements of this matrix are the local costs $C(j, i)$ of aligning a word $e_{m,j}$ from E_m to a word $e_{n,i}$ from E_n. Following [Matusov & Zens+ 04], we compute these local costs by interpolating the negated logarithms of the state occupation probabilities from the "source-to-target" and "target-to-source" training of the HMM model. These are marginal probabilities of the form $p_j(i, E_m|E_n) = \sum_{A:a_j=i} Pr(E_m, A|E_n)$ normalized over target positions i. For a given alignment $A \subset I_n \times I_m$, we define the costs of this alignment $C(A)$ as the sum of the local costs of all aligned word pairs. The goal is to find a minimum cost alignment fulfilling certain constraints. The whole procedure is similar to the approach for computing alignments between sentences in different languages as described in Section 4.3.2.2.

Two different alignments are computed using the alignment cost matrix C: the alignment $\tilde{a}$ used for reordering each secondary translation E_m, and the alignment $\bar{a}$ used to build the confusion network.

---

[a] A test corpus can be used directly because the alignment training is unsupervised and only automatically produced translations are considered.

6 Combination of multiple machine translation systems

The alignment $\tilde{a}$ between the translation E_m and the primary hypothesis E_n used for reordering is determined under the constraint that it must be a function of the words in the secondary translation E_m with minimal costs. It can be easily computed from the cost matrix C as:

$$\tilde{a}_j = \operatorname*{argmin}_{i} C(j,i) \tag{6.4}$$

The word order of the secondary hypothesis E_m is changed. The words $e_{m,j}$ in E_m are sorted by the indices $i = \tilde{a}_j$ of the words in E_n to which they are aligned. If two or more words in hypothesis E_m are aligned to the same word in hypothesis E_n, they are kept in the original order.

After reordering each secondary hypothesis E_m and the rows of the corresponding alignment cost matrix according to the permutation based on the alignment $\tilde{a}$, we determine $M - 1$ monotonic *one-to-one* alignments between E_n as the primary translation and $E_m, m = 1, \ldots, M; m \neq n$. This type of alignment will allow a straightforward construction of the confusion network in the next step of the algorithm. In case of many-to-one connections in $\tilde{a}$ of words in hypothesis E_m to a single word from hypothesis E_n, we only keep the connection with the lowest alignment costs. This means that for each position i in hypothesis E_n the unique alignment connection with a word in hypothesis E_m is found with the following equation:

$$\bar{a}_i = \operatorname*{argmin}_{j:\ \tilde{a}_j = i} C(j,i) \tag{6.5}$$

The use of the one-to-one alignment $\bar{a}$ implies that some words in the secondary translation will not have a correspondence in the primary translation and vice versa. We consider these words to be aligned with the empty word ε. In the corresponding confusion network, the empty word will be transformed to an ε-arc.

Using the flexible framework of alignment cost matrices described in Chapter 4, the alignments $\tilde{a}$ and $\bar{a}$ can be further improved to handle phenomena which are related to the fact that the alignment is computed between words in the same language. One problem we observed was the repetitions of identical words in the consensus translation. Such repetitions occur if two identical words from a secondary hypothesis E_m are aligned with the same word in the primary hypothesis E_n. This often happens with articles like "the", in cases when e.g. the secondary system tends to overproduce the articles which are then all aligned to a single article from the primary translation. For example, if "the big cat saw the green car" is aligned to the primary translation "the green car was seen by large cats", the reordered version of the first sentence based on the alignment with the second one is "the the green car saw big cat". In order to avoid such word repetitions, we extend the simple algorithm for computing the alignment $\tilde{a}$ in Equation 6.4 by introducing an additional constraint that

6.3 Word alignment algorithm

system hypotheses	1.	0.25	**would your like coffee or tea**						
	2.	0.35	have you tea or coffee						
	3.	0.10	would like your coffee or						
	4.	0.30	I have some coffee tea would you like						
alignment and reordering	have|**would** you|**your** $|**like** coffee|**coffee** or|**or** tea|**tea**								
	would|**would** your|**your** like|**like** coffee|**coffee** or|**or** $|**tea**								
	I|$ **would**|would you|**your** like|**like** have|$ some|$ coffee|**coffee** $|**or** tea|**tea**								
confusion network	$	would	your	like	$	$	coffee	or	tea
	$	have	you	$	$	$	coffee	or	tea
	$	would	your	like	$	$	coffee	or	$
	I	would	you	like	have	some	coffee	$	tea
voting	$	would	you	$	$	$	coffee	or	tea
	0.7	0.65	0.65	0.35	0.7	0.7	1.0	0.7	0.9
	I	have	your	like	have	some		$	$
	0.3	0.35	0.35	0.65	0.3	0.3		0.3	0.1
consensus translation	would you like coffee or tea								

Figure 6.3: Example of creating a confusion network for system combination from monotonic one-to-one word alignments of the reordered secondary MT hypotheses with the primary hypothesis (denoted with symbol |). The words of the primary hypothesis are printed in bold. The symbol $ denotes an empty word alignment or an ε-arc in the corresponding part of the confusion network.

identical words $e_{m,j} = e_{m,j'}$ in hypothesis E_m can not be all aligned to the same word $e_{n,i}$ in E_n. If two such connections are found, the one with the higher costs in the alignment cost matrix C is discarded (e.g. for $e_{m,j'}$) and another alignment point is determined. This is the point with the lowest costs in the same column of the matrix:

$$\tilde{a}_{j'} = \operatorname*{argmin}_{i': i' \neq i} C(j', i') \qquad (6.6)$$

In combination with the alignment strategy for insertions as described in [Matusov & Leusch+ 08] this additional constraint helps to avoid nearly all incorrect word repetitions in the produced consensus translations.

6.4 Confusion network generation and scoring

6.4.1 Single confusion network

The $M - 1$ monotonic one-to-one alignments determined as described in the previous section are used to transform the set of (reordered) hypotheses for a sentence to a confusion network. We follow the approach of Bangalore et al. [Bangalore & Bordel[+] 01] with some extensions. The construction of a confusion network is best explained by the example in Figure 6.3. Here, the original $M = 4$ MT hypotheses with their weights are shown, followed by the alignment of the reordered secondary hypotheses 2-4 to the primary hypothesis 1 (shown in bold). The alignment is shown with the | symbol, where the words of the primary hypothesis are to the right of this symbol. The symbol $ denotes an empty word alignment or an ε-arc in the corresponding part of the confusion network.

Starting from an initial CN state s_0, the primary hypothesis is processed from left to right and a new state s_k is produced for each word $e_{n,i}$. Then, an arc is created from the previous state to this state, for $e_{n,i}$ and for all words (or the null word) aligned to $e_{n,i}$. If there are insertions following $e_{n,i}$ (for example, "have some" in Figure 6.3), the states and arcs for the inserted words are also created (details are described in [Matusov & Leusch[+] 08]).

The weighted majority voting on a single confusion network is straightforward and analogous to the ROVER system of [Fiscus 97]. First, we sum up the probabilities of the arcs which are labeled with the same word and have the same start and the same end state. More formally, this can be described as follows. For each state $s_k, k = 0, \ldots, K$ in the confusion network, we say that a word is at position k if an arc labeled with this word exists between the states s_{k-1} and s_k. Each word e_{mk} (including the empty word) at position $k \geq 1$ that is hypothesized by MT system m is assigned a weight γ_m (e.g. the weights 0.25, 0.35, 0.1, 0.3 for the four systems in Figure 6.3). In our experiments, these weights give an a-priori estimation of the translation quality of the MT system with the index m. The weights are adjusted based on the performance of the involved MT systems on a held-out development set in terms of an automatic MT evaluation measure. Generally, a better consensus translation can be produced if the words hypothesized by a better-performing system get a higher probability.

The probability for a unique word e to appear at position k is obtained with the following equation:

$$p_k(e|F) = \frac{\sum\limits_{m=1}^{M} \gamma_m \cdot \delta(e_{mk}, e)}{\sum\limits_{\tilde{e}} \sum\limits_{m=1}^{M} \gamma_m \cdot \delta(e_{mk}, \tilde{e})} \tag{6.7}$$

According to Equation 6.7, the probability of a word e at position k is higher if the majority

6.4 Confusion network generation and scoring

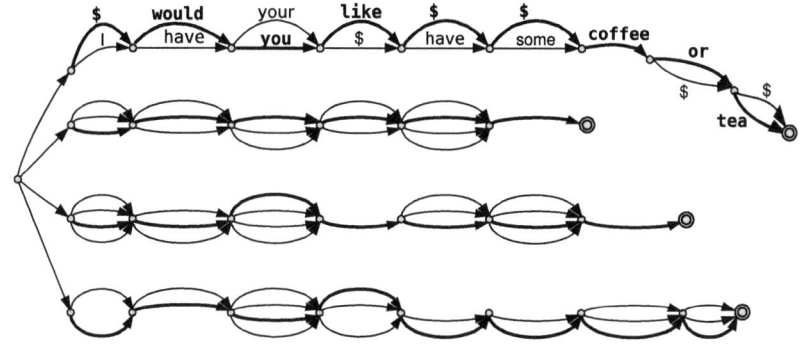

Figure 6.4: Union of several confusion networks, including the one shown in Figure 6.3. The thick lines represent the best paths in the individual confusion networks.

of the systems have produced e at this position. This implies that the output of at least 3 systems has to be combined in order to obtain meaningful system combination results. Note that the probability $p_k(e|F)$ is equal to 0 if the word e does not appear in the CN on position k.

Next, the consensus translation is extracted as the best path in the confusion network. The position-dependent probabilities $p_k(e|F)$ as given by Equation 6.7 are used to score each path. We define the consensus translation as the sequence $\hat{e}_1^K := \hat{e}_1, \ldots, \hat{e}_k, \ldots, \hat{e}_K$ [b] where, at each position k in the confusion network, the best word $\hat{e}_k$ is selected as given by the following equation:

$$\hat{e}_k = \underset{e}{\operatorname{argmax}} \{p_k(e|F)\} \qquad (6.8)$$

Note that the extracted consensus translation can be different from each of the original M translations. In the example in Figure 6.3, the weighted majority was obtained in the "voting" phase by the sequence $ would you like $ $ coffee or tea, which, after removal of the ε-arcs, becomes the consensus translation "would you like coffee or tea".

6.4.2 Union of confusion networks

In Section 6.3 it was mentioned that each translation E_m for a sentence F can be considered to be the primary hypothesis. Thus, a total of M confusion networks for each sentence can be generated. The consensus translation can be extracted only from one of these confusion networks as described above, e.g. from the CN corresponding to the primary hypothesis that

---
[b]with the ε-arcs removed from this sequence after its extraction.

6 Combination of multiple machine translation systems

was produced by a generally better performing MT system. However, the word order of the resulting consensus translation will follow the word order of the primary translation. This order may still be erroneous for some sentences. Because of that, a better strategy is to consider multiple primary hypotheses at once. Our experiments show that it is advantageous to unite the M confusion networks in a single lattice as shown in Figure 6.4. Then, the consensus translation can be selected from different alignment and reordering paths in this lattice. Note that each of the united CNs is reduced to the unique words at each position only, and each of these words has the "consensus" probability computed according to Equation 6.7.

Next, we formulate the decision criterion for extraction of the consensus translation for the case of multiple CNs. To this end, we re-write Equation 6.7 so that it expresses the probability for a unique word e to appear at position k in the CN that was generated using the primary hypothesis E_n:

$$p_k(e|F, E_n) = \frac{\sum_{m=1}^{M} \gamma_m \cdot \delta(e_{nmk}, e)}{\sum_{\tilde{e}} \sum_{m=1}^{M} \gamma_m \cdot \delta(e_{nmk}, \tilde{e})} \qquad (6.9)$$

Here, e_{nmk} is the word (or the empty word) from system m aligned to position k in the CN generated with the primary hypothesis E_n. Next, we use the probabilities $p_k(e|F, E_n)$ to extract the best word sequence according to the following criterion:

$$(\hat{I}, \hat{e}_1^{\hat{I}}) = \operatorname*{argmax}_{I, e_1^I} \left\{ \sum_{K', \bar{e}_1^{K'}: \; \bar{e}_1^{K'} \hat{=} e_1^I} \sum_{n=1}^{N} \prod_{k=1}^{K(n)} p_k(\bar{e}_k|F, E_n) \right\},$$

$$\text{with} \quad \bar{e}_k \in \{\varepsilon, e_1, \ldots, e_I\}, \; K' \leq \max_n K(n). \qquad (6.10)$$

Here, $K(n)$ is the length of the CN originating from the primary hypothesis E_n. The sequence $\bar{e}_1^{K'} := \bar{e}_1, \ldots, \bar{e}_k, \ldots, \bar{e}_{K'}$ represents a full path in one of the confusion networks. The expression $\bar{e}_1^{K'} \hat{=} e_1^I$ means that a sequence of real words and "empty" words (i.e. ε-arcs) $\bar{e}_1^{K'}$ would result in the sequence e_1^I containing only real words if the ε-arcs are removed from $\bar{e}_1^{K'}$. According to Equation 6.10, the probability of all paths $\bar{e}_1^{K'}$ in the union of the confusion networks is summed if each of these paths produces the same word sequence of non-empty words e_1^I. Thus, multiple identical word sequences are assigned a higher probability. Such identical sequences can occur because some of the individual system translations may be similar to each other in terms of word order. In such cases, the CNs resulting from these hypotheses (when they are considered as primary) are usually also similar. The sum over the identical hypotheses in the decision criterion can help to reach consensus not only on the word level, but on the level of sentence structure: the word order preferred by the weighted majority of the systems most probably will be used in the system combination translation.

After computing the sum over all lattice paths resulting in the same word sequence, we can extract not only the single best system combination hypothesis according to Equation 6.10, but also N-best hypotheses without duplicates. In a subsequent step, these N-best lists could be rescored with additional statistical models. However, the lattice representing a union of several confusion networks can also be directly scored with an n-gram language model, as described in Section 6.5.1.

6.5 Extensions

In this section some extensions to the basic algorithm are described. They either further improve the quality of the resulting consensus translations, or alleviate some of the constraints placed on the individual input translations, such as identical sentence segmentation across systems, which may be hard to achieve for translation of speech.

6.5.1 Using a language model

Experimental results show that the consensus translation computed by weighted majority voting often exhibits significantly better word choice than any of the individual system translations. However, a subjective analysis of the system combination output leads to the conclusion that the freedom to choose any word or the empty word at each position in the CN as well as the reordering of the secondary hypotheses often lead to insufficient fluency of the system combination translation. To improve the word order, we employ an n-gram LM. The lattice representing a union of several confusion networks can be scored directly using a language model. For LM scoring, a transformation of the lattice is required. The LM history has to be memorized, which means that the ε-arcs have to be removed. The resulting lattice is no longer a union of CNs, but a union of general lattices. This affects the probabilities $p_k(\bar{e}_k|F, E_n), k = 1, \ldots, k, \ldots, K'$ from Equation 6.10 for a single path $\bar{e}_1^{K'}$ in the CN corresponding to the primary hypothesis E_n. They are re-defined in terms of proper words only. For a single sentence hypothesis e_1^I which can be obtained from $\bar{e}_1^{K'}$ after ε-removal, we define the probability $p(e_1^I|F, E_n)$. It is computed from the probabilities $p_k(\bar{e}_k|F, E_n)$ by applying the ε-removal algorithm to the CN induced by the primary hypothesis E_n and already includes the sum over all paths which are labeled with e_1^I in this single CN. The language model probability can then be included in the decision criterion using log-linear interpolation. In

6 Combination of multiple machine translation systems

case of a trigram LM, the modified decision criterion is described with the following equation:

$$(\hat{I}, \hat{e}_1^{\hat{I}}) = \underset{I, e_1^I}{\operatorname{argmax}} \left\{ \alpha^I \sum_{n=1}^{N} p(e_1^I | F, E_n) \prod_{i=1}^{I} p^\lambda(e_i | e_{i-1}, e_{i-2}) \right\} \quad (6.11)$$

In Equation 6.11, the maximization is performed over all paths in the LM-scored system combination lattice, and the sum over n expresses again the sum over the identical paths e_1^I in each of the transformed confusion networks which are part of this lattice. The value λ is the LM scaling factor, and α is a word penalty. By modifying the value α the bias towards short sentences introduced by the LM scores can be avoided. The parameters λ and α can be optimized on a development set together with the system weights γ_m which are used to compute the probabilities $p(e_i | F, E_n)$ in Equation 6.9.

Whereas a general target LM can be successfully used for lattice scoring as shown by [Rosti & Matsoukas+ 07], in our experiments the translation fluency improves significantly by using an *adapted* LM learned on the outputs of the MT systems for the test corpus on which the system combination translation is to be determined. We attribute this in part to the fact that the systems we combine are all phrase-based systems. Using this special LM for lattice scoring gives bonus to n-grams from the original system hypotheses, in most cases from the original phrases. Presumably, many of these phrases have a correct word order, since they were extracted from the training data. Moreover, these phrases were selected as the best ones in translation, which means that a general LM has already given them high probability.

6.5.2 Handling of sentence segmentation differences

To apply the presented system combination algorithm to translations of speech, we have to keep in mind that the individual MT systems may translate different ASR output with different sentence segmentation (see Chapter 5). This poses an obstacle for MT system combination, since the hypotheses must be word-aligned at the sentence level. A straightforward solution of the problem is to take the sentence segmentation of the primary hypothesis as the "gold standard" segmentation, and re-segment the secondary hypotheses according to this segmentation. Here, we assume that the segmentation is given by a punctuation mark token (e. g. full stop or a question mark) in the primary hypothesis. Such segment boundaries could be inserted with e. g. the sentence segmentation algorithm presented in Chapter 5. The challenge of this approach is to consider all the secondary hypotheses simultaneously.

We developed a method for splitting multiple translation hypotheses for a whole speech document based on punctuation information and monotonic hypotheses alignment. We align the primary hypothesis with the other translations using the Levenshtein edit distance algorithm extended to multiple sequences. This approach is similar to the alignment used in [Bangalore & Bordel[+] 01]. First, we align two translations, then we align the third one to the alignment of the first two. If e. g. a word in the third hypothesis is identical to one of the two words representing a substitution in the first alignment, this is considered a "match" with no costs. The procedure is continued until all hypotheses are aligned. This alignment algorithm is efficient, but the solution is not globally optimal. However, in practice punctuation marks can be aligned rather well in most cases. We then transfer the punctuation marks from the primary hypothesis to the secondary ones based on the alignment and split all hypotheses at punctuation marks.

The approach can also be used to simultaneously split translations of long sentences (with more than 50-70 words each) into shorter subsentence units, provided that punctuation marks like commas are present in at least one of the translation hypotheses. Splitting of long sentences may be necessary because scoring "long" confusion networks for such sentences is computationally expensive due to the large number of paths which increases exponentially with sentence length.

6.5.3 TrueCasing

Some MT systems produce English words with their true case (e. g. starting names with a capital letter), while others only produce lowercase translations. Whereas it is of advantage to convert all words to lowercase in order to better estimate the word alignment, it is a good idea to preserve the case information when extracting the system combination translation from the confusion network or lattice. The advantage of this is that the decision on the case of a word can also be made using system combination. However, we have to make sure that if a certain word wins the weighted majority when the case information is ignored, the same word should have this majority when the case information is considered, i. e. if two versions of the same word produced by different MT systems are aligned to each other. To achieve this, we perform the summation in Equation 6.7 over the lowercase versions of each unique word e (i. e. we add together the weight γ_m of a lowercased and truecased version of e), but keep a separate arc in the lattice for each version of e, and assign this sum to it as its probability. In the subsequent lattice scoring, the language model will have the key role in deciding what version of the word is appropriate at this particular position. Promising results with this case-aware system combination approach in comparison with truecasing after system combination were reported in [Matusov & Leusch[+] 09].

6.6 Experimental results

The system combination approach presented in this chapter was evaluated on both small and large vocabulary text and speech translation tasks [Matusov & Ueffing[+] 06, Matusov & Leusch[+] 09]. Below, the results are reported for speech translation only on the Spanish-English TC-STAR large vocabulary task, the GALE large vocabulary task (translation of Chinese and Arabic broadcast news into English), as well as the BTEC small vocabulary speech translation task (translations from Chinese, Arabic, and Italian to English). We computed the error measures BLEU, TER, WER, PER as described in Chapter 3 using reference translations of manually and automatically transcribed speech.

The experiments can be roughly divided into the following parts. First, we analyze the influence of the individual system combination features on the quality of the consensus translation, as well as examine the potential of the presented approach. Then, we present the results of the experiments in which either structurally different or similar MT systems (or even variants of the same system) are combined. Further applications studied include multi-source system combination and combination of speech translation systems which process ASR word lattices with systems translating single best ASR output only.

6.6.1 TC-STAR Spanish↔English task

First, we describe the experimental results for the presented system combination algorithm on the TC-STAR EPPS task [TC-STAR 07]. We evaluate consensus translations of the TC-STAR partner systems for both Spanish-to-English and English-to-Spanish translation directions. The experiments were performed under two conditions:

- translating verbatim transcriptions which are the original manually created transcripts that reflect exactly what has been said by a parliament speaker;
- translating the output of an automatic speech recognition system (ASR) for the same speech for which the verbatim transcriptions had been produced.

We combined the output of six official systems from the 2007 TC-STAR evaluation. For the experiments, the official development and test data from that evaluation has been used (see Table A.8 in Appendix A). The evaluation was case-insensitive, with punctuation marks, and two manual reference translations were used.

Table 6.1 presents the evaluation results on the official TC-STAR 2007 test data for the English-to-Spanish translation direction. It contains the results for the individual systems A-F which participated in the 2007 evaluation, and their system combination using the algorithm

Table 6.1: TC-STAR 2007 evaluation results for the English-to-Spanish translation direction (including system combination).

Input	System	BLEU[%]	TER [%]	WER[%]	PER[%]
ASR	system A	41.1	45.1	47.0	35.7
(WER: 6.9%)	system B	40.8	44.1	45.4	35.7
	system C	39.8	45.1	46.5	36.3
	system D	38.8	47.2	49.1	37.0
	system F	38.1	45.1	46.0	37.1
	system E	38.0	45.1	48.3	37.4
	system combination	42.1	42.7	44.1	35.1
Verbatim	system B	52.4	34.9	36.7	27.9
	system C	52.4	35.1	37.2	28.0
	system A	51.8	36.0	37.9	28.8
	system F	51.7	34.7	36.4	28.2
	system E	49.9	37.0	39.2	29.8
	system D	49.3	37.6	39.8	30.0
	system combination	54.8	33.4	35.2	27.0

described in this chapter with all its features, in particular the union of confusion networks and the adapted LM. It can be observed that the system combination improves the BLEU score by 1% absolute for the ASR condition and more than 2% absolute for the Verbatim condition in comparison with the best individual system (system A and system B, respectively). These improvements are statistically significant at the 95% level. The other error measures also improved. For the ASR condition, the translations of individual systems differed in sentence segmentation, since it was performed automatically. To overcome these differences, they were first aligned at sentence level using the method described in Section 6.5.2. Since the sentence segmentation of the reference translation was different from the sentence segmentation of the hypotheses, the automatic re-segmentation of the MT output as described in Chapter 3 was applied before computing the evaluation measures.

The individual systems in Table 6.1 are ordered based on their BLEU score for the ASR condition. It is interesting to note that although all of these systems translate single best ASR output, they still differ in the ability to cope with recognition errors. Thus, the best system for the ASR condition scored only third on the verbatim condition. Nevertheless, the system combination approach is able to overcome some of the MT errors which were caused by ASR errors when the majority of the systems is able to overcome such errors (e.g. by omitting a

6 Combination of multiple machine translation systems

Table 6.2: The influence of individual system combination components on the quality of the consensus translation (TC-STAR 2007 test set, English-to-Spanish translation direction, verbatim condition). The best system combination result corresponding to the one in Table 6.1 is shown in bold.

	System	BLEU [%]	TER [%]	WER [%]	PER [%]
individual systems	worst single system	49.3	37.6	39.8	30.0
	best single system	52.4	34.9	36.7	27.9
consensus translation (single primary)	uniform weights	53.3	33.8	35.7	27.1
	+ system weight optimization	53.4	33.6	35.5	27.0
	+ adapted LM	53.9	33.8	35.6	27.3
consensus translation (union of CNs)	optimized weights	54.2	33.3	35.3	26.9
	+ adapted LM	**54.8**	**33.4**	**35.2**	**27.0**
	+ maximum (instead of sum)	54.8	33.5	35.3	27.1

translation of a wrongly recognized article or conjunction).

To assess the contribution of individual components of the presented system combination method, we performed several comparative experiments for the verbatim condition.

First, we created only one confusion network for each test sentence based on the HMM alignment described in Section 6.3 ("*single primary*" condition in Table 6.2). The translation hypothesis of the best performing system, as determined on the development set, was taken as the primary hypothesis. In the first experiment "*uniform weights*", we used a uniform distribution for the global system weights γ_m in Equation 6.7, i.e. the consensus word at a given position was selected by a simple majority voting. In case of a tie, when, for example, two alternative words were used by 3 systems each, the preference was given to the word used by the best performing system. Table 6.2 presents the result of this experiment. It is clear that this setup has already substantially improved all error measures, e.g. the BLEU score by 0.9% absolute and TER by 1.1% absolute.

In the second experiment, we optimized the six system weights on the development set automatically (see the "*system weight optimization*" condition in Table 6.2). The global system probabilities γ_m were optimized for BLEU using the CONDOR optimization tool [Berghen & Bersini 05]. For the optimization, the confusion networks can be kept fixed, since the parameters involved do not affect the alignment. In each step of the optimization algorithm, the confusion networks are scored using a set of system weights, and the consensus translation is extracted by finding the best path through the rescored lattice. Then, the

6.6 Experimental results

parameters are updated. The optimization algorithm converges after about 100-150 iterations.

The automatic optimization improved all error measures slightly. However, in contrast to the results on the development set, this improvement was not statistically significant. We attribute this to overfitting: in fact, the weight for two of the involved systems was automatically determined to be small. This can happen if the output of two systems is very similar on the majority of the sentences in the development set. If this similarity diminishes on another data set, the role of these systems in determining a consensus translation may be underestimated.

The next important improvement is due to the language model (see the line "adapted LM" in Table 6.2). We used a trigram language model trained on the six system translations for each of the 1 130 evaluation data sentences (see Table A.8 in Appendix), i.e. on 6780 sentences. As explained in Section 6.5.1, we expected a language model trained on the systems' translations to give preference to the n-grams from the original phrases produced by the involved MT systems. Indeed, we observed an absolute improvement of e.g. 0.5% in BLEU by scoring the single confusion network with this type of language model. However, the other measures degraded. For this experiments, the system combination parameters were again optimized for BLEU on the development set. These parameters were the system weights γ_m, the LM scaling factor λ and the word penalty α.

In the next condition "*union of confusion networks*", we combined the 6 confusion networks as described in Section 6.4. For these experiments, the weights were always optimized automatically on the development data. In the baseline experiment, we did not include the adapted LM. Nevertheless, we observed a significant improvement in BLEU from 53.4 to 54.2% in comparison to using a single confusion network. We attribute this improvement to the fact that the quality of the alignment and thus of the "voting" on the confusion network depends on the choice of the primary hypothesis. When all possible primary hypotheses are considered, the algorithm takes advantage of the "best" one on a sentence-by-sentence basis.

By scoring the union of confusion networks with the adapted LM we obtain a further gain in BLEU from 54.2 to 54.8% absolute, while the other error measures do not change significantly. Thus, using the adapted LM leads to better results when it is applied to the system combination lattice than to the confusion network based on a single primary hypothesis. This may indicate that the special language model has the power to discriminate between translations with good and bad word order which are present in the union of CNs. In contrast, the word order in a single CN is mostly dictated by the primary hypothesis, so that the adapted LM is not able to select better n-grams from the secondary hypotheses if they were broken in the alignment and reordering phase of the system combination algorithm.

Table 6.3: The influence of language model scores on the quality of the system combination translation (TC-STAR 2007 test set, English-to-Spanish translation direction, verbatim condition).

System	BLEU[%]	TER [%]	WER[%]	PER[%]
best single system	52.4	34.9	36.7	27.9
selection (with adapted LM)	53.6	34.5	36.5	27.8
baseline consensus translation	54.2	33.3	35.3	26.9
use general LM	53.7	34.1	36.2	27.4
use adapted LM	54.8	33.4	35.2	27.0

In the last line of Table 6.2, we show the result of a comparative experiment, in which the sum over all identical lattice paths in the decision criterion 6.11 is replaced by the maximum. Thus, we are interested in the best consensus translation according to system weights, LM and word penalty scores, but do not favor those paths which are present in multiple CNs derived from different primary hypotheses. The experiment shows a slight degradation of all error rates except BLEU. The small difference can be explained by the fact that on this task, the MT systems often produce sentences with similar word order. In such cases, the consensus with regard to the word order which can be achieved by computing the sum is not as important as the consensus with regard to the word choice.

Table 6.3 compares the effectiveness of the adapted LM (see Table 6.2) with the power of a regular 3-gram LM trained on the Spanish part of the bilingual training data. The condition "baseline consensus translation" corresponds to the condition "union of confusion networks, optimized weights" in Table 6.2. It can be observed that using a general LM did not improve the translation results, in contrast to using the adapted LM. The added general LM scores could not improve the word order of the consensus translations; this is especially reflected by the automatic metrics like BLEU and WER which are sensitive to fluency.

The second line of Table 6.3 presents the results of a comparative experiment, in which we select one of the individual system translations by rescoring. We created a word lattice with only 6 paths representing the original system translations and scored this lattice with system weights, the adapted LM and the word penalty. The model weights were optimized on the development set separately for this experiment. From the results in Table 6.3 we see that although this method improves the overall translation quality in comparison with the best single system, it is inferior to the approach in which a consensus translation is computed. This is an expected result, since the selection approach is not able to generate output different from the individual system translations.

Table 6.4: TC-STAR 2007 evaluation results for the Spanish-to-English translation direction.

Input	System	BLEU[%]	TER[%]	WER[%]	PER[%]
ASR	system A	44.8	40.6	43.9	30.5
(WER: 5.9%)	system B	44.7	40.3	43.3	30.0
	system C	44.5	40.5	43.9	30.2
	system D	43.8	40.3	43.1	30.5
	system E	43.4	41.9	44.8	31.9
	system F	43.1	42.4	45.3	31.9
	system combination	46.3	39.1	42.2	29.4
Verbatim	system C	54.4	32.7	35.5	25.1
	system D	54.1	32.8	35.3	25.4
	system B	53.5	33.2	35.9	25.0
	system F	53.1	33.8	36.3	25.7
	system A	52.8	34.2	37.2	26.1
	system E	52.2	34.6	37.2	26.7
	system combination	55.3	32.1	34.5	24.8

While it may be of value to analyze the contribution of each participating system to the final system combination translation, we should keep in mind that the system combination approach in many cases produces a new translation which is different from each of the original hypotheses. Our experiments show that the quality of this new translation is often significantly better than any of the original translations. Thus, on the English-to-Spanish verbatim evaluation data, for 582 out of 1167 sentences new translations were generated (for each of the remaining sentences, the consensus translation turned out to be identical to one of the systems' translations). Considering only these 582 sentences, the improvement due to the construction of a new consensus translation turned out to be from 49.1 to 50.7% in BLEU, whereas for the remaining 585 sentences, the improvement due to the mere selection of the "best" hypothesis was smaller: from 57.6 to 58.5%. Note that a genuine consensus translation is most often generated for sentences which are harder to translate.

Significant improvements in translation quality were also obtained for the inverse, Spanish-to-English translation direction (see Table 6.4). Here, the BLEU score improved by 1.5% absolute for the ASR condition and by 0.9% absolute for the verbatim condition. Again, some of the individual systems can translate ASR output better than others, and the presented system combination approach can partially take advantage of these system qualities.

On the Spanish-to-English 2007 TC-STAR evaluation data, verbatim condition, we tried to quantify the potential translation quality improvement that could be achieved with the

6 Combination of multiple machine translation systems

Table 6.5: The potential of the presented system combination approach (a subset of the official TC-STAR 2007 evaluation data, Spanish-to-English translation direction, verbatim condition).

System	BLEU[%]	TER[%]	WER[%]	PER[%]
worst single system	51.5	33.9	35.8	27.2
best single system	54.1	32.1	34.1	25.5
system combination	54.6	31.1	32.9	25.1
"human" system combination	58.0	29.7	31.5	24.2
"oracle" system combination	60.7	25.8	27.0	21.4

presented system combination approach. To this end, we selected a subset of 300 sentences from these data. We then let human experts with fluent knowledge of English put together the "consensus" translation. They had access neither to the source sentences nor to the reference translations, but were given only the 6 system translations for each sentence. Also, the experts were only allowed to use the words appearing in the original system translations. This means that the produced human system combination hypothesis can be viewed as an upper bound for the performance of the automatic system combination approach[c].

Table 6.5 shows the MT error measures for this experiment. Here, we include not only the "human system combination" as described above, but also the "oracle system combination" which is the path in the system combination CNs with the lowest WER. Naturally, the human system combination exhibits the best performance in comparison with the automatic system combination; however, the latter is able to explore more than one fourth of this potential. It is also interesting to note that the theoretically possible improvement with automatic system combination is even larger than the improvement obtained with the human system combination. We conclude from these results that the automatic system combination is an effective method, although refinements of the algorithm could have the potential to further improve the translation quality.

A larger set of experimental results on the TC-STAR task, including human evaluation, as well as the descriptions of the individual participating systems can be found in the joint TC-STAR journal publication on MT system combination in the project [Matusov & Leusch[+] 08].

Table 6.6 shows examples of how the translation quality can be improved with system combination. Here, the consensus translation is compared with the translation of the best individual system, as well as with a human reference translation.

---
[c]In practice, this upper bound cannot be even theoretically reached in every case because e.g. a human can delete a word present in every system translation.

Table 6.6: Examples of translation quality improvements resulting from system combination (TC-STAR Spanish-to-English verbatim evaluation condition).

single MT	it is the time to act and to make further forward the declarations of intent.
consensus MT	it is the time to act and leave for later the declarations of intent.
reference	it is time to act and to leave the declarations of intentions for the future.
single MT	history does not accept ... nor can expect us to other things happen.
consensus MT	history does not accept ... nor allows us to wait for other things happen.
reference	history does not accept ... nor allows us to wait for other things to take place.
single MT	we are seeing new forms of extremism wing of concern to all democrats.
consensus MT	we are seeing new forms of right-wing extremism concern to all democrats.
reference	we are observing new forms of right-wing extremism that worry all democrats.
single MT	therefore ask you are as more sophisticated possible in the use of the time.
consensus MT	please be as sophisticated possible in the use of the time.
reference MT	I therefore beg you to be as cautious as possible in the use of time.
single MT	are not two or three, ... they are transported , fifty-three companies.
consensus MT	they are not two or three, ... they are five hundred fifty three companies.
reference	they are not two or three, ... they are five hundred and fifty-three companies.
single MT	the commercial sky last month of July was clouded on Geneva.
consensus MT	the commercial sky is clouded on Geneva last July.
reference	the trade sky clouded over Geneva last month of July.
single MT	... necessary to alleviate and redress the unavoidable costs of the island.
consensus MT	... necessary to alleviate and correct the inevitable overspends of insularity.
reference	... necessary for alleviating and correcting the inevitable cost increments of insularity.

6.6.2 GALE Chinese-to-English and Arabic-to-English tasks

The presented system combination method was also successfully used in another important MT project, GALE [GALE 07]. Here, we present the results for Arabic-to-English on the 2007 MT evaluation data and for Chinese-to-English on the blind test data internally defined by the "Nightingale" (SRI) GALE team using documents from previous evaluations with 4 reference translations. The corpus statistics for these data and the development data can be found in Appendix in Tables A.10 and A.11, respectively.

For the Arabic-to-English translation direction, we combined 5 MT systems which were all

Table 6.7: System combination results for the Arabic-to-English translation of the broadcast news portion of the GALE 2007 evaluation data.

System	BLEU [%]	TER [%]
A	17.5	60.3
B	20.1	60.8
C	20.4	63.8
D	27.2	53.9
E	27.5	53.5
system combination	28.4	50.9

statistical MT systems. Whereas 3 out of 5 Arabic-to-English systems employed phrase-based search with a distance-based reordering model similar to the one described in Section 1.3, two of the systems were hierarchical phrase-based translation systems in the style of [Chiang 07].

For Chinese-to-English translation, 8 systems were combined:

- three purely phrase-based systems with differences in alignment training, Chinese word segmentation, and several extra features used in the log-linear model;
- a phrase-based MT system with reordering of source sentences based on syntactic chunks [Zhang & Zens[+] 07];
- a hierarchical phrase-based system in the style of [Chiang 07];
- a syntax-augmented hierarchical phrase-based translation system similar to the one described in [Zollmann & Venugopal 06];
- a hierarchical phrase-based system with a string-to-dependency LM in the style of [Shen & Xu[+] 08];
- a hybrid system combining a rule-based and a statistical translation system [Ueffing & Stephan[+] 08].

The experiments presented below were performed under evaluation conditions using the best available output of the individual MT systems. Here, we report the results on the broadcast news portion of the evaluation data. The broadcast news from different Chinese/Arabic television sources were first automatically recognized and then translated into English. The Chinese recognition character error rate on the test set was 6.2% for Chinese. For Arabic, the word error rate on the test set was 9.8%. The MT evaluation was case-sensitive and included punctuation marks. Only one reference translation was available for the Arabic-to-English task and four references were used for the Chinese-to-English task.

6.6 Experimental results

Table 6.8: System combination results for the Chinese-to-English translation of the broadcast news portion of the "Nightingale" blind test data. Comparison with the system combination approach of [Ayan & Zheng+ 08] (SRI).

System	BLEU [%]	TER [%]
A	26.6	63.9
B	27.1	66.9
C	29.1	64.2
D	29.5	62.3
E	29.6	63.6
F	30.0	63.4
G	30.1	63.1
H	30.1	62.7
system combination (RWTH)	32.5	59.1
system combination (SRI)		
general LM	31.4	60.0
adapted LM	31.9	59.0

Table 6.7 presents the results for the Arabic-to-English broadcast news translation. The table includes the results of the 5 individual systems, sorted by their BLEU score, and the result of the system combination using all of the features presented in this chapter (union of 5 CNs, 3-gram adapted LM, etc.). Whereas the BLEU score improves only by 0.9% absolute, the improvement in TER is much larger – from 53.5 to 50.9%. Most of the individual systems used the BLEU score as the optimization criterion to tune their parameters. Yet for system combination a better strategy was to use the combination of both measures $TER + (1.0 - BLEU)$ as the objective function. The system weights, the language model scaling factor, and the word penalty were optimized automatically on the development set with the goal of reducing this value. Using the combination of BLEU and TER was more stable in terms of generalization from the development to the evaluation data. In addition, the resulting hypotheses had a more reasonable average sentence length than when a single evaluation measure was used. The TER improvements in Table 6.7 are significant at the 95% level.

Table 6.8 shows the results for the combination of 8 systems for the Chinese-to-English translation direction. Here, we also compare the system combination approach presented in this thesis (RWTH) with the approach of [Ayan & Zheng+ 08] (SRI). As already mentioned, the alignment for the construction of CNs used in the approach of SRI is a two-pass strategy based on TER alignments extended with matching of synonyms. In the first pass, the primary hypothesis is determined as the best path in the initial system combination CN; in the second path, the individual system hypotheses are aligned to this primary hypothesis.

The results in Table 6.8 indicate that the absolute improvement in BLEU and TER due to RWTH system combination is highly significant and larger than on the Arabic-to-English task (e.g. 3.1% absolute in TER in comparison with the TER-best individual system E). We explain this by the fact that the individual Chinese-to-English systems have similar (good) BLEU and TER scores, whereas for Arabic-to-English, 2 systems clearly outperform the other three. Also, the translations of the Chinese-to-English systems have more differences to each other than their Arabic-to-English counterparts, since there are large structural differences in the models and algorithms implemented in these systems. This is important for system combination, since the concept of a consensus translation implies that different systems should make different errors.

The SRI system combination approach was tested on exactly the same data. It also resulted in significant improvements over the best single system. In its initial version, a general 4-gram LM was used to score the system combination confusion networks. However, after testing the adapted LM as suggested by the author of this thesis, SRI was able to improve their system (e.g. by reducing TER from 60.0 to 59.0%, see the last line of Table 6.8). This made the results of the RWTH and SRI system combination methods comparable in terms of TER, but the RWTH approach has a better BLEU score (32.5 vs. 31.9%) than the SRI approach.

Further experiments in which we combined the large vocabulary GALE systems on text data (newswire articles) were reported in [Matusov & Leusch[+] 09]. In particular, there it was shown experimentally that the proposed HMM alignment approach performs at least as well or better than the TER-based approach.

6.6.3 BTEC speech translation tasks

Additional system combination experiments were performed on the IWSLT 2008 Chinese-to-English and Arabic-to-English tasks [Paul 08]. The data for these tasks come from the Basic Travel Expression corpus (BTEC). It consists of tourism-related spoken utterances and their correct and automatic transcripts. In contrast to the experiments above, where systems from different research institutions had been combined, here we computed consensus translations from the outputs of RWTH-internal MT systems and even variants of the same system. Each system had used 20K sentence pairs (180K running words) from the BTEC corpus for training. As the development set for system combination, we used the IWSLT 2005 evaluation set. The official IWSLT 2008 evaluation set was used for testing. The system parameters were tuned on the development set to increase the BLEU score. The corpus statistics for these data are given in Appendix in Table A.4 for the Chinese-to-English task and in Table A.5 for the Arabic-to-English task. The evaluation was case-sensitive, using punctuation marks, and 7 reference translations were used. The following subsections describe the experimental findings in detail.

6.6.3.1 Chinese-to-English translation

For computing the consensus translations from Chinese to English, we combined the following statistical MT systems developed at Lehrstuhl für Informatik 6:

1. a "standard" phrase-based system with jump-based reordering [Mauser & Zens[+] 06].

2. an extension of system 1. that performs chunk-based reordering of the Chinese source sentences prior to translation [Zhang & Zens[+] 07].

3. a variant of system 1. that uses a different word segmentation of Chinese [Xu & Gao[+] 08] and additional language model data.

4. hierarchical phrase-based system in the style of [Chiang 07].

5. an extension of system 4. with a syntax-based feature that fires if a source or target phrase from the phrase table is a parse tree constituent [Vilar & Stein[+] 08].

Whereas better translation quality is expected when system combination is performed using systems developed independently and/or under different paradigms (e.g. rule-based vs. statistical translation), the experiments show that a significant improvement can also be obtained when variants of the same system(s) are combined. Table 6.9 shows the results of the individual systems mentioned above and the error rates of the consensus translation on the official 2008 IWSLT evaluation corpus (correct transcripts of read speech). These were all the official evaluation submissions. The system combination algorithm used all features described in this chapter (union of confusion networks, adapted LM); the system weights, the language model weight, and the word penalty were automatically optimized using the 2005 IWSLT test set as the development corpus.

In Table 6.9 it can be observed that the system combination significantly improves all automatic error measures in comparison with system 3 that scored best in terms of BLEU score. In particular, the BLEU score was improved by 1.7% absolute. The consensus translation also has better error measures than all other systems, except for TER which is lower for system 1 that produces, on average, shorter translations than other systems.

6 Combination of multiple machine translation systems

Table 6.9: System combination of 5 RWTH-internal systems on the BTEC Chinese-to-English task (correct transcripts of read speech), official IWSLT 2008 evaluation results.

System	BLEU [%]	TER [%]	WER [%]	PER [%]
system 1	42.5	36.6	45.3	40.6
system 2	42.6	39.9	47.8	42.4
system 3	44.3	40.3	47.3	42.0
system 4	41.2	41.5	48.1	42.7
system 5	41.4	40.6	47.3	42.8
system combination	46.1	37.7	43.9	39.4
+ N-best rescoring	48.1	35.7	42.7	38.6

In addition to extracting the best path from the confusion networks as described in Section 6.4, we conducted another experiment in which N-best translations were extracted from the system combination lattice for each test sentence. Clearly, for sentences whose translations were identical across all systems, there was only 1 hypothesis, whereas for sentences where individual systems strongly disagreed, the number of alternative system combination variants exceeded thousands. Setting the maximum number of hypotheses N to be 10000, the average number of hypotheses per sentence turned out to be 1560. These N-best lists were subsequently rescored with a number of statistical models, including cross-lingual triggers, sentence-level IBM model 1, deletion model, and other features. The scaling factors for these additional models were optimized together with the total system combination score on the development data using the Downhill Simplex algorithm. The details of the rescoring procedure are described in [Hasan & Ganitkevitch[+] 08]. From Table 6.9 we can infer that the system combination translation as extracted from the rescored N-best lists further improves all four translation error measures in comparison with the single best consensus translation. The total improvement in comparison with the BLEU-best system 3 is very large: 3.7% absolute in BLEU and 4.6% absolute in TER.

The reason for such large improvements due to N-best rescoring is that the N-best lists contain many hypotheses which are significantly different from each other. Among these hypotheses, there are many translations which are even better than the ones currently selected based on system weights, language model scores, or additional statistical models in rescoring. To investigate the potential of the presented system combination approach, for each sentence in the development corpus we selected the hypothesis from the N-best list with the lowest word error rate with respect to the multiple reference translations of the sentence ("*oracle consensus*"). We then evaluated the quality of these "oracle" translations for the whole

Table 6.10: Potential of the described system combination approach. BTEC Chinese-to-English task, IWSLT 2005 development corpus.

System	BLEU [%]	TER [%]	WER [%]	PER [%]
system 1	49.9	40.5	41.5	35.8
system 2	52.6	37.3	38.2	33.7
system 3	56.3	35.9	36.7	31.6
system 4	51.3	38.2	39.1	34.1
system 5	51.3	39.1	39.7	35.6
system combination	58.2	33.8	34.4	30.7
oracle selection	64.0	28.2	28.4	25.8
oracle consensus	66.1	26.0	26.0	24.7

development corpus. In a contrastive experiment, for each sentence the translation with the lowest WER was selected from the original 5 MT system outputs ("*oracle selection*").

Table 6.10 shows the oracle experiments on the IWSLT 2005 development corpus. The potential for improvement is significantly larger for the consensus-based combination of translation outputs than for simple selection of the best translation. The current system combination of the first-best MT outputs improves BLEU by 1.9% absolute and TER by 2.1% absolute as compared to the best single system 3. Yet the maximum improvement that could theoretically be achieved is from 56.3% to 66.1% in BLEU and from 36.7% to 26.0% in TER. Unfortunately, current statistical models that are used to score the system combination hypotheses are too weak to exploit even half of this improvement. Further research on enhanced methods for scoring system combination CNs and N-best lists therefore appears promising.

In [Matusov & Ueffing[+] 06], further "oracle" results were given for multi-source system combination using outputs of systems from different research groups. There, only 1000-best lists were used, but the results are astonishing: the BLEU score could theoretically improve by more than 43% relative. The results in Table 6.10 show that the potential for improvement is high even when, among others, variants of the same system participate in system combination.

The IWSLT 2008 evaluation showed that the presented approach works well not only on the correctly transcribed read speech data, but also on ASR output for the "challenge" condition: automatic transcripts of short tourism-related conversations recorded on the street with passers-by using a PDA. On this task, all of the systems from the list above were combined, with the exception of system 3, the training of which had not been finished on time. In Table 6.11 the results of this experiment are shown. The best individual system in

6 Combination of multiple machine translation systems

Table 6.11: System combination of 4 RWTH-internal systems on the BTEC Chinese-to-English task (ASR of spontaneous speech), official IWSLT 2008 evaluation results.

System	BLEU [%]	TER [%]	WER [%]	PER [%]
system 1	27.8	46.0	55.4	51.1
system 2	29.4	45.7	55.0	50.5
system 4	26.4	51.0	59.2	51.9
system 5	30.2	45.6	53.7	48.6
system combination	34.3	43.6	51.1	46.1

terms of BLEU and TER is system 5. The consensus translation improves all error measures significantly, e.g. the BLEU score by more than 4% absolute.

6.6.3.2 Arabic-to-English translation

For Arabic-to-English, the participants of the IWSLT 2008 evaluation had to translate correct transcripts and ASR output for read speech. Four statistical MT systems were employed at Lehrstuhl für Informatik 6, the output of which was then combined using the presented method. These systems were:

1. a "standard" phrase-based system with jump-based reordering [Mauser & Zens[+] 06] that used the MADA preprocessing and tokenization schemes for Arabic [Habash & Rambow 05].

2. a variant of system 1. that used a maximum-entropy based morphological tagger (MorphTagger, see [Mansour & Sima'an[+] 07]) to identify Arabic prefixes and suffixes and separate them from the stems in order to reduce the Arabic vocabulary size and, as the result, improve the translation performance.

3. a hierarchical phrase-based system in the style of [Chiang 07], using the MADA preprocessing.

4. the same hierarchical phrase-based system as in 3. trained using Arabic data preprocessed with MorphTagger.

The system weights, the scaling factor for the adapted LM and the word penalty were optimized on the development set. The final results obtained on the official IWSLT 2008 evaluation corpus are listed in Table 6.12. The best single system for both types of input (correct and automatic transcriptions) is system 2. The system combination improves the result on the correctly transcribed Arabic speech from 51.8 to 53.5% in BLEU and from 33.8 to 33.0% in TER. The improvements in BLEU are statistically significant. For the

Table 6.12: System combination of 4 RWTH-internal systems on the BTEC Arabic-to-English task (correct transcripts and ASR of read speech), official IWSLT 2008 evaluation results.

Input	System	BLEU[%]	TER[%]	WER[%]	PER[%]
correct text	system 1	50.0	33.7	39.7	36.0
	system 2	51.8	33.8	38.1	33.9
	system 3	49.2	36.6	41.3	36.7
	system 4	49.3	35.9	41.3	38.0
	system combination	53.5	33.0	37.6	33.9
ASR output	system 1	42.6	38.2	45.3	41.7
	system 2	44.0	38.0	43.4	39.4
	system 3	41.3	42.1	47.7	42.7
	system 4	41.3	40.7	47.2	43.9
	system combination	44.5	37.6	43.4	39.9

ASR condition, the improvement due to system combination is smaller: e. g. the BLEU score improves by 0.5% absolute. All of the improvements are smaller than for the Chinese-to-English translation using the same data (see Table 6.9). We attribute this to the fact that the differences between the individual Arabic-to-English MT systems were rather small. These differences were mostly related to the definition of the source language vocabulary and not to other more complex structures such as syntactic constraints, etc., as it was the case for the Chinese-to-English task.

These and the other experiments described above lead to the conclusion that significant improvements in translation quality due to consensus-based system combination can be achieved if the participating systems are substantially different, i. e. make different errors. At the same time, the majority of participating systems should have a similar level of performance as measured by (automatic) evaluation measures. If this is not the case, i. e. if only one system performs well, and two or three others are inferior to it, the words from the weaker systems will "outweigh" the words from the good quality system. Similar findings were made by [Macherey & Och 07] who performed experiments on selecting a subset of MT systems from a larger set for producing a consensus translation with the best possible quality.

When variants of the same or similar systems are combined, the condition that they should have similar performance in terms of an error measure can be satisfied more easily. For instance, the difference in BLEU scores of the individual Arabic-to-English MT systems in Table 6.12 does not exceed 3% absolute. However, the condition that the MT outputs should be significantly different is only partially satisfied. In contrast, when systems developed using

Table 6.13: Multi-source translation: improvements in translation quality when combining the output of 4 Chinese-to-English and 4 Arabic-to-English systems (correct transcripts of read speech, official IWSLT 2008 evaluation results).

System	BLEU [%]	TER [%]	WER [%]	PER [%]
best Chinese-to-English system	44.3	40.3	47.3	42.0
best Arabic-to-English system	51.8	33.8	38.1	33.9
system combination	56.2	31.7	36.0	32.6

different paradigms, algorithms, or data are combined, then they often do make different errors. However, in many cases some of these systems are usually significantly worse than the others at least in terms of automatic error measures, which makes a practical application of system combination a challenging task.

6.6.3.3 Multi-source translation

The content of the development and evaluation data for the 2008 IWSLT evaluation (read speech) was the same for Arabic and Chinese, i.e. they shared the same human reference translations. Therefore, it was interesting to perform an experiment on system combination of both Arabic-to-English and Chinese-to-English systems. Multi-source statistical machine translation was first performed by [Och & Ney 01], but the benefits of having source data in multiple languages for the same target language data were used in the process of training an MT system.

In the multi-source system combination experiment reported here, we combined a total of 8 systems – the four Chinese-to-English systems described in Section 6.6.3.1 (excluding system 3), and the four Arabic-to-English systems described in Section 6.6.3.2. The results of this experiment are given in Table 6.13. The improvement due to system combination as compared to the best individual system (the Arabic-to-English system 2) is quite significant, e.g. from 51.8 to 56.2% in BLEU. This result is by 2.7% absolute better than just the combination of the generally better-scoring Arabic-to-English systems. The large improvement is most probably explained by the structural differences between Chinese and Arabic. These differences make some sentences or sentence parts easier to translate for an Arabic-to-English system than for a Chinese-to-English system, and vice versa. Ideally, system combination should always select such easier and therefore more correct translations. In practice, this happens in many cases.

A similar experiment with equally convincing results using the participating systems of the IWSLT 2004 evaluation and Chinese and Japanese as the source languages was published in [Matusov & Ueffing[+] 06].

Table 6.14: The results of the system combination evaluation at the Workshop on Statistical Machine Translation 2009. The evaluation was performed by English-speaking humans who first edited individual automatically translated sentences. They had no access to either the source sentence or a reference translation. The goal was to produce well-formed sentences which express the same meaning as could be inferred from the original MT output. Then, the edited segments from different systems were compared to each other.

% of sentences where edited system output was judged to be acceptable:		
RWTH	[Rosti & Zhang+ 09]	[Hildebrand & Vogel 08]
32	27	25
% of sentences where edited RWTH system output was judged better/worse than:		
[Rosti & Zhang+ 09]		[Hildebrand & Vogel 08]
41/36		46/39

The system combination method described in this thesis was also used in the latest evaluation of the Workshop on Statistical Machine Translation (WMT 2009, see [Callison-Burch & Koehn+ 09]). In particular, the system was tested in a multi-source translation scenario, combining a total of 10 systems on a newswire data translation task: 3 Spanish-to-English, 3 German-to-English, and 4 French-to-English systems [Leusch & Matusov+ 09]. The RWTH approach obtained significant improvements over the best of those 10 systems (about 7% relative in BLEU and TER). Based on the results of a human evaluation, it also outperformed the other two system combination approaches participating in the evaluation: the sentence selection approach of [Hildebrand & Vogel 08] and the CN-based approach of [Rosti & Zhang+ 09]. The results of the human evaluation are summarized in Table 6.14.

6.6.4 Word lattice translation in context of MT system combination

Some state-of-the-art speech translation systems, including the ones described in Chapter 4, can translate either the single best recognition hypotheses or the word lattices of an ASR system. In Chapter 4 it was shown that word lattice input generally improves translation quality. In practice, however, the translation system may choose, for some sentences, the paths in the lattice with many recognition errors and thus produce inferior translations. These translations can be improved if we compute a consensus translation from the output of at least two different speech translation systems. From each system, we take the translation of the single best ASR output, and the translation of the ASR word lattice.

Table 6.15: Improvements in translation quality on the BTEC Italian-to-English task due to computing a consensus translation from the output of two MT systems which translate either single best ASR output or ASR word lattices.

System	Input	BLEU [%]	TER [%]	WER [%]	PER[%]
FSA	a) single best	53.9	32.8	36.9	28.6
	b) lattice	55.9	30.7	34.6	26.7
PBT	c) single best	54.7	31.6	36.6	27.5
	d) lattice	58.2	29.5	34.2	26.1
consensus a-d		58.9	28.5	32.9	25.0

The experiments to support this idea were performed on the BTEC Italian-to-English task using the same data as described in Chapter 4. The involved MT systems used about 60K sentence pairs (420K running words) for training (see Table A.2 in Appendix for the corpus statistics). The test corpus was the whole CSTAR'03 corpus of 506 tourism-related sentences[d]. The first-best recognition word error rate on this corpus was 22.3%.

In chapter 4, two different statistical MT systems capable of translating ASR word lattices have been compared, one implementing the joint probability model using WFSTs (FSA), and the other one using beam search and a log-linear model that combines phrase-based and word-based MT models, as well as the ASR features: the acoustic probability of a source word and its source LM probability (PBT). Both systems produced translations of better quality on the BTEC Italian-to-English speech translation task when using lattices instead of single best ASR output. To compute the consensus translation with the method described in this chapter, a total of 4 MT outputs was used: the single best Italian ASR output translated by the FSA and PBT systems and the word lattice ASR output translated by the same two systems. The system weights for this experiment were set manually, the better performing word lattice translations were assigned higher weights.

The objective error measures for the 4 translation hypotheses and the consensus translation are given in Table 6.15. The evaluation was performed without considering word case and punctuation marks, using 16 reference translations. With the consensus hypothesis, the TER was reduced from 29.5 to 28.5%; the other measures have also improved. Thus, the negative effect of recognition errors on the translation quality could be reduced beyond the reduction that can be obtained by using ASR word lattices.

---

[d]Only half of this corpus was used in the experiments in Chapter 4, the other half was set aside as the development set (cf. the development/test data statistics in Table 4.1).

Table 6.16: Examples of the errors made by a speech translation system which can be corrected after system combination.

single MT of the single best ASR	For short is recommend a good a general practice physician.
single MT of a lattice	For short is recommend as of that kind
consensus MT	For short recommend a good is a general practice physician.
reference	Please recommend a good general practitioner.
single MT of the single best ASR	How immigration?
single MT of a lattice	What's the sign?
consensus MT	Where's immigration?
reference	Which way is immigration?
single MT of the single best ASR	This is very nice.
single MT of a lattice	This is very delicious.
consensus MT	This is very beautiful.
reference	This is very beautiful.

Examples of the errors made by a lattice-based system that were corrected after system combination are shown in Table 6.16. In these cases, the best system that translates ASR word lattices erroneously follows a lattice path that contains more recognition errors than the single best ASR output. However, the other three systems avoid this erroneous path. Thus, the consensus translation also avoids these errors.

6.7 Conclusions

In this chapter, an algorithm for combining the outputs of multiple translation systems on the word level was presented. The method utilizes an enhanced statistical word alignment algorithm. The decision on how to align two translations of a sentence takes the context of a whole corpus of automatic translations into account. This high quality non-monotonic alignment is used for finding corresponding words and subsequent word reordering when confusion networks with translation alternatives are created. A consensus translation is extracted from these confusion networks using various probabilistic features which estimate the weight of each candidate word. This translation often has a significantly better quality than the original translations and may be different from any of them.

Experiments have shown that large and significant improvements can be obtained with the presented system combination method on a variety of translation tasks, including tasks with large vocabulary and spoken source language as input. The experimental findings lead to the following main conclusions:

- Word-level system combination in which a consensus translation is computed based on the word-level alignment of system hypotheses outperforms sentence-level system combination (selection) approaches.
- The HMM alignment for word-level system combination is a better choice than the alignment based on translation edit rate, because good-quality alignment links between synonyms and non-monotonic alignments can be obtained based on alignment and lexicon probabilities which were statistically learned on a whole corpus of translation outputs instead of a single sentence.
- To select the best path in the system combination lattice, it is important to use language model scores and possibly other features. An adapted n-gram LM trained on the system outputs gives a bonus to phrases appearing in the original system hypotheses and is therefore a good choice for lattice scoring. Nevertheless, the proposed statistical models do not yet explore the full potential of the hypotheses contained in the CNs, as the "oracle" experiments have shown.
- The largest improvements in translation quality as compared with the best-performing individual system can be obtained if the systems being combined are structurally different and often make different errors. At the same time, their performance in terms of automatic error measures should be of similar level.
- The presented system combination approach can be used effectively in the context of speech translation, and in particular in combination with the lattice-based translation of ASR output.

7 Scientific contributions

The aim of this thesis was to study and improve ways of combining NLP systems to produce high-quality translations of speech. In particular, the goal was to find effective solutions for coupling ASR and MT systems and explore how the ASR output can be automatically annotated to meet the MT requirements. Another important goal was to improve translation quality by combining multiple MT systems.

- For a tighter coupling of speech recognition and MT, algorithms for translation of multiple ASR hypotheses in the form of word lattices have been implemented. The decision on the ASR hypothesis that results in the best translation of the spoken utterance has been deferred to the MT search and is based on combination of ASR and MT model scores. In many cases, this can help to avoid passing recognition errors to the MT output. Two different translation models – a joint probability tuple-based model and a log-linear phrase-based model – have been proposed for lattice translation. They were compared theoretically and experimentally, and even combined. In addition, a consistent approach for training the joint probability model using word alignment cost matrices has been introduced and successfully used in practice.

- Experiments on several small and large vocabulary tasks have shown that significant improvements in translation quality can be obtained when the ambiguity of ASR is considered in MT search. The conditions under which these improvements are to be expected have been identified in the numerous experiments. Furthermore, a novel method was proposed that allows to pass the lattice-based improvements in translation quality to the MT systems which are not capable of translating lattices.

- For the phrase-based translation of word lattices, an algorithm has been introduced that utilizes confusion network slot information, yet translates the original ASR lattices using acoustic and source LM scores in the log-linear translation model. This algorithm makes it possible to efficiently perform both short-range and long-range phrase reordering given the lattice input. It was shown experimentally that such reordering can significantly improve lattice translation quality. The experiments have also shown the competitiveness of the proposed lattice translation algorithm as compared to the state-of-the-art translation of confusion networks and proved its advantages in terms of translation speed.

- To prepare the raw ASR output for translation, a novel sentence segmentation algorithm has been proposed and implemented. This algorithm exhibits state-of-the-art segmentation quality and at the same time is able to meet the requirements of an MT system concerning the minimum and maximum sentence lengths. The algorithm utilizes both language model and pause duration information, and also includes an explicit sentence length model. Furthermore, this algorithm was extended by a feature that penalizes sentence boundary candidates which split a frequent source phrase with a probable translation. To the best of our knowledge, this was the first time when a sentence segmentation algorithm was adapted to the subsequent MT processing and evaluated in terms of MT quality.

- In conjunction with the work on sentence segmentation, three different strategies for automatic prediction of punctuation marks have been investigated. It was shown that a MT system can be effectively used for producing punctuation marks in the target language. This approach is especially useful for lattice-based translation since it does not require any modifications of the original ASR lattices.

- A new algorithm has been proposed and implemented that enables automatic evaluation of speech translation hypotheses with sentence segmentation that differs from the manual reference segmentation. The algorithm re-segments the MT output based on the edit distance alignment with the reference, but takes multiple reference translations into account. The algorithm was used by the organizers of large-scale MT evaluation campaigns in the TC-STAR and GALE projects.

- With the goal of improving the ultimate speech translation quality, a method for combining the outputs of several MT systems has been proposed. The method computes a consensus translation on the word level and includes a novel statistical approach for aligning and reordering the translation hypotheses so that a confusion network for weighted majority voting can be created. In contrast to existing approaches, the context of a whole document of translations is taken into account to learn the alignments for a single sentence. In addition, a special language model was introduced for rescoring the system combination confusion networks. This LM is trained on the system hypotheses and assigns better scores to the phrases used by the individual MT systems. To the best of our knowledge, the proposed system combination approach was the first approach of this kind that obtained highly significant improvements in translation quality over the best single system on a multitude of text and speech translation tasks. Many of these improvements were obtained in official and highly competitive evaluations such as IWSLT, TC-STAR and GALE.

8 Future directions

The speech translation pipeline studied in this thesis provides several possible research directions which can be further investigated.

Translating multiple recognition hypotheses in the form of word lattices is not the only way of a tighter coupling between speech recognition and machine translation. Since currently the MT systems exhibit a worse quality of the output than most ASR systems, it is important to adapt them to speech data. This can be achieved by adding more spontaneous speech data (including high-confidence ASR output) to the MT training data. In addition, the phrase matching algorithms could be modified to allow for partial matches of phrases so that a spoken source phrase with a good translation could be matched even its transcription is not completely correct. Such "fuzzy" matching could be limited to only those words which are frequently misrecognized by a particular ASR system.

In this thesis, a phrase-based lattice translation algorithm that uses confusion network slots has been presented. The definition of slots allows for a more or less straightforward implementation of the lattice-based search using hierarchical phrase-based and even syntax-based MT models. Recently, syntax-based MT systems have shown a superior performance with respect to standard phrase-based systems on text data. However, this advantage diminishes on speech data and, in particular, on ASR output. The reason for this is the presence of recognition errors, as well as the often colloquial speaking style, the presence of hesitations, broken words, incomplete sentences, and other disfluencies. All of these phenomena make it hard to parse the spoken utterances. In turn, the mediocre parsing has a strong negative impact on the performance of syntax-based MT systems. One of the future research directions could be the detection and removal or correction of disfluencies, as well as adaptation of parsing techniques to speech data. In addition, some syntax constraints could be placed on the ASR output by using e.g. an additional syntax-based language model to rescore the ASR lattices.

The lattice translation algorithms proposed in this thesis make it possible to process not only multiple ASR output, but also any type of ambiguous input to MT, such as alternative preprocessing, morphological decomposition, etc. A challenge is to combine this type of

8 Future directions

ambiguity with the ambiguity of ASR hypotheses. In particular, it would be important to develop ways of detecting special entities in ASR word lattices (such as named entities, numbers, word sequences with predefined standard translations, etc.) and transferring the dedicated translations of these entities into the MT hypotheses.

The sentence segmentation algorithm presented in this thesis could be further improved with additional features which take the MT context at a hypothesized sentence boundary into account. The presented phrase coverage feature is a first step in this direction. The automatic punctuation prediction could be extended beyond commas (e.g. to quotation marks). Its quality could probably be significantly improved by including source-side prosodic features in the target-side punctuation prediction using the MT system. It would be also of advantage if a punctuation-mark-aware syntax-based component could be used to assess the sentence structure of the target language translation hypothesis. In addition, better ways of evaluating the quality of punctuation mark prediction in the target language are necessary in order to enable a better placement of punctuation marks without a degradation of the MT quality of the actual words and phrases.

The future work on MT system combination may include improving the word confidence estimation and scoring of the confusion networks. It would be also interesting to consider phrases and other syntactic and semantic structures and constraints explicitly in the alignment and rescoring steps of the presented algorithm. On one side, it is important to preserve the structures which the individual systems may provide. Examples of such structures are marked translations of named entities or chunks which have a high translation confidence. It would be of advantage to transfer this information to the consensus translation even if only one system output provides it. On the other hand, it would probably be useful to rescore the system combination lattices with dependency-based and other syntactically motivated language models. These models could help to better explore the rather high potential of the system combination approach proposed in this thesis.

A Corpora

This appendix contains corpus statistics for the bilingual parallel training corpora, as well as the development and test data used to train and evaluate the MT systems employed for the experiments in this thesis. The individual translation tasks for which the corpus statistics are listed below are described in the chapters where the experiments on these tasks have been reported.

A.1 LC-STAR Spanish-to-English and Spanish-to-Catalan tasks

Table A.1: Training corpus statistics of the LC-STAR Spanish-to-English and Spanish-to-Catalan speech translation tasks (MT systems for word lattice translation experiments described in Chapter 4).

		\multicolumn{4}{c}{LC-STAR}		
		Spanish	English	Spanish	Catalan
Train	Sentences	\multicolumn{2}{c	}{39 018}	\multicolumn{2}{c}{41 885}
	Running words	427 014	456 198	534 215	544 731
	Vocabulary	10 821	9 303	11 834	12 163

A.2 BTEC speech translation tasks

Table A.2: Corpus statistics of the MT training data for the Italian-to-English and Chinese-to-English BTEC tasks (MT systems for word lattice translation experiments described in Chapter 4).

	Italian	English
Sentences	66 107	
Running words	410 275	427 402
Vocabulary	15 983	10 971

	Chinese	English
Sentences	40 000	
Running characters	415 972	377 341
Vocabulary	3 557	9 569

A.2 BTEC speech translation tasks

Table A.3: Corpus statistics of the IWSLT 2006 training data and development, test and evaluation corpora after preprocessing (MT system for sentence segmentation and punctuation prediction experiments described in Chapter 5).

		Chinese	English
Train	Sentences	40 000	
	Running words	295 579	377 355
	Vocabulary	11 170	9 570
Dev 2005	Sentences	506	
	Running words	3 208	3 767
	Vocabulary	928	843
	OOVs (running words)	67 (2.1%)	179 (4.7%)
Dev 2006	Sentences	489	
	Running words	5 214	6 362
	Vocabulary	1 137	1 012
	OOVs (running words)	126 (2.4%)	296 (4.7%)
Test 2006	Sentences	500	
	Running words	5 550	7 353
	Vocabulary	1 328	1 223
	OOVs (running words)	172 (3.1%)	204 (2.8%)

A Corpora

Table A.4: Corpus statistics of the IWSLT 2008 development and evaluation data for the Chinese-to-English task (as used for the system combination experiments in Chapter 6).

		Chinese	English
Dev 2005	Sentences	506	
	Running words	3 208	3 767
	OOVs (running words)	2.1%	–
Test 2008	Sentences	507	
read	Running words	2 585	3 440
speech	OOVs (running words)	3.9%	–
	single best ASR WER	16.4%	–
Test 2008	Sentences	504	
spontaneous	Running words	2 513	3 107
speech	OOVs (running words)	2.9%	–
	single best ASR WER	14.2%	–

Table A.5: Corpus statistics of the IWSLT 2008 development and evaluation data for the Arabic-to-English task (as used for the system combination experiments in Chapter 6).

		Chinese	English
Dev 2005	Sentences	506	
	Running words	3 208	3 767
	OOVs (running words)	6.2%	–
Test 2008	Sentences	507	
read	Running words	2 585	3 440
speech	OOVs (running words)	9.9%	–
	single best ASR WER	27.2%	–

A.3 TC-STAR Spanish-English speech translation tasks

Table A.6: Corpus statistics of the TC-STAR English-to-Spanish MT training data (MT system used for the sentence segmentation and punctuation prediction experiments described in Chapter 5).

		English	Spanish
Train:	Sentences	1 176 274	
	Running words	33 677 837	34 991 944
	Running words without punct. marks	30 611 047	31 764 903
	Vocabulary	75 171	130 014
Dev:	Sentences	1 194	
	Running words	30 439	31 889
	Running words without punct. marks	28 083	29 071
	OOVs (running words)	147	237
Test:	Sentences	1 155	
	Running words	30 695	30 669
	Running words without punct. marks	27 894	27 957
	OOVs (running words)	80	151

Table A.7: Corpus statistics of the TC-STAR Spanish-to-English MT training data (MT system used in word lattice translation experiments described in Chapter 4).

		Spanish	English
Train:	Sentences	1 276 215	
	Running words (no punctuation marks)	33 924 077	32 763 312
	Vocabulary	126 295	70 769

A Corpora

Table A.8: Corpus statistics of the TC-STAR Spanish-to-English development and test corpora used for the system combination experiments in Chapter 6.

		EPPS English → Spanish		EPPS Spanish → English		CORTES Spanish → English	
Dev:	Sentences	1 122		699		753	
	Running words	28 390	30 503	24 275	25 240	27 707	29 617
	Vocabulary	4 139	4 886	4 376	3 582	4 479	3 480
Test:	Sentences	1 130		828		642	
	Running words	27 278	25 745	28 015	25 137	27 470	24 993
	Vocabulary	3 723	5 695	4 719	4 914	4 067	4 261

A.4 GALE Arabic-to-English and Chinese-to-English tasks

Table A.9: Corpus statistics for the bilingual training data of the Chinese-to-English and Arabic-to-English MT systems (GALE large data track). These systems were used for sentence segmentation and soft boundary experiments in Chapter 5.

Language pair		Source	Target
Chinese to English	Sentence pairs	7M	
	Running words	199M	213M
	Vocabulary	223K	351K
Arabic to English	Sentence pairs	4M	
	Running words	126M	125M
	Vocabulary	421K	337K

Table A.10: Corpus statistics of the development (DEV07) and evaluation (EVAL07) data used by the Nightingale team in the GALE 2007 evaluation to perform system combination experiments (Arabic-to-English task, see Chapter 6).

Broadcast news		Arabic	English
DEV07	Sentences	565	
	Running words	13 583	17 787
	Running words without punct. marks	13 018	16 165
EVAL07	Sentences	666	
	Running words	16 543	21 718
	Running words without punct. marks	15 877	19 530

A Corpora

Table A.11: Corpus statistics of the development and test data used by the Nightingale team in the GALE 2008 evaluation to perform system combination experiments (Chinese-to-English task, see Chapter 6).

Broadcast news		Chinese	English
Test08	Sentences	529	
(development set	Running words	12 295	15 718
for system combination)	Running words without punct. marks	11 656	14 026
Dev08	Sentences	483	
(blind test set	Running words	11 156	14 087
for system combination)	Running words without punct. marks	10 578	12 698

B Additional examples

The following examples from the TC-STAR Spanish-to-English EPPS 2007 test set (translation of word lattice ASR output, see Section 4.5.2.2) illustrate the automatic sentence segmentation and punctuation prediction performed using the algorithms described in Chapter 5, as well as the re-segmentation to match the reference sentence boundaries using the extended edit distance alignment presented in Chapter 3. The automatically inserted segment boundaries are shown with symbol [s], the symbol # stands for the boundaries inserted for correspondence with the reference translation boundaries. One of the two reference translations is shown in the right column. Severe translation errors caused by recognition errors are underlined; the words erroneously assigned to a wrong reference segment and their corresponding reference words are printed in italic.

Examples 1-2 show a very good quality of the re-segmentation for the evaluation, even when the majority of the hypothesis words at the boundaries are not identical to the reference words. In each of the examples 3 and 4, one of the two inserted reference boundaries is also placed correctly. However, in example 3 the phrase "*this whole*" is assigned to a wrong segment because it does not align well with the reference phrase "*all of the*" expressing almost the same meaning. In example 4, the same happens with the phrase "*this point*". These re-segmentation errors do not affect the error rates because the n-grams of the misplaced phrases do not match reference n-grams. The same conclusions can be made about examples 5 and 6.

In contrast, the re-segmentation errors in example 7 negatively influence the error rates, but they are caused by differences in word order between hypothesis and reference which the edit distance alignment can not handle. Example 8 illustrates the bad quality of the reference translation which does not include the repetition "*does anybody wish*" made by the speaker. In example 9, the misplaced word at a segment boundary is a translated recognition error. With the exception of example 7, all of the examples show that the positions of the automatically inserted segment boundaries are reasonable.

B Additional examples

	Machine translation of ASR output	Reference translation
1.	# it was not possible to reach an agreement with parliament at first reading, # the council's desire to get rid of the projects of European interest, not the we share ...	It was not possible to reach an agreement with parliament on the first reading. # We do not share the council's intention to do away with projects of European interest ...
2.	# seeking progress towards its full and effective <u>wish</u>, of course, # by requesting that was voted on a resolution on this subject. [s]	They are asking that progress be made towards full and effective membership, of course. # They also ask that a resolution be voted on in this respect.
3.	[s] *This whole* # investment of resources and illusion it can not come now under # the product must be a guarantee powerful, which will serve to maintain and strengthen what we have built up until now [s] #	*All of the* investment of resources and expectation cannot be left to fall away now. # Life Plus has to be a powerful guarantee for the maintenance and strengthening of what we have constructed up to now.
4.	# I believe that there are various aspects which we introduced new # in the first place, it has been great emphasis on the aspects of the management of natural resources, which has this project # *this point.* [s]	In my opinion, we have introduced several new aspects. # Firstly, in this project there has been a great deal of insistence on the management of natural resources.

	Machine translation of ASR output	Reference translation
5.	# , [s] several members of the socialist group requested by an intermediary ... calling for the release of the gentlemen <u>formalise</u> without charge [s] *because* # I believe that it is good to apply the treaty in all its extremes levels #	Through my intermediary, several colleagues from the socialist group ... asking for the release of Messrs. Foreman and Hoedt without charges. # *Or* I believe that it is good to implement the treaty in all its respects.
6.	... as well as a substantial agreement on the objectives of this piece of legislation [s] *indeed* # , the security of supply ... will oblige us to an approach multi-dimensional in energy policy. [s]	... as well as there being substantial coincidence on the goals of this piece of legislation. # *In effect*, the security of supply ... compels us to make a multi-dimensional focus on energy policy.
7.	... and as an opposition coloured that required <u>exit</u> contradictory *had* # only then, with a high popularity and a good command no doubt of the communication. [s] # *Television* ...	... and a varied opposition that demanded solutions from him that were contradictory amongst themselves. # He only then *had* a high degree of popularity and a doubtless mastery in *television* communication.
8.	[s] For the agenda for Wednesday, the socialist group has requested that it be removed the questions to the council *does anybody wish* # to explain if Mister Poettering, if you ask me if I may *does anybody wish* to explain the request of the socialist group. [s]	For the agenda for Wednesday, the socialist group requested the questions session to the council be suppressed. # Mister Poettering, *could anyone previously care* to explain, if I may be allowed, the request from the socialist group?
9.	I would ask you, ladies and gentlemen, that we observe a minute's silence in memory and memory of our colleague. [s] <u>To</u> # thank you very much. [s]	I would ask you, dear colleagues for us to observe one minute of silence in memory and remembrance of our colleague. # many thanks.

B Additional examples

C Symbols and acronyms

C.1 Key mathematical symbols

$f_1^J = f_1, ..., f_j, ..., f_J$	source language sentence (also F)
$e_1^I = e_1, ..., e_i, ..., e_I$	target language sentence
$t_1^K = t_1, ..., t_k, ..., t_K$	sequence of bilingual tuples for a sentence pair (f_1^J, e_1^I)
$x_1^T = x_1, ..., x_\tau, ..., x_T$	acoustic observations for the spoken source sentence
$E_1, ..., E_m, ...E_M$	translations of the same source sentence by M different MT systems
$A \subseteq J \times I$	word alignment (general)
$a_1^J = a_1, ..., a_j, ..., a_J$	word alignment (mapping)
$j(k)$	source word index of the k-th alignment link in a monotonic alignment
$i(k)$	target word index of the k-th alignment link in a monotonic alignment
$C(i, j)$	local word alignment costs
$w_1^N = w_1, ..., w_n, ..., w_N$	general word sequence
$n_1^K = n_1, ..., n_k, ..., n_K$	sentence boundaries (the values are word indices)
$Pr(\cdot)$	general probability distribution with no specific assumptions
$p(\cdot)$	model-based probability distribution
λ	model scaling factor
$h(\cdot)$	component of log-linear model
s_1^K	segmentation into K phrase pairs
i_k	end position of kth target phrase
j_k	end position of kth source phrase
b_k	start position of kth source phrase
$\tilde{e}$	target phrase
$\tilde{f}$	source phrase
$|\tilde{e}|$	length of the phrase $\tilde{e}$

C Symbols and acronyms

$\tilde{e}^i$	the ith word of phrase $\tilde{e}$
$q_{TM}(\cdot)$	weighted translation model score
$q_{LM}(\cdot)$	weighted language model score
$q_{DM}(\cdot)$	weighted distortion model score
$E(j,j')$	translation candidates for source phrase $f_j, \ldots, f_{j'}$
$\text{\textlangle s\textrangle}$	sentence start or sentence end symbol
ε or \$	empty word
$Q(\ldots)$	auxiliary quantity
$\delta(\cdot,\cdot)$	Kronecker delta

C.2 Acronyms

ASR	automatic speech recognition
BLEU	bilingual evaluation understudy
BTEC	basic travel expression corpus
CN	confusion network
EM	expectation-maximization
EPPS	European Parliament Plenary Sessions
EU	European Union
FSA	finite state automaton; also the acronym for the tuple-based MT system described in Chapter 4.
FST	finite state transducer
GALE	Global Autonomous Language Exploitation
GIATI	Grammatical Inference and Alignments for Transducer Inference
HMM	hidden Markov model
IBM	International Business Machines corporation
IWSLT	International Workshop on Spoken Language Translation
LDC	Linguistic Data Consortium
LM	language model
MT	machine translation
NIST	National Institute of Standards and Technology
NLP	natural language processing
OOV	out of vocabulary
PBT	phrase based translation; also the acronym for the phrase-based log-linear MT system used in the experiments for this thesis.
PER	position independent word error rate
POS	part-of-speech
SCSS	source cardinality-synchronous search
SMT	statistical machine translation
TC-STAR	Technology and Corpora for Speech to Speech Translation

C Symbols and acronyms

TER translation edit rate
WER word error rate
WFST weighted finite state transducer

Bibliography

[Akiba & Federico[+] 04] Y. Akiba, M. Federico, N. Kando, H. Nakaiwa, M. Paul, J. Tsujii: Overview of the IWSLT 2004 Evaluation Campaign. Proc. *International Workshop on Spoken Language Translation*, pp. 1–12, Kyoto, Japan, September 2004.

[Alabau & Sancis 07] V. Alabau, F. Sancis, A. abd Casacuberta: Using Word Posterior Probabilities in Lattice Translation. Proc. *International Workshop on Spoken Language Translation*, pp. 131–136, Trento, Italy, October 2007.

[Allauzen & Mohri[+] 03] C. Allauzen, M. Mohri, B. Roark: Generalized algorithms for constructing statistical language models. Proc. *Annual Meeting of the Association for Computational Linguistics*, pp. 40–47, Sapporo, Japan, July 2003.

[Arranz & Castell[+] 03] V. Arranz, N. Castell, J. Giménez: Development of Language Resources for Speech-to-Speech Translation. Proc. *RANLP 2003*, Borovets, Bulgaria, September 2003.

[Ayan & Zheng[+] 08] N.F. Ayan, J. Zheng, W. Wang: Improving Alignments for Better Confusion Networks for Combining Machine Translation Systems. Proc. *22nd International Conference on Computational Linguistics (Coling 2008)*, pp. 33–40, Manchester, UK, August 2008.

[Bangalore & Bordel[+] 01] S. Bangalore, G. Bordel, G. Riccardi: Computing Consensus Translation from Multiple Machine Translation Systems. Proc. *IEEE Automatic Speech Recognition and Understanding Workshop*, Madonna di Campiglio, Italy, December 2001.

[Bangalore & Riccardi 00a] S. Bangalore, G. Riccardi: Finite-State Models for Lexical Reordering in Spoken Language Translation. Proc. *6th International Conference on Spoken Language Processing (ICSLP)*, Vol. 4, pp. 422–425, Beijing, China, October 2000.

[Bangalore & Riccardi 00b] S. Bangalore, G. Riccardi: Stochastic Finite-State Models for Spoken Language Machine Translation. Proc. *Workshop on Embedded Machine Translation Systems, NAACL*, pp. 52–59, Seattle, WA, May 2000.

[Beeferman & Berger[+] 98] D. Beeferman, A. Berger, J. Lafferty: Cyberpunc: a Lightweight Punctuation Annotation System for Speech. Proc. *IEEE International Conference on*

Acoustics, Speech, and Signal Processing (ICASSP), pp. 689–692, Seattle, WA, USA, May 1998.

[Berger & Brown[+] 96] A.L. Berger, P.F. Brown, S.A.D. Pietra, V.J.D. Pietra, J.R. Gillett, A.S. Kehler, R.L. Mercer: Language Translation Apparatus and Method of Using Context-based Translation Models, United States Patent 5510981, April 1996.

[Berghen & Bersini 05] F.V. Berghen, H. Bersini: CONDOR, a New Parallel, Constrained Extension of Powell's UOBYQA Algorithm: Experimental Results and Comparison with the DFO Algorithm. *Journal of Computational and Applied Mathematics*, Vol. 181, pp. 157–175, 2005.

[Bertoldi 05] N. Bertoldi: *Statistical Models and Search Algorithms for Machine Translation*. Ph.D. thesis, Università degli Studi di Trento, Italy, Feb. 2005.

[Bertoldi & Zens[+] 07] N. Bertoldi, R. Zens, M. Federico: Speech Translation by Confusion Network Decoding. Proc. *IEEE International Conference on Acoustics, Speech, and Signal Processing*, pp. 1297–1300, Honululu, HI, USA, April 2007.

[Besacier & Mahdhaoui[+] 07] L. Besacier, A. Mahdhaoui, V.B. Le: The LIG Arabic/English Speech Translation System at IWSLT07. Proc. *International Workshop on Spoken Language Translation*, pp. 137–141, Trento, Italy, October 2007.

[Bozarov & Sagisaka[+] 05] A. Bozarov, Y. Sagisaka, R. Zhang, G. Kikui: Improved Speech Recognition Word Lattice Translation by Confidence Measure. Proc. *Interspeech*, pp. 3197–3200, Lisbon, Portugal, September 2005.

[Brown & Cocke[+] 88] P.F. Brown, J. Cocke, S.D. Pietra, V.J.D. Pietra, F. Jelinek, R.L. Mercer, P.S. Roossin: A Statistical Approach to Language Translation. Proc. *COLING*, pp. 71–76, Budapest, Hungary, August 1988.

[Brown & Cocke[+] 90] P.F. Brown, J. Cocke, S.A. Della Pietra, V.J. Della Pietra, F. Jelinek, J.D. Lafferty, R.L. Mercer, P.S. Roossin: A Statistical Approach to Machine Translation. *Computational Linguistics*, Vol. 16, No. 2, pp. 79–85, June 1990.

[Brown & Della Pietra[+] 93] P.F. Brown, S.A. Della Pietra, V.J. Della Pietra, R.L. Mercer: The Mathematics of Statistical Machine Translation: Parameter Estimation. *Computational Linguistics*, Vol. 19, No. 2, pp. 263–311, June 1993.

[Callison-Burch & Flournoy 01] C. Callison-Burch, R. Flournoy: A Program for Automatically Selecting the Best Output from Multiple Machine Translation Engines. Proc. *Machine Translation Summit VIII*, pp. 63–66, September 2001.

[Callison-Burch & Koehn[+] 09] C. Callison-Burch, P. Koehn, C. Monz, J. Schroeder: Findings of the 2009 Workshop on Statistical Machine Translation. Proc. *Fourth Workshop on*

Statistical Machine Translation, pp. 1–28, Athens, Greece, March 2009. Association for Computational Linguistics.

[Casacuberta & Llorens[+] 01] F. Casacuberta, D. Llorens, C. MartíÃĆÂŋnez, S. Molau, F. Nevado, H. Ney, M. Pastor, D. Picó, A. Sanchis, E. Vidal, J.M. Vilar: Speech-to-Speech Translation based on Finite-State Transducer. Proc. *IEEE International Conference on Acoustics, Speech, and Signal Processing*, pp. 613–616, Salt Lake City, Utah, May 2001.

[Casacuberta & Vidal 04] F. Casacuberta, E. Vidal: Machine Translation with Inferred Stochastic Finite-state Transducers. *Computational Linguistics*, Vol. 30, No. 2, pp. 205–225, 2004.

[Cattoni & Bertoldi[+] 07] R. Cattoni, N. Bertoldi, M. Federico: Punctuating Confusion Networks for Speech Translation. Proc. *Interspeech*, pp. 2453–2456, Antwerp, Belgium, August 2007.

[Chiang 07] D. Chiang: Hierarchical Phrase-based Translation. *Computational Linguistics*, Vol. 33, No. 2, pp. 201–228, 2007.

[Crego & Mariño[+] 05] J.M. Crego, J.B. Mariño, A. de Gispert: Reordered Search and Tuple Unfolding for Ngram-based SMT. Proc. *10th Machine Translation Summit*, pp. 283–289, Phuket, Thailand, September 2005.

[de Gispert & Mariño 02] A. de Gispert, J. Mariño: Using X-grams for Speech-to-Speech Translation. Proc. *International Conference on Spoken Language Processing*, pp. 1885–1888, Denver, CO, USA, September 2002.

[Doddington 02] G. Doddington: Automatic Evaluation of Machine Translation Quality Using N-gram Co-occurrence Statistics. Proc. *ARPA Workshop on Human Language Technology*, pp. 128–132, San Diego, 2002.

[Dyer & Muresan[+] 08] C. Dyer, S. Muresan, P. Resnik: Generalizing Word Lattice Translation. Proc. *ACL-08: HLT*, pp. 1012–1020, Columbus, OH, USA, June 2008.

[Eck & Hori 05] M. Eck, C. Hori: Overview of the IWSLT 2005 Evaluation Campaign. Proc. *International Workshop on Spoken Language Translation*, pp. 11–32, Pittsburgh, PA, USA, October 2005.

[Evermann & Woodland 00] G. Evermann, P.C. Woodland: Large Vocabulary Decoding and Confidence Estimation Using Word Posterior Probabilities. Proc. *IEEE International Conference on Acoustics, Speech, and Signal Processing (ICASSP)*, Vol. 3, pp. 1655–1658, Istanbul, Turkey, June 2000.

[Fiscus 97] J.G. Fiscus: A Post-Processing System to Yield Reduced Word Error Rates: Recognizer Output Voting Error Reduction (ROVER). Proc. *IEEE Automatic Speech*

Recognition and Understanding Workshop, pp. 347–352, Santa Barbara, USA, December 1997.

[Fügen & Kolss 07] C. Fügen, M. Kolss: The Influence of Utterance Chunking on Machine Translation Performance. Proc. *Interspeech*, pp. 2837–2840, Antwerp, Belgium, August 2007.

[GALE 07] GALE: Global Autonomous Language Exploitation (GALE). http://www.darpa.mil/ipto/programs/gale/index.htm, 2007.

[Habash & Rambow 05] N. Habash, O. Rambow: Arabic Tokenization, Part-of-speech Tagging and Morphological Disambiguation in One Fell Swoop. Proc. *43rd Annual Meeting of the Association for Computational Linguistics*, pp. 573–580, Morristown, NJ, USA, June 2005.

[Hahn & Lehnen[+] 08] S. Hahn, P. Lehnen, C. Raymond, H. Ney: A Comparison of Various Methods for Concept Tagging for Spoken Language Understanding. Proc. *International Conference on Language Resources and Evaluation*, pp. 2947–2950, Marrakech, Morocco, May 2008.

[Hakkani-Tür & Riccardi 03] D. Hakkani-Tür, G. Riccardi: A General Algorithm for Word Graph Matrix Decomposition. Proc. *IEEE International Conference on Acoustics, Speech, and Signal Processing (ICASSP)*, pp. 596–599, Hong Kong, April 2003.

[Hasan & Ganitkevitch[+] 08] S. Hasan, J. Ganitkevitch, H. Ney, J. Andrés-Ferrer: Triplet Lexicon Models for Statistical Machine Translation. Proc. *Conference on Empirical Methods in Natural Language Processing*, pp. 372–381, Honolulu, Hawaii, October 2008.

[He & Yang[+] 08] X. He, M. Yang, J. Gao, P. Nguyen, R. Moore: Indirect-HMM-based Hypothesis Alignment for Combining Outputs from Machine Translation Systems. Proc. *Conference on Empirical Methods in Natural Language Processing*, pp. 98–107, Honolulu, Hawaii, October 2008.

[Hildebrand & Vogel 08] A.S. Hildebrand, S. Vogel: Combination of Machine Translation Systems via Hhypothesis Selection from Combined N-best Lists. Proc. *Eighth Conference of the Association for Machine Translation in the Americas (AMTA)*, pp. 254–261, Waikiki, Hawaii, USA, October 2008.

[Hillard 08] D. Hillard: *Automatic Sentence Structure Annotation for Spoken Language Processing*. Ph.D. thesis, University of Washington, Seattle, Washington, USA, January 2008.

[Hoffmeister & Plahl[+] 07] B. Hoffmeister, C. Plahl, P. Fritz, G. Heigold, J. Lööf, R. Schlüter, H. Ney: Development of the 2007 RWTH Mandarin LVCSR System. Proc. *IEEE Automatic*

Speech Recognition and Understanding Workshop (ASRU), pp. 455–458, Kyoto, Japan, December 2007.

[Huang & Papineni 07] F. Huang, K. Papineni: Hierarchical System Combination for Machine Translation. Proc. *Joint Conference on Empirical Methods in Natural Language Processing and Computational Natural Language Learning (EMNLP-CoNLL)*, pp. 277–286, Prague, Czech Republic, June 2007.

[Huang & Zweig 02] J. Huang, G. Zweig: Maximum Entropy Model for Punctuation Annotation from Speech. Proc. *International Conference on Spoken Language Processing*, pp. 917–920, Denver, CO, USA, September 2002.

[Jayaraman & Lavie 05] S. Jayaraman, A. Lavie: Multi-Engine Machine Translation Guided by Explicit Word Matching. Proc. *10th Annual Conference of the European Association for Machine Translation (EAMT)*, pp. 143–152, Budapest, Hungary, May 2005.

[Kanthak & Ney 04] S. Kanthak, H. Ney: FSA: An Efficient and Flexible C++ Toolkit for Finite State Automata Using On-Demand Computation. Proc. *42nd Annual Meeting of the Association for Computational Linguistics (ACL)*, pp. 510–517, Barcelona, Spain, July 2004.

[Kanthak & Vilar[+] 05] S. Kanthak, D. Vilar, E. Matusov, R. Zens, H. Ney: Novel Reordering Approaches in Phrase-Based Statistical Machine Translation. Proc. *ACL Workshop on Building and Using Parallel Texts*, pp. 167–174, Ann Arbor, Michigan, June 2005.

[Kendall 70] M.G. Kendall: *Rank Correlation Methods*. Charles Griffin & Co Ltd, London, UK, 1970.

[Kim & Woodland 01] J. Kim, P. Woodland: The Use of Prosody in a Combined System for Punctuation Generation and Speech Recognition. Proc. *Eurospeech*, pp. 2757–2760, Aalborg, Denmark, September 2001.

[Kneser & Ney 95] R. Kneser, H. Ney: Improved Backing-off for m-gram Language Modeling. Proc. *IEEE International Conference on Acoustics, Speech and Signal Processing*, pp. 181–184, Detroit, Michigan, USA, May 1995.

[Koehn 04] P. Koehn: Pharaoh: a Beam Search Decoder for Phrase-Based Statistical Machine Translation Models. Proc. *6th Conference of the Association for Machine Translation in the Americas (AMTA 04)*, pp. 115–124, Washington DC, September/October 2004.

[Koehn & Hoang[+] 07] P. Koehn, H. Hoang, A. Birch, C. Callison-Burch, M. Federico, N. Bertoldi, B. Cowan, W. Shen, C. Moran, R. Zens, C. Dyer, O. Bojar, A. Constantine, E. Herbst: Moses: Open Source Toolkit for Statistical Machine Translation. Proc. *45th*

Annual Meeting of the Association for Computational Linguistics (ACL): Poster Session, pp. 177–180, Prague, Czech Republic, June 2007.

[Kumar & Byrne 03] S. Kumar, W. Byrne: A Weighted Finite State Transducer Implementation of the Alignment Template Model for Statistical Machine Translation. Proc. *Human Language Technology Conference (HLT-NAACL)*, pp. 142–149, Edmonton, Canada, May/June 2003.

[Lee 06] Y.S. Lee: IBM Arabic-to-English Translation for IWSLT 2006. Proc. *International Workshop on Spoken Language Translation (IWSLT) 2006*, pp. 45–52, Kyoto, Japan, November 2006.

[Lee & Roukos[+] 06] Y.S. Lee, S. Roukos, Y. Al-Onaizan, K. Papineni: IBM Spoken Language Translation System. Proc. *TC-STAR Workshop on Speech-to-Speech Translation*, pp. 13–18, Barcelona, Spain, June 2006.

[Leusch & Matusov[+] 09] G. Leusch, E. Matusov, H. Ney: The RWTH System Combination System for WMT 2009. Proc. *Fourth Workshop on Statistical Machine Translation*, pp. 56–60, Athens, Greece, March 2009.

[Leusch & Ueffing[+] 05] G. Leusch, N. Ueffing, D. Vilar, H. Ney: Preprocessing and Normalization for Automatic Evaluation of Machine Translation. Proc. *ACL Workshop on Intrinsic and Extrinsic Evaluation Measures for Machine Translation and/or Summarization*, pp. 17–24, Ann Arbor, Michigan, June 2005.

[Levenshtein 66] V.I. Levenshtein: Binary Codes Capable of Correcting Deletions, Insertions and Reversals. *Soviet Physics Doklady*, Vol. 10, No. 8, pp. 707–710, February 1966.

[Liu & Shriberg[+] 04] Y. Liu, E. Shriberg, A. Stolcke, D. Hillard, M. Ostendorf, B. Peskin, M. Harper: The ICSI-SRI-UW Metadata Extraction System. Proc. *International Conference on Spoken Language Processing*, pp. 577–580, Jeju Island, Korea, October 2004.

[Lööf & Gollan[+] 07] J. Lööf, C. Gollan, S. Hahn, G. Heigold, B. Hoffmeister, C. Plahl, D. Rybach, R. Schlüter, H. Ney: The RWTH 2007 TC-STAR Evaluation System for European English and Spanish. Proc. *Interspeech*, pp. 2145–2148, Antwerp, Belgium, August 2007.

[Macherey & Och 07] W. Macherey, F.J. Och: An Empirical Study on Computing Consensus Translations from Multiple Machine Translation Systems. Proc. *Joint Conference on Empirical Methods in Natural Language Processing and Computational Natural Language Learning (EMNLP-CoNLL)*, pp. 986–995, Prague, Czech Republic, June 2007.

[Mangu & Brill+ 00] L. Mangu, E. Brill, A. Stolcke: Finding Consensus in Speech Recognition: Word Error Minimization and Other Applications of Confusion Networks. *Computer Speech and Language*, Vol. 14, pp. 373–400, 2000.

[Mansour & Sima'an+ 07] S. Mansour, K. Sima'an, Y. Winter: Smoothing a Lexicon-based POS Tagger for Arabic and Hebrew. Proc. *Workshop on Computational Approaches to Semitic Languages: Common Issues and Resources*, pp. 97–103, Prague, Czech Republic, June 2007.

[Mariño & Banchs+ 06] J.B. Mariño, R. Banchs, J.M. Crego, A. de Gispert, P. Lambert: N-gram Based Machine Translation. *Computational Linguistics*, Vol. 32, No. 4, December 2006.

[Mathias & Byrne 06] L. Mathias, W. Byrne: Statistical Phrase-based Speech Translation. Proc. *IEEE International Conference on Acoustics, Speech, and Signal Processing (ICASSP)*, pp. 561–564, Toulouse, France, May 2006.

[Matusov & Hillard+ 07] E. Matusov, D. Hillard, M. Magimai-Doss, D. Hakkani-Tür, M. Ostendorf, H. Ney: Improving Speech Translation by Automatic Boundary Prediction. Proc. *Interspeech*, pp. 2449–2452, Antwerp, Belgium, August 2007.

[Matusov & Hoffmeister+ 08] E. Matusov, B. Hoffmeister, H. Ney: ASR Word Lattice Translation with Exhaustive Reordering is Possible. Proc. *Interspeech*, pp. 2342–2345, Brisbane, Australia, September 2008.

[Matusov & Kanthak+ 05a] E. Matusov, S. Kanthak, H. Ney: Efficient Statistical Machine Translation with Constrained Reordering. Proc. *Conference of the European Association for Machine Translation*, pp. 181–188, Budapest, Hungary, May 2005.

[Matusov & Kanthak+ 05b] E. Matusov, S. Kanthak, H. Ney: On the Integration of Speech Recognition and Statistical Machine Translation. Proc. *Interspeech*, pp. 3177–3180, Lisbon, Portugal, September 2005. ISCA Best Student Paper Award.

[Matusov & Leusch+ 05] E. Matusov, G. Leusch, O. Bender, H. Ney: Evaluating Machine Translation Output with Automatic Sentence Segmentation. Proc. *International Workshop on Spoken Language Translation*, pp. 148–154, Pittsburgh, PA, USA, Oct. 2005.

[Matusov & Leusch+ 08] E. Matusov, G. Leusch, R.E. Banchs, N. Bertoldi, D. Dechelotte, M. Federico, M. Kolss, Y.S. Lee, J.B. Mariño, M. Paulik, S. Roukos, H. Schwenk, H. Ney: System Combination for Machine Translation of Spoken and Written Language. *IEEE Transactions on Audio, Speech and Language Processing*, Vol. 16, No. 7, pp. 1222–1237, September 2008.

Bibliography

[Matusov & Leusch[+] 09] E. Matusov, G. Leusch, H. Ney: *Learning To Combine Machine Translation Systems*, chapter 13, pp. 257–276. Neural Information Processing Series. MIT Press, 2009.

[Matusov & Mauser[+] 06] E. Matusov, A. Mauser, H. Ney: Automatic Sentence Segmentation and Punctuation Prediction for Spoken Language Translation. Proc. *International Workshop on Spoken Language Translation (IWSLT)*, pp. 158–165, Kyoto, Japan, November 2006.

[Matusov & Ney[+] 05] E. Matusov, H. Ney, R. Schlüter: Phrase-based Translation of Speech Recognizer Word Lattices Using Loglinear Model Combination. Proc. *IEEE Automatic Speech Recognition and Understanding Workshop*, pp. 110–115, San Juan, Puerto Rico, November 2005.

[Matusov & Peters[+] 03] E. Matusov, J. Peters, C. Meyer, H. Ney: Topic Segmentation Using Markov Models on Section Level. Proc. *IEEE Automatic Speech Recognition and Understanding Workshop*, pp. 471–476, St. Thomas, Virgin Islands, USA, December 2003.

[Matusov & Ueffing[+] 06] E. Matusov, N. Ueffing, H. Ney: Computing Consensus Translation from Multiple Machine Translation Systems Using Enhanced Hypotheses Alignment. Proc. *11th Conference of the European Chapter of the Association for Computational Linguistics (EACL)*, pp. 33–40, Trento, Italy, April 2006.

[Matusov & Zens[+] 04] E. Matusov, R. Zens, H. Ney: Symmetric Word Alignments for Statistical Machine Translation. Proc. *COLING: The 20th International Conference on Computational Linguistics*, pp. 219–225, Geneva, Switzerland, August 2004.

[Matusov & Zens[+] 06] E. Matusov, R. Zens, D. Vilar, A. Mauser, M. Popović, S. Hasan, H. Ney: The RWTH Machine Translation System. Proc. *TC-STAR Workshop on Speech-to-Speech Translation*, pp. 31–36, Barcelona, Spain, June 2006.

[Mauser & Zens[+] 06] A. Mauser, R. Zens, E. Matusov, S. Hasan, H. Ney: The RWTH Statistical Machine Translation System for the IWSLT 2006 Evaluation. Proc. *International Workshop on Spoken Language Translation (IWSLT) 2006*, pp. 103–110, Kyoto, Japan, November 2006.

[Mohri 97] M. Mohri: Finite-state Transducers in Language and Speech Processing. *Computational Linguistics*, Vol. 23, No. 2, 1997.

[Mohri & Pereira[+] 00] M. Mohri, F.C.N. Pereira, M. Riley: Weighted Finite-State Transducers in Speech Recognition. Proc. *ISCA Workshop, ASR2000*, Paris, France, September 2000.

Bibliography

[Ney 99] H. Ney: Speech Translation: Coupling of Recognition and Translation. Proc. *IEEE International Conference on Acoustics, Speech, and Signal Processing*, pp. 517–520, Phoenix, Arizona, USA, March 1999.

[Nießen & Vogel+ 98] S. Nießen, S. Vogel, H. Ney, C. Tillmann: A DP Search Algorithm for Statistical Machine Translation. Proc. *36th Annual Meeting of the Association for Computational Linguistics (ACL 1998) and the 17th International Conference on Computational Linguistics (CoLing 1998)*, pp. 960–967, Montreal, Canada, August 1998.

[Nirenburg & Frederking 94] S. Nirenburg, R. Frederking: Toward Multi-Engine Machine Translation. Proc. *ARPA Workshop on Human Language Technology*, pp. 147–151, Plainsboro, NJ, March 1994.

[Nomoto 04] T. Nomoto: Multi-Engine Machine Translation with Voted Language Model. Proc. *42nd Annual Meeting of the Association for Computational Linguistics (ACL)*, pp. 494–501, Barcelona, Spain, July 2004.

[Och 03] F.J. Och: Minimum Error Rate Training in Statistical Machine Translation. Proc. *41st Annual Meeting of the Association for Computational Linguistics (ACL)*, pp. 160–167, Sapporo, Japan, July 2003.

[Och & Ney 01] F.J. Och, H. Ney: Statistical Multi-Source Translation. Proc. *Machine Translation Summit*, pp. 253–258, Santiago de Compostela, Spain, Sept. 2001.

[Och & Ney 02] F.J. Och, H. Ney: Discriminative Training and Maximum Entropy Models for Statistical Machine Translation. Proc. *40th Annual Meeting of the Association for Computational Linguistics (ACL)*, pp. 295–302, Philadelphia, PA, July 2002.

[Och & Ney 03] F.J. Och, H. Ney: A Systematic Comparison of Various Statistical Alignment Models. *Computational Linguistics*, Vol. 29, No. 1, pp. 19–51, March 2003.

[Och & Tillmann+ 99] F.J. Och, C. Tillmann, H. Ney: Improved Alignment Models for Statistical Machine Translation. Proc. *Joint SIGDAT Conference on Empirical Methods in Natural Language Processing and Very Large Corpora*, pp. 20–28, University of Maryland, College Park, MD, June 1999.

[Ostendorf & Favre+ 08] M. Ostendorf, B. Favre, R. Grishman, D. Hakkani-Tür, M. Harper, D. Hillard, J. Hirschberg, H. Ji, J.G. Kahn, Y. Liu, S. Maskey, E. Matusov, H. Ney, A. Rosenberg, E. Shriberg, W. Wang, C. Wooters: Speech Segmentation and Spoken Document Processing. *IEEE Signal Processing Magazine*, Vol. 25, No. 3, pp. 59–69, May 2008.

[Papineni 02] K.A. Papineni: The NIST `mteval` Scoring Software. http://www.itl.nist.gov/iad/894.01/tests/mt/resources/scoring.htm, 2002.

Bibliography

[Papineni & Roukos⁺ 02] K. Papineni, S. Roukos, T. Ward, W.J. Zhu: Bleu: a Method for Automatic Evaluation of Machine Translation. Proc. *40th Annual Meeting of the Association for Computational Linguistics (ACL)*, pp. 311–318, Philadelphia, PA, July 2002.

[Paul 08] M. Paul: Overview of the IWSLT 2008 Evaluation Campaign. Proc. *International Workshop on Spoken Language Translation (IWSLT)*, pp. 1–17, Hawaii, USA, October 2008.

[Paul & Doi⁺ 05] M. Paul, T. Doi, Y. Hwang, K. Imamura, H. Okuma, E. Sumita: Nobody is Perfect: ATR's Hybrid Approach to Spoken Language Translation. Proc. *International Workshop on Spoken Language Translation (IWSLT)*, pp. 55–62, Pittsburgh, USA, October 2005.

[Paulik & Rao⁺ 08] M. Paulik, S. Rao, I. Lane, S. Vogel, T. Schulz: Sentence Segmentation and Punctuation Recovery for Spoken Language Translation. Proc. *IEEE International Conference on Acoustics, Speech and Signal Processing*, pp. 5105–5108, Las Vegas, Nevada, USA, April 2008.

[Pereira & Riley 96] F.C.N. Pereira, M.D. Riley: Speech Recognition by Composition of Weighted Finite Automata. Proc. *Finite-State Language Processing*, pp. 431–453. MIT Press, 1996.

[Plahl & Hoffmeister⁺ 08] C. Plahl, B. Hoffmeister, M.Y. Hwang, D. Lu, G. Heigold, J. Lööf, R. Schlüter, H. Ney: Recent Improvements of the RWTH GALE Mandarin LVCSR System. Proc. *Interspeech*, pp. 2426–2429, Brisbane, Australia, Sept. 2008.

[Popović & Ney 06] M. Popović, H. Ney: POS-based Word Reorderings for Statistical Machine Translation. Proc. *International Conference on Language Resources and Evaluation*, pp. 1278–1283, Genoa, Italy, May 2006.

[Press & Teukolsky⁺ 02] W.H. Press, S.A. Teukolsky, W.T. Vetterling, B.P. Flannery: *Numerical Recipes in C++*. Cambridge University Press, Cambridge, UK, 2002.

[R. Costa-jussà & Crego⁺ 07] M. R. Costa-jussà, J.M. Crego, D. Vilar, J.A. R. Fonollosa, J.B. Mariño, H. Ney: Analysis and System Combination of Phrase- and N-Gram-Based Statistical Machine Translation Systems. Proc. *Human Language Technologies 2007: The Conference of the North American Chapter of the Association for Computational Linguistics; Companion Volume, Short Papers*, pp. 137–140, Rochester, New York, April 2007.

[Rabiner & Juang 93] L. Rabiner, B.H. Juang: *Fundamentals of Speech Recognition*. Prentice Hall, Englewood Cliffs, NJ, 1993.

[Rao & Lane⁺ 07] S. Rao, I. Lane, T. Schulz: Optimizing Sentence Segmentation for Spoken Language Translation. Proc. *Interspeech*, pp. 2845–2848, Antwerp, Belgium, August 2007.

[Rosti & Ayan+ 07] A.V. Rosti, N.F. Ayan, B. Xiang, S. Matsoukas, R. Schwartz, B. Dorr: Combining Outputs from Multiple Machine Translation Systems. Proc. *Human Language Technology Conference / North American Chapter of the Association for Computational Linguistics Annual Meeting (HLT-NAACL)*, pp. 228–235, Rochester, NY, USA, April 2007.

[Rosti & Matsoukas+ 07] A.V. Rosti, S. Matsoukas, R. Schwartz: Improved Word-Level System Combination for Machine Translation. Proc. *45th Annual Meeting of the Association of Computational Linguistics*, pp. 312–319, Prague, Czech Republic, June 2007.

[Rosti & Zhang+ 08] A.V. Rosti, B. Zhang, S. Matsoukas, R. Schwartz: Incremental Hypothesis Alignment for Building Confusion Networks with Application to Machine Translation System Combination. Proc. *Third Workshop on Statistical Machine Translation*, pp. 183–186, Columbus, Ohio, June 2008. Association for Computational Linguistics.

[Rosti & Zhang+ 09] A.V. Rosti, B. Zhang, S. Matsoukas, R. Schwartz: Incremental Hypothesis Alignment with Flexible Matching for Building Confusion Networks: BBN System Description for WMT09 System Combination Task. Proc. *Fourth Workshop on Statistical Machine Translation*, pp. 61–65, Athens, Greece, March 2009. Association for Computational Linguistics.

[Saleem & Jou+ 04] S. Saleem, S.C. Jou, S. Vogel, T. Schultz: Speech Translation: Coupling of Recognition and Translation. Proc. *International Conference on Spoken Language Processing*, pp. 41–44, Jeju Island, Korea, Oct. 2004.

[Saon & Picheny 07] G. Saon, M. Picheny: Lattice-based Viterbi Decoding Techniques for Speech Translation. Proc. *IEEE Automatic Speech Recognition and Understanding Workshop, CD ROM, IEEE Catalog No. 01EX544*, pp. 386–389, Kyoto, Japan, December 2007.

[Schmidt & Vilar+ 08] C. Schmidt, D. Vilar, H. Ney: Using a Bilingual Context in Word-Based Statistical Machine Translation. Proc. *International Workshop on Pattern Recognition in Information Systems*, pp. 144–153, Barcelona, Spain, June 2008.

[Shen & Delaney+ 07] W. Shen, B. Delaney, T. Anderson, R. Slyh: The MIT-LL/AFRL IWSLT-2007 MT System. Proc. *International Workshop on Spoken Language Translation*, pp. 95–102, Trento, Italy, October 2007.

[Shen & Delaney+ 08] W. Shen, B. Delaney, T. Anderson, R. Slyh: The MIT-LL/AFRL IWSLT-2008 MT System. Proc. *International Workshop on Spoken Language Translation (IWSLT)*, pp. 69–76, Hawaii, USA, October 2008.

[Shen & Xu+ 08] L. Shen, J. Xu, R. Weischedel: A New String-to-Dependency Machine Translation Algorithm with a Target Dependency Language Model. Proc. *46th Annual*

Meeting of the Association for Computational Linguistics (ACL), pp. 577–585, Columbus, Ohio, USA, June 2008.

[Snover & Dorr+ 06] M. Snover, B. Dorr, R. Schwartz, L. Micciula, J. Makhoul: A Study of Translation Edit Rate with Targeted Human Evaluation. Proc. *7th Conference of the Association for Machine Translation in the Americas (AMTA 06)*, pp. 223–231, Cambridge, Massachusetts, USA, August 2006.

[Stolcke 02] A. Stolcke: SRILM – An Extensible Language Modeling Toolkit. Proc. Proc. *International Conference on Spoken Language Processing*, pp. 901–904, Denver, CO, September 2002.

[Stolcke & Shriberg+ 98] A. Stolcke, E. Shriberg, R. Bates, M. Ostendorf, D. Hakkani, M. Plauche, G. Tür, Y. Lu: Automatic Detection of Sentence Boundaries and Disfluencies Based on Recognized Words. Proc. *International Conference on Spoken Language Processing*, pp. 2247–2250, Sidney, Australia, December 1998.

[TC-STAR 07] TC-STAR: European Research Project TC-STAR – Technology and Corpora for Speech-to-Speech Translation. http://www.tc-star.org, 2007.

[Tidhar & Küssner 00] D. Tidhar, U. Küssner: Learning to Select a Good Translation. Proc. *COLING: The 18th International Conference on Computational Linguistics*, pp. 843–849, Saarbrücken, Germany, August 2000.

[Tillmann & Ney 00] C. Tillmann, H. Ney: Word re-ordering and DP-based search in statistical machine translation. Proc. *COLING: The 18th International Conference on Computational Linguistics*, pp. 850–856, Saarbrücken, Germany, July 2000.

[Tillmann & Vogel+ 97] C. Tillmann, S. Vogel, H. Ney, A. Zubiaga, H. Sawaf: Accelerated DP Based Search for Statistical Translation. Proc. *European Conference on Speech Communication and Technology*, pp. 2667–2670, Rhodes, Greece, September 1997.

[Ueffing & Stephan+ 08] N. Ueffing, J. Stephan, E. Matusov, L. Dugast, G. Foster, R. Kuhn, J. Senellart, J. Yang: Tighter Integration of Rule-Based and Statistical MT in Serial System Combination. Proc. *22nd Intl. Conference on Computational Linguistics (COLING)*, pp. 913–920, Manchester, UK, August 2008.

[Utiyama & Finch+ 08] M. Utiyama, A. Finch, H. Okuma, M. Paul, H. Cao, H. Yamamoto, K. Yasuda, E. Sumita: The NICT/ATR Speech Translation System for IWSLT 2008. Proc. *International Workshop on Spoken Language Translation*, pp. 77–84, Hawaii, USA, October 2008.

Bibliography

[Vidal 97] E. Vidal: Finite-State Speech-to-Speech Translation. Proc. *IEEE International Conference on Acoustics, Speech, and Signal Processing (ICASSP)*, Vol. 1, pp. 111–114, Munich, Germany, April 1997.

[Vilar & Stein[+] 08] D. Vilar, D. Stein, H. Ney: Analysing Soft Syntax Features and Heuristics for Hierarchical Phrase Based Machine Translation. Proc. *International Workshop on Spoken Language Translation 2008*, pp. 190–197, Waikiki, Hawaii, October 2008.

[Vogel & Ney[+] 96] S. Vogel, H. Ney, C. Tillmann: HMM-Based Word Alignment in Statistical Translation. Proc. *COLING: The 16th International Conference on Computational Linguistics*, pp. 836–841, Copenhagen, Denmark, August 1996.

[Vogel & Och[+] 00] S. Vogel, F.J. Och, C. Tillmann, S. Nießen, H. Sawaf, H. Ney: Statistical Methods for Machine Translation. In W. Wahlster, editor, *Verbmobil: Foundations of Speech-to-Speech Translation*, pp. 377–393. Springer Verlag, Berlin, Heidelberg, New York, 2000.

[Wessel & Schlüter[+] 01] F. Wessel, R. Schlüter, K. Macherey, H. Ney: Confidence Measures for Large Vocabulary Continuous Speech Recognition. *IEEE Transactions on Speech and Audio Processing*, Vol. 9, No. 3, pp. 288–298, March 2001.

[Xu & Gao[+] 08] J. Xu, J. Gao, K. Toutanova, H. Ney: Bayesian Semi-Supervised Chinese Word Segmentation for Statistical Machine Translation. Proc. *22nd International Conference on Computational Linguistics*, pp. 1017–1024, Manchester, UK, August 2008.

[Xu & Matusov[+] 05] J. Xu, E. Matusov, R. Zens, H. Ney: Integrated Chinese Word Segmentation in Statistical Machine Translation. Proc. *International Workshop on Spoken Language Translation*, pp. 141–147, Pittsburgh, PA, USA, October 2005.

[Zens 08] R. Zens: *Phrase-based Statistical Machine Translation: Models, Search, Training*. Ph.D. thesis, RWTH Aachen University, Aachen, Germany, February 2008.

[Zens & Bender[+] 05] R. Zens, O. Bender, S. Hasan, S. Khadivi, E. Matusov, J. Xu, Y. Zhang, H. Ney: The RWTH Phrase-based Statistical Machine Translation System. Proc. *International Workshop on Spoken Language Translation*, pp. 155–162, Pittsburgh, PA, USA, October 2005.

[Zens & Matusov[+] 04] R. Zens, E. Matusov, H. Ney: Improved Word Alignment Using a Symmetric Lexicon Model. Proc. *International Conference on Computational Linguistics*, pp. 36–42, Geneva, Switzerland, August 2004.

[Zens & Ney 04] R. Zens, H. Ney: Improvements in Phrase-Based Statistical Machine Translation. Proc. *Human Language Technology Conference / North American Chapter* of the Association for Computational Linguistics Annual Meeting (HLT-NAACL), pp. 257–264, Boston, MA, May 2004.

[Zens & Ney 06] R. Zens, H. Ney: Discriminative Reordering Models for Statistical Machine Translation. Proc. *Human Language Technology Conference / North American Chapter of the Association for Computational Linguistics Annual Meeting (HLT-NAACL): Workshop on Statistical Machine Translation*, pp. 55–63, New York City, NY, June 2006.

[Zens & Ney 07] R. Zens, H. Ney: Efficient Phrase-table Representation for Machine Translation with Applications to Online MT and Speech Translation. Proc. *Human Language Technology Conference / North American Chapter of the Assoc. for Computational Linguistics Annual Meeting*, pp. 492–499, Rochester, NY, April 2007.

[Zhang & Matusov[+] 09] Y. Zhang, E. Matusov, H. Ney: Are Unaligned Words Important for Machine Translation? Proc. *13th Annual Meeting of the European Association for Machine Translation*, pp. 226–233, Barcelona, Spain, May 2009.

[Zhang & Zens[+] 07] Y. Zhang, R. Zens, H. Ney: Improved Chunk-level Reordering for Statistical Machine Translation. Proc. *International Workshop on Spoken Language Translation*, pp. 21–28, Trento, Italy, October 2007.

[Zhou & Besacier[+] 07] B. Zhou, L. Besacier, Y. Gao: On Efficient Coupling of ASR and SMT for Speech Translation. Proc. *International Conference on Acoustics, Speech and Signal Processing*, Vol. IV, pp. 101–104, Honolulu, Hawaii, USA, April 2007.

[Zimmerman & Hakkani-Tur[+] 06] M. Zimmerman, D. Hakkani-Tur, J. Fung, N. Mirghafori, L. Gottlieb, E. Shriberg, Y. Liu: The ICSI+ Multilingual Sentence Segmentation System. Proc. *Interspeech*, pp. 117–120, Pittsburgh, PA, USA, September 2006.

[Zollmann & Venugopal 06] A. Zollmann, A. Venugopal: Syntax Augmented Machine Translation via Chart Parsing. Proc. *SMT Workshop, HLT-NAACL 2006*, pp. 138–141, New York City, NY, June 2006.

I want morebooks!

Buy your books fast and straightforward online - at one of world's fastest growing online book stores! Environmentally sound due to Print-on-Demand technologies.

Buy your books online at
www.morebooks.shop

Kaufen Sie Ihre Bücher schnell und unkompliziert online – auf einer der am schnellsten wachsenden Buchhandelsplattformen weltweit! Dank Print-On-Demand umwelt- und ressourcenschonend produziert.

Bücher schneller online kaufen
www.morebooks.shop

KS OmniScriptum Publishing
Brivibas gatve 197
LV-1039 Riga, Latvia
Telefax: +371 686 204 55

info@omniscriptum.com
www.omniscriptum.com

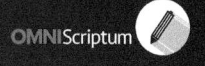

MIX
Papier aus verantwortungsvollen Quellen
Paper from responsible sources
FSC® C105338

Printed by Books on Demand GmbH, Norderstedt / Germany